Protestants and the Cult of the Saints

Habent sua fata libelli

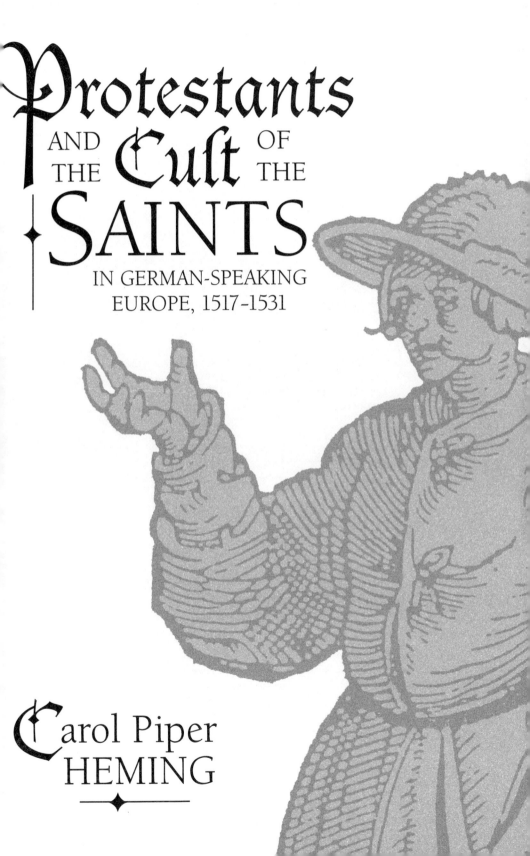

Protestants
AND THE Cult OF THE
SAINTS

IN GERMAN-SPEAKING
EUROPE, 1517–1531

Carol Piper
HEMING

Library of Congress Cataloging-in-Publication Data

Heming, Carol Piper, 1945–
    Protestants and the cult of the saints in German-speaking Europe, 1517–1531 / by
Carol Piper Heming.
        p. cm. — (Sixteenth century essays & studies ; v. 65)
Includes bibliographical references (p.   ) and index.
    ISBN 1-931112-23-1 (casebound) — ISBN 1-931112-24-X (pbk.)
    1. Christian saints—Cult—History—16th century. 2. Protestant churches—Doc-
trines—History—16th century. 3. Reformation—Europe, German-speaking.
4. Europe, German-speaking—Church history—16th century. I. Title. II. Series.

    BX4818.3 .H46 2003
    235'.2'094309031—dc21   2002153252

Cover art: From the cover page of Diepold Peringer's *A Sermon Preached by the Peasant from Wöhrd-by-Nuremberg, on the Sunday before Carnival, about Free Will and Also
about the Invocation of the Saints* (1524).

Cover design by Teresa Wheeler
Printed by McNaughton & Gunn, Inc., Saline, Michigan
Set in Linotype AG Duc De Berry and Monotype Bembo

To Charles G. Nauert,
with gratitude and affection

CONTENTS

Preface ix

Abbreviations xiii

CHAPTER 1
Presence of the Saints 1

CHAPTER 2
Religion and the Saints 13

CHAPTER 3
Society and the Saints 36

CHAPTER 4
Reformers and the Saints. 53

CHAPTER 5
Virgin Mary among the Saints 66

CHAPTER 6
Ubiquity of the Saints 75

CHAPTER 7
Persistence of the Saints 105

APPENDIX 1
Disputations, Diets, and Colloquies. 111

APPENDIX 2 113

APPENDIX 3
Key to Works Cited in this Appendix 117
Scriptural References Used against the Saints and Images. 122

Bibliography 147

Index 159

PREFACE

The subject of the cult of the saints is likely to stir up immediate notions of icons, shrines, and relics—or of prayers and miraculous cures—but it is far less likely to be understood as the complex, multilayered belief system that it had become by the late fifteenth and early sixteenth century. While the reformers' responses to the cult of the saints are generally painted in pronouncements on *adiaphora*—or, more dramatically, in incidents of iconoclasm—less attention has been accorded the contemporary objections to the saints and their trappings as part of a fundamental reevaluation of appropriate expressions of Christian piety.[1]

One of the aims of this study is to begin an examination of the framework underpinning the cult of the saints on the eve of the Reformation. Although much work has been done on the evolution of the medieval cult,[2] historians have typically treated the cult of the saints during the fifteenth and sixteenth centuries as one aspect of the more inclusive topic of popular religion.[3] It is clearly the case that customs and beliefs concerning the saints were part and parcel of the externalization of religion

---

[1] The centrality of the issue of Christian piety to the Reformation is addressed prominently by Carlos M. N. Eire in *War against the Idols: The Reformation of Worship from Erasmus to Calvin* (Cambridge: Cambridge University Press, 1986; reprint, 1998). Luther's concern with piety as expressed in his early vernacular publications aimed at the "simple folk" is stressed by Bernd Moeller, "Das Berühmtwerden Luthers," *Zeitschrift für Historische Forschung* 15 (1988): 65–92, esp. 73. The present study owes much to Eire's examination of the issue of piety and to his interpretation of the cult of the saints.

[2] See, for example, Peter Brown, *The Cult of the Saints: Its Rise and Function in Latin Christianity* (Chicago: University of Chicago Press, 1981); Stephen Wilson, ed., *Saints and Their Cults: Studies in Religious Sociology, Folklore and History* (Cambridge: Cambridge University Press, 1983); Donald Weinstein and Rudolph M. Bell, *Saints & Society: The Two Worlds of Western Christendom, 1000–1700* (Chicago: University of Chicago Press, 1982); André Vauchez, *Sainthood in the Later Middle Ages*, trans. Jean Birrell (Cambridge: Cambridge University Press, 1997); Barbara Abou-El-Haj, *The Medieval Cult of Saints: Formations and Transformations* (Cambridge: Cambridge University Press, 1994).

[3] See, for example, Margaret Aston, *Faith and Fire: Popular Religion and Unpopular Religion, 1350–1600* (Rio Grande, Ohio: Hambledon, 1993); Peter Burke, *Popular Culture in Early Modern Europe* (New York: New York University Press, 1978); Keith Thomas, *Religion and the Decline of Magic* (New York: Charles Scribner's Sons, 1977); Bernd Moeller, "Religious Life in Germany on the Eve of the Reformation," in *Pre-Reformation Germany*, ed. Gerald Strauss (New York: Harper & Row, 1972), 13–42; Steven D. Sargent, "Miracle Books and Pilgrimage Shrines in Late Medieval Bavaria," *Historical Reflections/Réflexions historiques* 15 (1986): 455–71; Steven D. Sargent, "Saints' Cults and Naming Patterns in Bavaria, 1400–1600," *Catholic Historical Review* 76 (October 1990): 673–96; and a number of works by Robert Scribner, including, *Popular Culture and Popular Movements in Reformation Germany* (London: Hambledon, 1987) and "Ritual and Popular Religion in Catholic Germany at the Time of the Reformation," *Journal of Ecclesiastical History* 35 (January 1984): 47–77.

which characterized popular expression around 1500. That the cult of the saints was, in addition, an intricate construct that reformers confronted over and over throughout the early Reformation era is one of the principal arguments of this study.

One reason this is so is that the cult of the saints stood at the intersection of many early modern byways.[4] Linking the spiritual and the physical, the pagan and the Christian, the dead and the living, the cult of the saints penetrated numerous boundaries—the very boundaries that reformers were striving to reinforce. In the sample of Reformation-era pamphlets analyzed in this study, individual opponents of the veneration of the saints often began by placing emphasis upon a single issue—usually a point of Scripture. The topic of the saints, once introduced, however, almost invariably opened a floodgate through which a variety of related objections proceeded to flow.

One typical case is a piece by Lutheran reformer Johannes Brenz, *Sermon on the Saints*, preached at Swäbische Hall on the Feast Day of St. James, 25 July 1523, and published as a pamphlet in that same year.[5] Brenz begins this sermon by noting that at times Scripture holds up the saints as examples. Citing passages from the Epistle of St. James, from Hebrews, and from Romans, he points to the powerful faith demonstrated by such figures as Abraham and Elias (or Elijah).[6] Brenz then goes on to note: "Such good models are altered by perverse, selfish, foolish, indeed, godless people who no longer praise the faith of the saints, but the saints themselves. They hold them up as gods in whom we should place our faith, as helpers, as intercessors.... In short, the veneration of the saints today is idolatry."[7]

Later in the sermon, Brenz points out the paganlike qualities of contemporary saint veneration[8] and devotes much of the rest of the sermon to the necessity of invoking Christ as the only intercessor and to the impropriety of venerating dead saints at the expense of the living: "One honors Saint Peter, Saint James, and the mother of Jesus Christ, all dead, not with fasts, sacrifices, pilgrimages, or fires. Rather, such honor belongs to the living."[9] While Brenz's point of departure in the sermon is clearly an endorsement of what he sees as the scriptural model of honor due dead saints, his message concerns numerous examples of the rampant disregard of this very same model. He closes his sermon with a pointed condemnation of a piety that had overstepped what he considers appropriate boundaries: "This is a

---

[4] For a more detailed discussion of this point, see chap. 3 below.

[5] Johannes Brenz, *Ein Sermon von den Heiligen* [Ulm: Matthias Hoffischer, 1523], Köhler 87/233.

[6] James 5:17–18; Rom. 4; Heb. 11. This and all other scriptural citations throughout the text and appendixes are from the Authorized (or King James) Version of the Bible.

[7] Brenz, *Sermon von den Heiligen*, Aii.

[8] Brenz, *Sermon von den Heiligen*, Aii^v.

[9] Brenz, *Sermon von den Heiligen*, Aiii^v–Biii. Quotation is from Bii^v.

common model found in the invocation of saints. It is with God as it is with a prince; if you want something from the prince, you first must make friends with [him] through his chancellor or marshal. But this model is repudiated by Christ himself in Matt. 20 and Luke 22."[10]

A second critical element that helps explain the continuing intrusion of the cult of the saints into the reformers' activities, sermons, and writings is the fact that the cult was intricately plaited into the elaborate tapestry of early modern piety. Carlos Eire notes, for example, that "the cult of the saints materialized in two forms: artistic representation and relics."[11] When reformers expressed concerns over the issue of "artistic representation" of the saints, they invariably pointed to the scriptural prohibitions of images. Frequently, however, they were also compelled to demonstrate the complexity of the pattern of saint invocation and veneration by taking up such related topics as the paganlike shrines that housed saints' images, the unseemly pilgrimages to those shrines, the resources squandered upon such images, and so forth.[12] Likewise, the issue of relics linked the cult of the saints to far broader concerns about the shrines where the relics were housed, the monastics who most commonly were the guardians of such relics, and the indulgences earned through their veneration. Eire, for instance, underscores the pervasive reach of the cult of the saints in the following observation: "Since relics were a source of indulgences when properly venerated, the relic-mania of the late Middle Ages was also intricately connected with indulgences. This relationship, in turn, helped intensify two types of devotion: the pilgrimage and the relic collection."[13] Thus, the present study touches on a variety of aspects of early modern devotion in order to define the construct

[10]Brenz, *Sermon von den Heiligen*, Biii. Scriptural references are to Matt. 20:25–28: "But Jesus called unto him, and said, 'Ye know that the princes of the Gentiles exercise dominion over them, and they that are great exercise authority upon them. / But it shall not be so among you: but whosoever will be great among you, let him be your minister; / And whosoever will be chief among you, let him be your servant: / Even as the Son of man came not to be ministered unto, but to minister, and to give his life a ransom for many' "; and Luke 22:25–26: "And he said unto them, 'The kings of the Gentiles exercise lordship over them; and they that exercise authority upon them are called benefactors. / But ye shall not be so: but he that is greatest among you, let him be as the younger; and he that is chief, as he that doth serve.' "

[11]Eire, *War against the Idols*, 13. Eire reiterates the intimate connection between images, relics, and the cult of the saints throughout the study, noting, for instance, that "the cult of images was principally an extension of the cult of the saints, and from its earliest days served as a physical reminder alongside the relic..." (18). In addition, he refers to the cult of the saints as the "theological foundation" of the "veneration of images" (59).

[12]See, for example, Andreas Karlstadt, *Von Abtuhng der Bylder und das keyn Betdler unther den Christen seyn soll* (Wittenberg: Nickell Schyrlentz, 1522), Köhler 434/1175. In this pamphlet, Karlstadt proceeds from biblical proscriptions of images to condemnations of such pilgrimage sites as Grimmental, Rome, and Wilsnack (Aiiiᵛ).

[13]Eire, *War against the Idols*, 15.

that comprised the cult of the saints as well as to recognize more fully the reasons for the cult's seeming ubiquity.

One of the numerous problems facing historians of the early Reformation era has to do with appropriate terminology. How does one refer to those who ultimately became Protestants in the period prior to the Second Diet of Speyer of 1529 when the term Protestant originated? This anachronistic term is used both in the title of the study and in the bulk of the text—despite reservations due to the historical inaccuracy—because the term Protestants is more understandable and less ambiguous than any other term available.[14]

I am grateful to the numerous colleagues, friends, and family members who helped see this project through to completion. First and foremost, thank you to Charles G. Nauert, professor emeritus from the University of Missouri–Columbia, who generously rendered advice and encouragement first throughout the writing of the dissertation and then during the preparation of the manuscript for publication. His patience, perseverance, and calm assurance were as important as his professional advice.

Thank you, Richard Bienvenu, Barbara Bank, Kerby Miller, and Mark Smith of UMC for advice, support, inspiration, and your scholarly example. Of the many individuals who helped facilitate my research, I am particularly grateful to Michelle Caver, Linda Naru, and Marilyn Grush at the Center for Research Libraries, Chicago; June DeWeese, Josephine Johnson, and Sue Halaweh at Ellis Library, Columbia; and Pat Downing and Lori Fitterling at J. C. Kirkpatrick Library, Warrensburg, Missouri. Thanks also to Brian Sebastian and Kevin Kile of UMC for their assistance with Latin texts.

To the professionals at Truman State University Press, many thanks for making this experience rewarding and pleasant. I am grateful to Ray Mentzer for his assistance in transforming a dissertation into a monograph, to Nancy Rediger for working minor miracles, and to Paula Presley for her consummate professionalism, enormous heart, and consideration and understanding when I needed them most.

Finally, thank you to my colleagues and friends at Central Missouri State University who supported my efforts, and to my wonderful family—thanks for being there, Dwight, Val, Raoul, and Jurgentje.

---

[14]The most likely alternatives are evangelicals or Evangelicals. I use the term evangelicals at times in the text, but only when no confusion would result.

ABBREVIATIONS

CT   *Concordia triglotta: Die symbolischen Bücher der evangelisch-lutherischen Kirche, deutsch-lateinisch-englisch, als Denkmal der vierhundertjährigen Jubelfeier der Reformation, anno Domini 1917.* St. Louis: Concordia, 1921. Numerals refer to page.

Köhler   Köhler, Hans-Joachim, Hildegard Hebenstreit-Wilfret, and Christoph Weisman, eds. *Flugschriften des frühen 16. Jahrhunderts.* Microfiche Serie 1978. Zug: Inter Documentation Co., 1978–87. When citing pamphlets from this collection, the modified titles and publication information provided by Köhler is used. In addition, updated information is used concerning authorship and publication data provided in the available volumes of Hans-Joachim Köhler, *Bibliographie der Flugschriften des 16. Jahrhunderts* Tübingen: Bibliotheca Academica, 1991–. Numerals refer to fiche and pamphlet.

LW   Luther, Martin. *Luther's Works.* Edited by Helmut T. Lehmann. Philadelphia: Muhlenberg, 1955. Numerals refer to volume and page.

Plass   *What Luther Says: An Anthology.* Compiled by Ewald Plass. St. Louis: Concordia, 1959. Numerals refer to entry and page.

WA   Luther, Martin. *D. Martin Luthers Werke: Kritische Gesamtausgabe.* Weimar: Böhlau, 1883. Numerals refer to volume, part, and page.

WA-T   Luther, Martin. *Tischreden.* In *D. Martin Luthers Werke: Kritische Gesamtausgabe.* Weimar: H. Böhlau, 1912. Numerals refer to volume and item.

WA Br. Luther, Martin. *D. Martin Luthers Briefwechsel, D. Martin Luthers Werke: Kritische Gesamtausgabe.* Weimar: H. Böhlau, 1930. Numerals refer to volume and page.

 resence

Presence OF THE SAINTS

Throughout the sixteenth century, religious issues first split, then splintered western Christendom. Disputes concerning both belief and practice reached their most active state of ferment in the presses and pulpits of central Europe. Pamphlets—likely more than ten thousand[1]—and sermons, many of which became pamphlets themselves, propagandized and polemicized, revealing and promoting the burning controversies of an era in religious turmoil. Certain matters aroused discussion not only among the learned, but among countless ordinary people as well: the nature of the Eucharist, the efficacy of works, the source of authority, the number of sacraments, pedobaptism, clerical celibacy, Christian liberty, communion in two kinds, the value of the contemplative life, even the very definition of church.

Compared to these issues, questions involving the cult of the saints may seem minor. In a letter to evangelicals in Erfurt, Martin Luther refers to arguments over the veneration of the saints as "superfluous concerns," distractions created by Satan himself,[2] while Huldrich Zwingli considered the dispute over saints' images a "childish matter," particularly in comparison with the far more significant debate over the nature of the mass.[3]

Several modern historians have contributed to this dismissal of the cult of the saints. In 1924, Johan Huizinga wrote: "The Reformation attacked the cult of the saints, and nowhere in the whole contested area did it meet with less resistance."[4]

---

[1] Steven Ozment, "Pamphlet Literature of the German Reformation," in *Reformation Europe: A Guide to Research*, ed. Steven Ozment (St. Louis: Center for Reformation Research, 1982), 85.

[2] "Epistel oder Unterricht von den Heiligen," 10 July 1522, WA 10(2):165–66.

[3] Zwingli at the Second Zurich Disputation, 27 October 1523, quoted in Charles Garside, Jr., *Zwingli and the Arts* (New Haven: Yale University Press, 1966), 161; *Die Akten der zweiten Disputation vom 26.–28. Oktober 1523*, in *Huldreich Zwinglis sämtliche Werke*, vol. 2, *Werke 1523*, Corpus Reformatorum (Zurich: Theologischer, 1982), 733.

[4] Johan Huizinga, *The Waning of the Middle Ages: A Study of the Forms of Life, Thought and Art in France and the Netherlands in the Dawn of the Renaissance* (Garden City, N.Y.: Doubleday Anchor Books, 1954), 177. Cf. Johan Huizinga, *The Autumn of the Middle Ages*, trans. Rodney J. Payton and Ulrich Mammitzsch (Chicago: University of Chicago Press, 1996), 202.

Lionel Rothkrug, Bernd Moeller, and other twentieth-century historians have at least implicitly concurred with Huizinga's contention that in Protestant areas "the saints fell without a blow being struck in their defence."[5] Many others have reiterated Hermann Heimpel's well-known pronouncement, that "the iconoclasts who destroyed the images were the very men who had donated them."[6] Such scholarship serves to underpin the conclusion that the saints retained few devotees in areas where Luther, Zwingli, John Calvin, and other reformers claimed victory.

In contrast, Merry E. Wiesner writes in 1992: "The veneration of the saints was in theory prohibited, though it is clear from local records that Protestant women continued to pray to female saints, especially during childbirth, for centuries after the Reformation."[7] This statement clearly reflects an altered discourse produced by the expansion of research in women's, gender, and popular history in the decades since Huizinga wrote his masterful work. Focus upon the religious attitudes of the laity, particularly of members of the lower orders, has generated considerable interest in historical analysis of issues surrounding popular piety. As Carlos Eire notes, "Protestant theologians attacked Catholic piety vigorously, but the success of their polemic depended largely on its acceptance by the laity. The war against Catholic worship was as much a layman's struggle as a theologian's."[8] Any number of recent scholars have acknowledged and addressed the persistence of traditional religious practices among the laity in Protestant regions.[9] In the case of the veneration of the saints, moreover, several historians cite evidence that supports the suggestion that

[5] Huizinga, *Waning*, 177; cf. Huizinga, *Autumn*, 202. See also Lionel Rothkrug, *Religious Practices and Collective Perception: Hidden Homologies in the Renaissance and Reformation* (Waterloo, Ont.: University of Waterloo, 1980); Bernd Moeller, "Imperial Cities and the Reformation," in *Imperial Cities and the Reformation: Three Essays*, Bernd Moeller, ed. and trans. H. C. Erik Midelfort and Mark U. Edwards (1972; repr., Durham, N.C.: Labyrinth Press, 1982), 58–59. Cf. Weinstein and Bell, *Saints and Society*, esp. chap. 6.

[6] Hermann Heimpel, "Characteristics of the Late Middle Ages in Germany," in *Pre-Reformation Germany*, ed. Strauss, 69.

[7] Merry E. Wiesner, "Studies of Women, the Family, and Gender," in *Reformation Europe: A Guide to Research II*, ed. William S. Maltby (St. Louis: Center for Reformation Research, 1992), 165. See also Lyndal Roper, *The Holy Household: Women and Morals in Reformation Augsburg*, Oxford Studies in Social History (Oxford: Oxford University Press, 1989; 1991), 261.

[8] Eire, *War against the Idols*, 6.

[9] See Robert Kolb, *For All the Saints: Changing Perceptions of Martyrdom and Sainthood in the Lutheran Reformation* (Macon, Ga.: Mercer University Press, 1987); Steven Ozment, *Protestants: The Birth of a Revolution* (New York: Doubleday, 1992); Robert Scribner, "The Image and the Reformation," in *Disciplines of Faith: Studies in Religion, Politics and Patriarchy*, ed. Jim Obelkevich, Lyndal Roper, and Raphael Samuel (New York: Routledge & Kegan Paul, 1987); Scribner, *Popular Culture and Popular Movements*; Gerald Strauss, *Luther's House of Learning: Indoctrination of the Young in the German Reformation* (Baltimore: Johns Hopkins University Press, 1978), among others.

women may have been especially reluctant to abandon entirely a piety that included invocation of the saints.[10]

When one begins to examine the status of the cult of the saints during the early Reformation era, two central questions immediately emerge. First, why did Reformation leaders so strongly and, despite their many intricate differences, so universally denounce the cult of the saints? Second, did the holy patrons, in fact, disappear from Protestant areas without benefit of champion or defender? Or does evidence suggest a more persistent veneration of the saints, at least among certain members of society?

In addressing the first question, one can gain considerable insight by examining relevant sermons and propaganda pieces. An analysis of approximately 180 pamphlets published between 1500 and 1530—works which deal with the saints (in part or in whole)—reveals an interesting phenomenon. An assessment of the writers' objections[11] exposes as a sub-text many of the very same issues which the reformers considered to be the weightier, more profound areas of contention.

Foremost among the criteria for judging the veneration of saints was *sola Scriptura*, the authority of Scripture alone. Some saints were apocryphal; others wholly traditional. Indeed, even saints who bore the imprimatur of scriptural authority would themselves have disapproved of the veneration paid them, as both Luther and Zwingli frequently admonished their followers. In addition, the commandment condemning the use of images loomed large, although many other scriptural passages were pressed into service against the saints as well.[12]

Tangential to scriptural concerns was the association of saints with the cloister. Although clearly the major objection of reformers to the cloister had to do with the propriety of vows, especially the vow of chastity, the devotion of monks and nuns to the saints caused apprehension. The prolific pamphleteer and disaffected Franciscan

---

[10] In her work on Augsburg, Lyndal Roper notes the outbreak of a riot in 1523 sparked by Protestant outrage at the continued invocation of St. Margaret by pregnant women; *Holy Household*, 233–34. In her article on Nordic Lutheranism, Grethe Jacobson writes that the cults of the Virgin and of St. Margaret persisted in Protestant Iceland, while the invocation of St. Margaret by women in childbirth continued into the eighteenth century in Denmark; idem, "Nordic Women and the Reformation," in *Women in Reformation and Counter-Reformation Europe: Public and Private Worlds*, ed. Sherrin Marshall (Bloomington: Indiana University Press, 1989), 60–61. Susan Karant-Nunn finds similar devotion to St. Margaret in Protestant Zwickau. Karant-Nunn furthermore contends that Huizinga's assertion concerning the uncontested demise of the saints "needs examining, not only as it may apply to Zwickau"; idem, *Zwickau in Transition, 1500–1547: The Reformation as an Agent of Change* (Columbus: Ohio State University Press, 1987), 204. Eire, *War against the Idols*, 114, mentions an attempt at iconoclasm in Aeschi put down by "a contingent of armed women."

[11] Or, in some cases, writer' defense. A small percentage of the pamphlets examined were written by defenders of traditional religious practices.

[12] See appendix 3.

Johann Eberlin von Günzburg, for example, seemed particularly antipathetic to the relationship between the cloistered and the saints.[13] Monks featured prominently as object lessons in pamphlets aimed at the popular classes. One typical work, a pamphlet by Hans Staygmeyer, is a dialogue between a monk and a baker.[14] As the dialogue unwinds, the two discuss the burning issues of the time: fasting, oral confession, communion in two kinds, and penance. Ultimately, the baker convinces the monk of the error of his ways through the use of Scripture, and the monk expresses gratitude for his enlightenment. The baker's final word of advice to the monk is to leave the order, for "you are not baptized in the name of Peter or Paul, but in Christ's name."[15] Staygmeyer here raises a stock complaint among reformers that the saints were inappropriately superseding Christ in the hearts of their devotees.

To the scriptural objections must be added criticisms that are largely socioeconomic in nature. Religious and socioeconomic issues blended in intriguing ways as the Reformation unfolded: the foremost example of this is, of course, the Peasants' War of 1525–26. For their part, reformers often complained that the saints devoured funds and energies better spent on more worthwhile causes. One anonymous pamphleteer, for instance, draws this contrast, "Christ teaches that charity should be extended to the poor.… The pope teaches the buying of indulgences; the building of churches, cloisters, and cells; chapels, altars, vigils, masses, anniversary masses; pilgrimages to the wooden saints."[16] In a sermon preached on St. Hilaria's Day (12 August) in 1523, pamphleteer Caspar Adler sounds a positively Erasmian note when he criticizes the many who travel "to the saints, to St. Wolfgang, [St.] Leonard, Regensburg, Aachen, and leave wife and child in need."[17]

Two further areas of criticism reflect a similar focus upon the dangers the cult of the saints posed for the laity, particularly those of the lower socioeconomic orders. The first has to do with the association of saint worship with superstition. Of this, Steven Ozment writes: "Protestants believed that nothing so exploited lay fears and

---

[13] See, for example, Johann Eberlin, *Ein klägliche Klag an den christlichen römischen Kaiser Carolum von wegen Doktor Luthers und Ulrich von Hutten. Der erst [bis XV.] Bundgenoß* [Augsburg: Jörg Nadler, 1521], esp. Fiii^{r-v} and Iii–Iiii, Köhler, 232–33/648. See also, Eberlin, *Wider die falsch scheinende[n] Geistlichen unter dem christlichen Haufen* ([Augsburg: Melchior Ramminger], 1524), Köhler 49/136.

[14] Hans Staygmeyer, *Ein schöner Dialogus oder Gespräch von einem Mönch und Becken* [Augsburg: Philipp Ulhart, 1524], Köhler 4/17.

[15] Staygmeyer, *Ein schöner Dialogus*, Bi^v. This and all other translations from the German are mine unless otherwise noted.

[16] *Ein klärlich Anzeigung und Ausweisung eins christlichen und unchristlichen Lebens* [Speyer: Jakob Schmidt, 1523], Bi^v–Bii, Köhler 223/624.

[17] Caspar Adler, *Ein Sermon von der Schul Christi* ([Augsburg: Sigmund Grimm], 1523), bii, Köhler 45/125. Cf. Desiderius Erasmus, "A Pilgrimage for Religion's Sake," in *Colloquies*, trans. Craig R. Thompson, Collected Works of Erasmus, vol. 40 (Toronto: University of Toronto Press, 1997), 619–74. On Erasmus's critique of medieval piety, see Eire, *War against the Idols*, 28–53.

COVER OF HANS STAYGMEYER'S *DIALOGUE BETWEEN A MONK AND A BAKER* (1524).

superstition as that body of belief and religious practice which related to the dead. [Pamphilus] Gengenbach and [Nikolaus] Manuel summarized it with a phrase that must surely have embodied the most profound contemporary animosities: *Totenfresserei*—'feeding upon the dead.'"[18] While the dead responsible for this feeding frenzy included those for whom soul masses were endowed and indulgences purchased, the dead saints generated an equal amount of concern.[19] Luther, in fact, set out to reclaim the word saint to apply to all believers in Christ, living and dead: "I and others were so steeped in our monasticism and unbelief that we were frightened if a man considered himself, or was called, a saint on earth. For our thoughts about saints were directed only toward the blessed in heaven, even though Scripture constantly uses this term with reference to the living on earth."[20] In his letter to the evangelicals at Erfurt, Luther implicitly connects saint worship with superstition,[21] while in other writings he does so more explicitly.[22] Controversialists of the era, such as Johann Eberlin and Hartmuth von Cronberg, and preachers, such as Nikolaus Hausmann, Wolfgang Zeuner, and Paul Lindenau, further contributed to the body of literature connecting the saints to superstition.[23] The desire to put an end to superstition, to sever the link between this world and the beyond—a link forged by the saints—is a theme that resounds throughout the early Reformation era.[24]

Finally, in a culture moving rapidly, in Peter Burke's words, from "Carnival to Lent,"[25] the saints, and traditional religion in general, were frequently labeled as contributors to an undesirable disorder and lack of discipline. Many works substantiate this connection, but Andreas Karlstadt (admittedly an unlikely critic of disorder) provides the best summary. In his pamphlet on the Sabbath and holidays, he declares the saints' days to be the invention of the devil and the devil's son (that is,

[18] Steven Ozment, *The Reformation in the Cities: The Appeal of Protestantism to Sixteenth-Century Germany and Switzerland* (New Haven: Yale University Press, 1975), 95–96.

[19] For an explanation of the association of the word saint with the dead only, see Stephen Wilson's introduction to *Saints and Their Cults*, 1–53.

[20] Luther's exposition of John 14:25–26, WA 45:616–17, Plass 3977/1246.

[21] WA 10(2):166–67. In the same letter, he also notes that the saints are all those "in Christ," whether living or dead (166).

[22] "Probably the papists took this custom of praying to the saints from the heathen." WA-T 5:6351, Plass 4000/1254.

[23] See, for example, Johann Eberlin, *Das Lob der Pfarrer von dem unnützen Kosten* [Augsburg: Sigmund Grimm und Marx Wirsung, 1522], Köhler 7/32; idem, *Ein Sermon zu den Christen in Erfurt* [Erfurt: Johannes Loersfeld], 1524, Köhler 53/149; Harmuth von Cronberg, *Ein christliche Schrift und Vermahnung an alle Stände des Römischen Reichs* [Zwickau: Jörg Gastel, 1523], Köhler 231/643; and Nikolaus Hausmann, Wolfgang Zeuner, and Paul Lindenau, *Unterricht und Warnung an die Kirch zu Zwickau* (Zwickau: [Jörg Gastel, 1525]), Köhler 290/841.

[24] Keith Thomas uses Max Weber's phrase "the disenchantment of the world" to refer to this phenomenon; Thomas, *Religion and the Decline of Magic*, 657.

[25] Burke, *Popular Culture in Early Modern Europe*, esp. chap. 8.

the pope). He continues, "I want to put an end to the injuries which the fathers [*Haußväter*] endure, in which some of their workforce leaves and through popish tyranny becomes smaller; for the servant is responsible to work six days for his master. But the saints' days of the priests destroy the duty and obedience of the servant and replace this obedience with masterful occasions for all sorts of trouble, such as slander, drunkenness, swearing, stealing, murder, and all sorts of evil things that would take many more words to describe."[26]

In exploring the question of whether the cult of the saints readily disappeared in the early Reformation era, one must immediately confront the innumerable condemnations of the practice of venerating the saints that appear in sermons and tracts from the period. Analysis of pamphlets published by a variety of clerics and propagandists reveals a significant interest in and concern about this issue throughout the period. Such evidence clearly begs the question: would writers bent on reform devote this sort of unremitting attention to a practice that had abruptly ceased "without a blow being struck in [its] defence"? Furthermore, as "superfluous" or "childish" as they may have considered the veneration of the saints, reformers such as Luther and Zwingli frequently found themselves expending great energies dealing with that very issue. The years 1522 and 1523 are notable in this regard.

In 1522, for example, the violent iconoclasm being carried out in Wittenberg by the "false brethren" Andreas Karlstadt and Gabriel Zwilling provoked Luther to return from exile to attempt to defuse the situation.[27] In a series of eight sermons, known collectively as the Invocavit sermons, Luther devoted considerable attention to the question of saints' images.[28] In the sermon delivered on Tuesday, 11 March, in a portion subtitled "Concerning Images," Luther explains that while images are not necessities for Christians, neither are they forbidden. He continues: "We can have them or not although it would be better if we did not have them at all. I am also not favorably disposed toward them."[29] He criticizes the iconoclasts' violent methods, however, telling them they were likely to defeat their own purposes, that they would only strengthen devotion rather than eliminate it.[30] In a sermon delivered the next day, Luther further elaborates on the issue of images, explaining that while they were generally misused (that is, worshiped, venerated, or prayed to),

---

[26] Andreas Karlstadt, *Von dem Sabbat und geboten Feiertagen* [Konstanz: Johann Schäffler, 1524], D2–D3, Köhler 70/186.

[27] Mark U. Edwards, Jr., *Luther and the False Brethren* (Stanford: Stanford University Press, 1975), 6–33.

[28] Martin Luther, *Acht Sermone D. Martin Luthers, von ihm gepredigt zu Wittenberg in der Fastenzeit 9–16 März 1522*, in *Ausgewählte Schriften*, vol. 1, *Aufbruch zur Reformation*, ed. Karin Bornkamm and Gerhard Ebeling (Frankfurt a/M: Insel, 1982), 270–307; WA 10(3):1–65.

[29] Luther, *Acht Sermone*, in *Ausgewählte Schriften*, ed. Bornkamm and Ebeling, 1:284.

[30] Luther, *Acht Sermone*, in *Ausgewählte Schriften*, ed. Bornkamm and Ebeling, 1:286.

occasionally they were used properly (as objects of inspiration only). For this reason, the iconoclasts should show judicious restraint.[31]

Only four months after preaching the Invocavit sermons, Luther once again attempted to moderate a growing rift, this time in the university city of Erfurt. The factions in this case were radicals headed by his friend Johannes Lang and traditionalists led by his old teacher, the Augustinian Bartholomaeus von Usingen.[32] Fearing that the situation would escalate to the extremes experienced in Wittenberg, Luther dispatched an open letter to the congregation at Erfurt. His topic: the veneration of the saints. Once again Luther admonished the radicals to tread lightly and to allow the "weak," who still relied upon the saints spiritually, to come around gradually.[33] While Luther's moderation may have been generated by his own gradual weaning from reliance on the saints,[34] one is also tempted to infer that Luther considered the "nonessential" saints a somewhat more formidable lot than his words might otherwise imply.[35]

In the meantime, the problem of the saints was becoming a contentious issue among the Swiss as well. In his classic biography of Huldrich Zwingli, Samuel Macauley Jackson writes: "The year 1522 is that in which the Reformation began in Zürich."[36] Jackson refers not so much to Zwingli's arrival in Zürich—he had

---

[31] Luther, *Acht Sermone*, in *Ausgewählte Schriften*, ed. Bornkamm and Ebeling, 1:288–90.

[32] For brief accounts of the situation in Erfurt, see James MacKinnon, *Luther and the Reformation*, vol. 3, *Progress of the Movement (1521–29)* (New York: Russell & Russell, 1962), 105–7; E. G. Schwiebert, *Luther and His Times: The Reformation from a New Perspective* (St. Louis: Concordia, 1950), 543; Heinrich Bornkamm, *Luther in Mid-Career 1521–1530*, ed. and with a foreword by Karin Bornkamm, trans. E. Theodore Bachmann (Philadelphia: Fortress, 1983), 99–100; Martin Brecht, *Martin Luther*, vol. 2, *Shaping and Defining the Reformation 1521–1532*, trans. James L. Schaaf (Minneapolis: Fortress, 1990), 77–78. More detailed accounts appear in Ulman Weiss, *Ein fruchtbar Bethlehem: Luther und Erfurt* (Berlin: Evangelische, 1982), 68–81; and Erich Kleineidam, *Universitas Studii Erffordensis: Überblick über die Geschichte der Universität Erfurt*, part 3, *Die Zeit der Reformation und Gegenreformation 1521–1632*, Erfurter theologische Studien (Leipzig: St. Benno, 1983), 2–35.

[33] WA 10(2):166.

[34] Bornkamm, *Luther in Mid-Career*, 99, citing letters to Johannes Lang, 29 May 1522, WA Br. 2:548; and to Adam Kraft, 28 July 1522, WA Br. 2:582.

[35] Other evidence of Luther's outspokenness against iconoclasm can be seen in his "Letter to the Princes of Saxony concerning the Rebellious Spirit," in which he addresses Thomas Müntzer's activities at Allstedt in 1524, WA 15:210–21; "Letter to the Christians at Strassburg in Opposition to the Fanatic Spirit," in which he addresses Karlstadt's influence in Strassburg in 1524, WA 15:391–97; and *Against the Heavenly Prophets in the Matter of Images and Sacraments*, pt. 1, 1524–25, in which he once again admonishes Karlstadt, WA 18:62–125. The fact that furor over the cult of the saints did not completely die down either in Wittenberg or in Erfurt after Luther's intervention is further evidence of the tenacity of the belief.

[36] Samuel Macauley Jackson, *Huldreich Zwingli: The Reformer of German Switzerland: 1484–1531* (New York: G. P. Putnam's Sons, 1901), 158. For a more recent biography of Zwingli, see G. R. Potter, *Zwingli* (Cambridge: Cambridge University Press, 1976).

been in the city since late 1518—as to the confrontation between old believers and reformers that began coming to a head in that year. Central among the issues disputed was the cult of the saints.

Zwingli had likely first seriously pondered the issue of veneration of the saints between 1516 and 1518 while he served as pastor at Einsiedeln, a tenth-century Marian shrine which, by the sixteenth century, had become the principal pilgrimage site in southern Germany and Switzerland. By 1521 Zwingli was preparing to publish some sermons on saint worship which apparently never saw print.[37] The issue did, however, generate controversy in July 1522 when Zwingli and the Franciscan Franz Lambert of Avignon engaged in a public debate over the intercession of the saints. Zwingli won the debate although Lambert was said to have been "tainted" with Reformation ideas and thus to have "made but a feeble opposition."[38]

In the following year the question of the saints arose even more prominently during the first and second Zurich Disputations of January and October.[39] Of the sixty-seven *Schlußreden* (articles for debate) issued by Zwingli before the January Disputation, three deal specifically with the saints.[40] Like Luther, Zwingli strove to effect change gradually and legally. He disapproved of violent iconoclasm, believing that images should be removed only with the approval of civic authorities. Nonetheless, incidents of iconoclasm proliferated throughout 1523.

One major impetus seems to have been a blistering pamphlet, published sometime prior to October, by the cleric Ludwig Hätzer.[41] Reminiscent of Andreas Karlstadt's earlier work on iconoclasm,[42] Hätzer's pamphlet is an outline of thirty-one scriptural admonitions against the making and use of images. In addition, Hätzer responds to a number of arguments mounted by the defenders of images,

---

[37] Jackson, *Huldreich Zwingli*, 153; Potter makes no mention of these.

[38] Jackson, *Huldreich Zwingli*, 170; Potter notes that Lambert defended veneration of images in a debate in Zurich on 21 July 1522 (82 n. 3); Potter further notes that Lambert was regarded by some as an adherent of Luther at the time (248). Ultimately, Lambert became evangelical. For a brief biographical sketch of Lambert, see Johannes Schilling, *Klöster und Mönche in der hessischen Reformation,* Quellen und Forschungen zur Reformationsgeschichte (Gütersloh: Gütersloher, 1997), 190–91.

[39] On the first Zurich Disputation, see Potter, *Zwingli,* 197–203; Jackson, *Huldreich Zwingli,* 179–98; and Garside, *Zwingli and the Arts,* 96–98. On the second Zurich Disputation, see Potter, *Zwingli,* 130–33; Jackson, *Huldreich Zwingli,* 199–210; and Garside, *Zwingli and the Arts,* 129–45.

[40] Articles 19, 20, and 21 deal with the saints; article 20 is by far the longest of the *Schlußreden.* See Ulrich Zwingli, *Huldrych Zwingli: Writings,* vol. 1, *The Defense of the Reformed Faith,* trans. E. J. Furcha (Allison Park, Penn.: Pickwick, 1984), 128–34, 135–76, 177–83; idem, *Auslegen und Gründe der Schlußreden 14 July 1523,* in idem, *Sämtliche Werke,* 2:157–66; 166–230; 231–39.

[41] Ludwig Hätzer, *Ein Urteil Gottes unsers Ehegemahl, wie man sich mit allen Götzen und Bildnissen halten soll uß der heiligen Gschrift gezogen* (Zurich: C. Froschauer, 1523), Köhler 244/675. For a useful discussion of the significance of the Hätzer pamphlet, see Garside, *Zwingli and the Arts,* 108–15.

[42] Karlstadt, *Von Abtuhung der Bylder.*

again citing Scripture. For Hätzer, no distinction between the proper use of images and improper idolatry existed. To those who tried to draw such a distinction, he responds: "Say you godless what you will. Even if you do not venerate them, Christians shall have no images. Thus says God. So you then say you honor the saints. You do that, however, without God's word or commandment, for he wants you to honor no one else."[43]

It was thus a charged atmosphere that surrounded the Second Zurich Disputation. Summoned by the Great Council on 26 October 1523, the participants took up the topics of images and the mass. The meetings lasted for three days, the first of which was devoted to the issue of saints' images. Indeed, discussion of saints' images—by Zwingli and by others in Zurich—extended well beyond the pivotal year of 1524. In 1525 and 1526, for instance, Zwingli produced two highly significant works dealing, at least in part, with the topic. In *Commentary on True and False Religion*, he takes up the intercession of the saints and the use of images in two separate sections,[44] while in his *Answer to Valentin Compar*, he produces his self-proclaimed definitive treatise on the subjects.[45] Furthermore, throughout the decade, Zwingli was called upon to address these issues numerous times.[46] In January 1528 he and other reformers participated in the Bern Disputation, and once again the saints were at issue. Of the ten *Acts of the Disputation*, produced after the Zwinglian victory of 27 January, two concerned the saints: one proclaimed Christ the only mediator, and another declared images unscriptural.[47] Despite such successes, the appeal of many traditional practices, including veneration of the saints, refused to melt away. Ironically, in 1530, the year before Zwingli's untimely death, the Zurich City Council found itself confronting the dilemma of backsliders. Among the problems the council complained about was the "news that concerning our Christian order and contrary to it in certain areas in castles, churches, chapels, and other

---

[43] Hätzer, *Ein Urteil Gottes*, Biiii^v.

[44] Huldrich Zwingli, *Von wahrem und falschem Glauben* (Zurich: C. Froschauer, 1526), Köhler 911/2265; idem, *De vera et falsa religione commentarius*; idem, *Sämtliche Werke*, vol. 3, *Werke 1524–März 1525*, 590–912.

[45] Huldrich Zwingli, *Ein Antwort, Valentino Compar gegeben* (Zurich: Hans Hager, [1525]), Eiii^v, Köhler 305–6/881; idem, *Sämtliche Werke*, vol. 4, *Werke April 1525–März 1526*, 84. For a detailed analysis of the work, see Garside, *Zwingli and the Arts*, 161–78.

[46] See, for example, Zwingli, *Ein Gegenwurf und Widerwehr wider Hieronymum Emser* (Zurich: C. Froschauer, 1525), Köhler 137/372, Eiiii^v–Gi^v; idem, *Adversus Hieronymum Emserum antibolon*, 20 August 1524, in idem, *Sämtliche Werke*, 3: 269–76; idem, *Ein christenliche, fast nützliche und tröstliche Epistel an die Gläbigen zu Eslingen* (n. p., 1526), Köhler 306/883; idem, *Sämtliche Werke*, vol. 5, *Werke April 1526–Juni 1527*, 272–85; idem, *Die erst kurze Antwort über Ecken sieben Schlusreden* (n. p., 1526), Aii^v–Aiv, Köhler 57/160; idem, *Sämtliche Werke*, 5:188–92.

[47] Bern, Disputation (1528), *Ratschlag haltender Disputation zu Bern* [Zurich: C. Froschauer, 1528], articles vi and vii, Bi^v, Köhler 1805/4620.

establishments in our territory, idols, images, altars, and paintings still remain, and in some areas at suspicious times lights appear, especially near certain chapels or households; with such lights various pilgrimages and offerings are still going on."[48]

Like Zwingli, Luther continued to wrestle with the cult of the saints and other traditional religious practices throughout the early Reformation era. Distress over such issues resulted in the first Saxon visitation of 1527–28[49] and the subsequent publication of the small and large catechisms of 1529. In the preface to the *Small Catechism*, Luther voices his concerns for his followers: "The deplorable, miserable condition which I discovered lately when I, too, was a visitor, has forced and urged me to prepare this Catechism, or Christian doctrine, in this small, plain, simple form. Mercy! Good God! what manifold misery I beheld! The common people, especially in the villages, have no knowledge whatever of Christian doctrine, and, alas! many pastors are altogether incapable and incompetent to teach."[50] While his commentary on the First Commandment in the *Small Catechism* is sparse—"We should fear, love, and trust in God above all things"[51]—in the *Large Catechism* he expounds at some length:

> Besides, consider what, in our blindness, we have hitherto been practising and doing under the Papacy. If any one had toothache, he fasted and honored St. Apollonia; if he was afraid of fire, he chose St. Lawrence as his helper in need; if he dreaded pestilence, he made a vow to St. Sebastian or [St. Roche], and a countless number of such abominations, where every one selected his own saint, worshiped him, and called for help to him in distress.... For all these place their heart and trust elsewhere than in the true God, look for nothing good to Him nor seek it from Him.[52]

---

[48] Zurich, Bürgermeister, Rat und Grosser Rat, *Christenlich Ansehung des gemeinen Kilchgangs zu Hörung göttlichs Wort* (Zurich, 1530), Aiiii^v, Köhler 1600/4135.

[49] On the visitation, see Brecht, *Martin Luther*, 2:259–73; Mackinnon, *Luther and the Reformation*, 3:290–97; Schwiebert, *Luther and His Times*, 615–19.

[50] Martin Luther, *Small Catechism*, in *Concordia* or *Book of Concord: The Symbols of the Evangelical Lutheran Church* (St. Louis: Concordia, 1950), 158; idem, *Der kleine Catechismus für die gemeine Pfarrherr und Prediger*, WA 30(1):239–425.

[51] Luther, *Small Catechism*, 159. In references to the Decalogue, I have followed the Lutheran/Roman Catholic numeration, which places the prohibition of images in the First Commandment. Except for Lutherans, all English-speaking Protestants (plus all followers of Jewish tradition, all Reformed Protestants, and all Eastern Orthodox) define the prohibition of graven images as the Second Commandment.

[52] Martin Luther, *Large Catechism*, in *Concordia*, 170; idem, *Deudsch Catechismus [Der Große Katechismus]*, WA 30(1):123–238.

In view of such language, it seems likely that what reformer Philipp Melanchthon labels "childish, and needless works" in article 20 of the *Augsburg Confession* were, even as late as 1530, practices still familiar and comforting to at least some of the evangelical flock.[53] Thus, despite the best efforts of the likes of Luther or Zwingli—or of the more radical reformers such as Karlstadt, Zwilling, Lang, and Hätzer—by the end of the early Reformation era, the cult of the saints remained a formidable presence—one that few historians have sufficiently recognized or acknowledged.

[53] *Augsburg Confession*, "Article XX: Of Good Works," in *Concordia*, 15; *CT* 53.

$\mathcal{R}$eligion AND THE SAINTS

CHAPTER 2

ASSOCIATIONS WITH THE ORDERS

Unlike Huldrich Zwingli, Martin Luther and numerous other reformers emerged from the institution of monasticism.[1] While the issue of when Luther severed his ties entirely with the ideals of the regular life is the subject of some debate, it is unquestionably the case that Luther's views on the orders evolved over time and frequently seemed inconsistent, much as did his views on the saints themselves.[2] Nonetheless, almost surely from 1521 on—and certainly after his marriage to former nun Katharina von Bora in 1525—Luther's assessment of monasticism became more and more critical. In a 1522 sermon dealing with works, Luther clearly begins to connect monasticism with works righteousness, saying, for instance: "Therefore, it is the first mistake that we use the saints' lives as a model and bind their lives up with rules, as the orders do."[3] While Luther's critiques of monasticism are numerous and complex,

---

[1]Johannes Schilling, *Klöster und Mönche*, 128, makes this point about Luther. In addition to Luther, among those reformers whose works are cited in this study, the following had been regular clergymen: Nikolaus von Amsdorf (Augustinian), Ambrosius Blarer (Benedictine), Johannes Bugenhagen (Premonstratensian), Martin Bucer (Dominican), Johannes Culsamer (Augustinian), Johann Eberlin (Franciscan), Johannes Fritzhans (Franciscan), Kaspar Güttel (Augustinian), Heinrich von Kettenbach (Franciscan), Johannes Lang (Augustinian), Wenzeslaus Linck (Augustinian), Johann Locher (Franciscan), Johannes Lonicer (Augustinian), Sebastian Mayer (Franciscan), Melchior Mirisch (Augustinian), Johannes Oecolampadius (briefly in a Brigittine cloister), Simon Reuter (possibly Cistercian or Carthusian), Michael Sattler (Benedictine), Konrad Schmid (Johannite), and Michael Stifel (Augustinian).

[2]A certain amount of consensus converges around the date of the appearance of Luther's work *On Monastic Vows*, written while he was in exile at the Wartburg in 1521 (*De Votis monasticis Martini Lutheri iudicium*, WA 8:564–669). Bernhard Lohse discusses this and other research issues in *Mönchtum und Reformation: Luthers Auseinandersetzung mit dem Mönchsideal des Mittelalters*, Forschungen zur Kirchen- und Dogmengeschichte (Göttingen: Vandenhoeck & Ruprecht, 1963), 201–12. Lohse traces the development of Luther's views on monasticism from 1509 to 1521, noting the conflicts between Luther's holding fast to tradition in some ways, while at the same time departing from orthodoxy in others (201–370). "Luther's attitude toward the cult of the saints bore a close resemblance to his critique of monasticism," as noted by David Bagchi, *Luther's Earliest Opponents: Catholic Controversialists, 1518–1525* (Minneapolis: Fortress, 1991), 152.

[3]Luther, *Predigt am Johannistage*, 24 June 1522, WA 10(3):202.

of interest here are his conclusions about the manner in which monasticism had falsely shaped his own and other monks' interpretation of and devotion to the saints, and how the practices of the cloistered and the mendicants had influenced the devotion of the laity.

In an exposition of John 14:25–26 written in 1537, for instance, Luther comments on his previously faulty notions of sainthood: "Thus I and others were so steeped in our monasticism and unbelief that we were frightened if a man considered himself, or was called, a saint on earth."[4] In an earlier work on Gal. 5:19 (1531), Luther had likewise reflected on his blindness as a monastic to the true nature of sainthood: "I am glad and thank God that he has given me in superabundant measures what I once asked as a monk. I have seen, not one saint but many...."[5] In the same year, he wrote to his mother, Margarethe: "Dear mother...be thankful that God has brought you to such understanding and has not left you in the papal error that we were taught, built from our works and monks' holiness: to consider this sole consolation, our Savior, not as a consoler, but rather as a grim judge and tyrant, so that we must flee to Mary and the saints and cannot expect any grace or consolation from him."[6] In these three passages, Luther calls attention to what he perceived to be an intimate link between the orders and abuses involving the saints—a link which numerous other evangelical writers, as well as Erasmian humanists—also pointed to and exploited. Indeed, one of the frequently cited objections to the cult of the saints was its relationship to and misappropriation by the increasingly discredited regular clergy, particularly the mendicants who had enthusiastically promoted popular religious practices, including veneration of the saints. Zwingli, while never a monk, likewise connects monasticism with abuses of the cult of the saints. In one instance, he sums up a variety of complaints about monks and their idols in this brief remark: "Which monks have become so poor that they have built no shrines for their images?"[7] Furthermore, in the second edition of a work entitled *On the Origin of Errors*, published in 1529, Zwingli's soon-to-be successor, Heinrich Bullinger, fixes blame directly on monastics for creating a piety that focused inappropriately on the bodies of dead saints.[8]

---

[4] WA 45:616–17, Plass 3977/1246.

[5] WA 40(2):104, Plass 3992/1251.

[6] Martin Luther to Margarethe Luther, 20 May 1531, WA Br. 6:103–6, no. 1820. Margarethe died approximately one year later (30 June 1531).

[7] Zwingli, *Von wahrem und falschem Glauben*, 278ᵛ, in idem, *Sämtliche Werke*, 3:901.

[8] Eire, *War against the Idols*, 86–88, makes this point; he writes: "[Bullinger] asserts that Christian image worship developed when the bodies of the saints and martyrs began to be revered, and he places the blame on monastic piety, with its emphasis on physical holiness" (87–88). While Bullinger was not himself a monk, he taught monks in the Cistercian cloister school in Kappel and later was instrumental in converting the abbot and the monks to the Reformed faith.

REPRESENTATIVES OF VARIOUS ORDERS, FROM A DERISIVE PAMPHLET CALLED
"THE PAPACY AND ITS MEMBERS" (1526). ORDERS FROM LEFT TO RIGHT INCLUDE: BRIGGITINE,
CISTERCIAN, FRANCISCAN, DOMINICAN, JOHANNITE, ANTONITE, AND BENEDICTINE.

Ain fraintlich troſt

liche vermanung an alle frum

men Chaſten/zu Augſpurg Am Leech/Dariñ
auch angezaygt wirt/waʒd der Doc.
Martini Luther von Got
geſandt ſey.
Durch Johann Eberlin
von Ginʒburg·

J. E.
m. w. Wittemberg.

COVER OF A PAMPHLET BY JOHANNES EBERLIN IN SUPPORT OF MARTIN LUTHER (1522).

On Christmas day 1523, a new arrival to the reformers' cause, Georg von Polenz, bishop of Samland, shocked his congregation at Königsberg cathedral by delivering the first of many evangelical sermons. In his Christmas sermon, the bishop devotes a section to the way in which the cloistered abused the saints, stressing in particular the error of their focus on works: "Monks, priests, or nuns…exert themselves to buy from such supposed saints their good works and through [the saints'] merits and invocation expect to become blessed."[9] Often evangelical writers objected to the saints in part because of the manner in which veneration of them, as encouraged and practiced by monastics, along with the vows taken by members of orders, unquestionably fostered works righteousness.[10] Rarely, in fact, does one encounter an evangelical pamphlet dealing with the orders that fails to point out the connection of monastics to idols, pilgrimages, relics, indulgences, and other such notorious trappings associated with the cult of the saints and thus with salvation by works.

Pamphleteer and former Franciscan Johann Eberlin, for one, lumps together and lambasts the "numerous instances of superstition, magic, worship of idols, orders, pilgrimages, prayers, blessings, and vows to various saints,"[11] while Sebastian Mayer connects the monks not only with costly images but also with a variety of "foolish" relics, including "the cord with which Judas hanged himself," "the tail of the donkey that Christ rode," "hay from the crib in Bethlehem," "the bit from St. George's horse," and "a piece of shoelace from a supposed saint."[12] The Hessian Johannes Ferrarius, rector of the newly founded Marburg University, calls the various orders to task because of their appeals to "emergency helpers, prayers to saints, shrines, pilgrimages, and similar misleading abuses and unsavory temptations to their neglected folds";[13] he goes on to celebrate the fact that the city's monastery, with its abuses such as "pilgrimages and idolatrous images" was, by 1527, quite literally being converted into the first Protestant university.[14] He closes his pamphlet by expressing gratitude that thus "we will be set free from such unchristian abominations as monks, priests,

---

[9] Georg von Polenz, Bf. Von Samland, *Ein Sermon in der Domkirch zu Königsberg gepredigt* [Augsburg: Melchior Ramminger, 1524], Bii[v], Köhler 461/1244.

[10] See, for example, Luther, *Sermon in der Kaufmannskirche zu Erfurt gepredigt von Kreuz und Leiden eines rechten Christenmenschen*, WA 10(3):362–63, 367. Johannes Schilling writes: "Luther objected to viewing the virtue of Bernard, of Francis, and of Dominic as examples because they were not saved as a result of their vows but as a result of their faith; *Klöster und Mönche*, 130, citing WA 6:540.

[11] Eberlin, *Ein Sermon zu den Christen in Erfurt*, Aiiii[v].

[12] Sebastian Mayer, *Widerrufung an ein löblich Freistadt Straßburg* ([Augsburg: Philipp Ulhart], 1524), C[v], Köhler 147/405. Cf. Ambrosius Blarer, *Wahrhaft Verantwortung an einen ehrsame weisen Rat zu Konstanz anzeigendem warum es aus dem Kloster gewichen* ([Augsburg: Simprecht Ruff], 1523), Ciiii[v]–Diii, Köhler 83/224.

[13] [Johannes (Montanus) Ferrarius], *Was der durchleüchtige Fürst Philipp, Landgraf zu Hessen, mit den Klosterpersonen, Pfaffherren und Bildnissen in seinem Fürstentume fürgenommen hat* (n.p., 1528), Biiii[v]–Bv, Köhler 1496/3937. *Nothelfer* were special "helper saints" called upon in emergencies.

[14] Ferrarius, *Was der durchleüchtige Fürst Philipp*, Aiii.

idols, and the like."[15] Luther himself makes the point explicitly in his exposition of the First Commandment in the *Large Catechism*: "There is also a false worship and extreme idolatry, which we have hitherto practised, and is still prevalent in the world, upon which also all ecclesiastical orders are founded, and which concerns the conscience alone, that seeks in its own works help, consolation, and salvation...."[16]

Particularly notorious for their abuses of the saints were the begging orders, "the false prophets and false teachers,"[17] who were often heavily criticized by evangelical and humanist reformers alike. In the list of grievances presented at the Diet of Worms, the *Stationierer*, a begging order infamous for its sale of relics, was cited as being especially economically burdensome to the empire:

> It is not a small burden that the *Stationierer* who collect [money] here and there throughout the land, take in much money with their writing and begging, and offer huge indulgences. The people ... bring money to them; therefore, they take it and sinfully and shamefully use it up. Also, in part, the poor innocent people, who otherwise would give them nothing, because of reprimands from the saints, whose sealed messages they [that is, the *Stationierer*] quote, offensively and contrary to Christian belief, consider giving to them. The bishop allows this. At first we had only St. Anthony's message to be concerned with;[18] now messages come from the Holy Ghost, St. Hubert, St. Cornelius, St. Bernard, St. Valentine, and their envoys.[19]

Similarly, the Antonites—derisively referred to as *Thonies Pfaffen*—were chided for their encouragement of pilgrimages, their sale of indulgences, and their devotion to relics, "even though they themselves could not agree whether the relics were human or pig bones."[20] The Augustinian Johannes Lonicer, who later became a professor at Marburg, pointedly addresses his instruction against the invocation of saints to the Barefoot Franciscans, warning that "life, hope and salvation can be found neither in

---

[15] Ferrarius, *Was der durchleüchtige Fürst Philipp*, Bv.

[16] *Large Catechism*, in *Concordia*, 170; *CT* 585.

[17] Nikolaus Kattelsburger, *Ein Missive oder Sendbrief von den falschen Lehren* ([Augsburg: Philipp Ulhart], 1524), Aii^{r-v}, Köhler 725/1845.

[18] A reference to St. Anthony's *Brief* (or letter), a legendary message delivered to earth from St. Anthony, who is sometimes referred to as St. Anthony Messenger.

[19] *Die Beschwerung, damit päpstliche Heiligkeit das Heilige Römische Reich und gemeine teutsche Nation beschweren* (n.p., n.d.), A2^v, Köhler 1776/4574. Cf. the very similar complaints made against the *Stationierer* and a like order, the *Terminierer*, in the *Gravamina* from the First Diet of Nuremberg, 1522–23; *Deutscher Nation beschwerd von den Geistlichen* [Strassburg: Johann Schott, 1523], Köhler 983/2488, Aiii^v.

[20] *Die deutsche Vigile der gottlosen Papisten, Münch und Pfaffen* [Lübeck: Johan Balhorn, 1526 or 1527?], in *Flugschriften aus den ersten Jahren der Reformation*, ed. Otto Clemen (Leipzig: von Rudolf Haupt, 1907–11), 3:141–43.

Ein Dialogus oder gespräch zwischē
einem Prior) Leyēbruder vō Bettler ōz wort gōttes belanget

Gemacht durch Baltasar
Stanberger zū Weimar in dem Fürstlichē
schloß/ dem armen leyen zū trost.

:Leyenbrū. Prior : Bettler.

COVER OF BALTHASAR STANBERGER'S *DIALOGUE BETWEEN A PRIOR,
A LAY BROTHER, AND A BEGGAR* (1522).

Mary, nor Peter, nor Paul, nor Francis, nor Dominic, nor in any other saint, but only in Jesus Christ."[21]

While the begging orders took the brunt of this sort of criticism, other regular clergy also faced attack, not simply for their ignorance and error, but also for their self-interested misuse of the saints. Diepold Peringer provides an effective metaphor, designed specifically to appeal to the peasants: "These idols [that is, the saints] are nothing other than decoy birds of the shorn bands [that is, the monks].... I cannot even say this in better German (for I am a peasant) than decoy birds.... From these decoy birds they have given their whores feasts and nice clothing."[22] In another pamphlet published in the same year, Peringer rages against the out and out fraud often perpetrated by the monks: "For a long time we have clung to the saints and pushed God under our feet; it is pitiful that we were so blind and have not sought consolation where we should have. But our priests and monks have led us astray and have tricked us with fraudulent figures. In one they poured oil in the back of the head so that it poured out from the eyes; in another one, blood, so that it sweat blood, and so forth. About this they say: 'Look, isn't that a great miracle!' Thus the poor, wretched peasants have been taken in and have invoked the saints and abandoned God."[23]

Probably the most notorious fraud of the period—the infamous Bern incident of 1509—involved the mendicants, specifically the Franciscans and the Dominicans. The episode grew out of a dispute between the two orders over the Immaculate Conception of the Virgin Mary. The Franciscans urged adoption of the doctrine as part of the official teaching of the church, while the Dominicans opposed this. In a pamphlet attributed to Johann Eberlin, an artisan explains the story to a Dominican, a priest, and a peasant:

> A good, poor journeyman tailor, named Hans Jetzer, came to Bern and asked to be taken into the Order [of Preachers, i.e., the Dominican Order], and they agreed. As the [members of the Order] noticed Hans's simplemindedness, they thought he would make a good Franciscan.[24] They decided to have a ghost appear to him in the night, hoping to get rid of him. When the good brother failed to catch on, one of the broth-

---

[21]Johannes Lonicer, *Berichtbüchlin* (n.p., n.d.), Aiiii^v, Köhler 225/631.

[22]Diepold Peringer, *Ein Sermon von der Abgötterei durch den Bauern, der weder schreiben noch lesen kann, gepredigt* [Nuremberg: Hans Hergot, 1524], Aiii^v, Köhler 1493/3922.

[23][Diepold Peringer], *Ein Sermon, gepredigt vom Bauern zu Wöhrd bei Nürnberg von dem freien willen des Menschen, auch von Anrufung der Heiligen* [Augsburg: Silvan Otmar, 1524], iii, Köhler 375/1045.

[24]This is a rather sardonic reference to the rivalry between the Dominicans and the Franciscans. The point seems to be that upon recognizing Jetzer's simplemindedness, the Dominicans wished him upon the Franciscans.

ers put on women's clothing and appeared to him saying that "she" was the Virgin Mary, and that he should make a public announcement that she was born in original sin and that it hurt her very much when people said otherwise. The good brother was still taken in and told his superiors about the message. Soon the announcement was made to the people. Then they [the Dominicans] thought they had won the first game, and as they continued to see the simplemindedness of their brother, they decided to make a Francis out of him. They gave him a drink that put him into such a deep sleep that he was aware of nothing. One of them had prepared some etching acid *[Ätzwasser]* and etched five wounds into his hands, feet, and side. Then they woke him up and told the poor drip *[den armen Tropfen]* that Christ had imprinted him with wounds, as he had St. Francis.[25]

Ultimately, the fraud was exposed, the four perpetrators executed by fire as heretics, and "the poor drip" immured.[26]

Upon hearing this story, Eberlin's peasant responds to the artisan-narrator: "God help us! That is a wild tale! ... *I will no longer have much respect for the saints.* You have just told me two stories, about Grimmental[27] and about the tailor from Bern. I suspect the Barefoot monks have also done as much with their Francis."[28]

One important objection to the saints, therefore, quite plainly revolved around the manner in which the monks had misused and abused them, largely for gain. A further objection, which likewise involved the relationship of the orders to the saints, is equally apparent in pamphlet literature: the cult of the saints, in David Bagchi's apt words, "had multiplied the objects of Christian worship and charity beyond necessity."[29] This particular criticism seems most common in Lutheran literature, but it also appears in Swiss works. For instance, in the *Schlußreden*, Zwingli writes:

---

[25] *Ein Gespräch zwischen vier Personen, wie sie ein Gezänk haben von der Wallfahrt im Grimmental, was für Unrat oder Büberei daraus entstanden sei* (Erfurt: Wolfgang Stürmers, 1523 or 1524), in *Die Wahrheit muss ans Licht! Dialoge aus der Zeit der Reformation*, ed. Rudolf Bentzinger (Frankfurt a/M: Röderberg, 1983), 274.

[26] *Ein Gespräch*, in *Die Wahrheit*, ed. Bentzinger, 275. For other references to the Bern incident, see [Eberlin], *Ein klägliche Klag*, Niiii^v; Hans Ulem, *Merkt ihr Laien, habt euch in Hut, secht der Geistlichen Übermut* (n.p., n.d.), Aiii^{r–v}, Köhler 843/2117; *Im Land zu Meißen bei Freiburg im Jahr 1522 ist ein solch Wundergeburt von einer Kuh kommen* [Augsburg: Melchior Ramminger, 1523], Aiii^v, Köhler 7/30.

[27] The claim was that the statue of the Virgin Mary at Grimmental was weeping because people were no longer flocking there on pilgrimages. The artisan discloses that the weeping came from water being poured into the head and holes made in the eyes with needles to make beads of water, looking like tears, drip from the eyes of the statue; *Ein Gespräch zwischen vier Personen*, 271–72.

[28] *Ein Gespräch zwischen vier Personen*, 275–76; emphasis added.

[29] This is an obvious reference to Luther's nominalist (Occamist) roots; Bragchi, *Luther's Earliest Opponents*, 157. Schilling argues similarly that Luther claimed, "Christ is divided up by the orders," and

"After [Christ] alone we are to carry the cross without hesitation and not after Dominic, Benedict, Francis, Anthony or Bernard.... Should Francis or Dominic or any of the others be among us today they would undoubtedly say, 'O you fools. What are you doing? Do you not know that you are not to have any other teacher, father and leader but God alone. Why do you attach yourselves to us who all our lives adhered to God only?'"[30]

One of the most thorough discussions of the divisive nature of the orders' allegiance to the various saints is Andreas Karlstadt's *Instruction on Vows.*[31] In fact, at least one-third of this relatively long (sixty-three-page) pamphlet is devoted to the subject, with Karlstadt consistently stressing the following theme: "Monks and nuns bind themselves not only to God but to saints, with oaths or vows, and thus have erring and divided hearts."[32] Similar, if less extensive, commentaries poured from the pens of numerous other writers, lay and clerical alike. The Strasbourg knight Matthias Wurm, for instance, chastises the monastics for making vows not only to God, but to St. Dominic, St. Francis, St. Bernard, St. Clare, St. Nicholas, and so forth,[33] while Johann Eberlin criticizes his former order by charging that the Franciscans often honored St. Francis more than they did Christ.[34] Nikolaus Kattelsburger cautions that the Lord warns his children that if their sects or orders "are not planted in God's word, but rather one in [the rule of] St. Francis, another in that of Dominic, a third in that of Bernard, then their kingdom is not grounded in Christ."[35] Other writers simply warn monastics to follow Christ's rule rather than

---

that neither Francis nor Dominic, nor any other saint was crucified for us, nor are we baptized in their names; Schilling, *Klöster und Mönche*, 155. Cf. Nikolaus Grebel and Johann Schweblin, *Ein Sermon auf Misericordia Domini zu(o) Pfortzhaim im Spital* ([Augsburg: Melchior Raminger], 1524), in *Städtische Predigt in der Frühzeit der Reformation: Eine Untersuchung deutscher Flugschriften der Jahre 1522 bis 1529*, ed. Bernd Moeller and Karl Stackman (Göttingen: Vandenhoeck & Ruprecht, 1996), 81; *Ein Sendbrief von einer ehrbaren Frau im ehelichen Stand an ein Klosterfrauen* [Augsburg: Heinrich Steiner, 1524], D, Köhler 170/466. See also 1 Cor. 1:13: "Is Christ divided? was Paul crucified for you? or were ye baptized in the name of Paul?"

[30] Zwingli, "Twenty-Seventh Article," *Writings*, ed. Furcha, 1:208; *Der siben und zwentzgist Artickel*, in idem, *Sämtliche Werke*, 2:256.

[31] Andreas Karlstadt, *Von Gelübden Unterrichtung* (Wittenberg: [Nickel Schirlentz], 1521), Köhler 134/362.

[32] Karlstadt, *Von Gelübden Unterrichtung*, Cii.

[33] Matthias Wurm, *Trost Klostergefangner* (n.p., n.d.), Ciiii^v–Di, Köhler 154–55/424.

[34] [Eberlin], *Ein klägliche Klag*, Niiii. See similar charges in Balthasar Stanberger, *Ein Dialogus oder Gespräch zwischen einem Prior, Laienbruder und Bettler, das Wort Gottes belangend* (n.p., n.d.), Fi, Köhler 1003/2546; Heinrich Spelt, *Ein wahre Deklaration oder Erklärung der Profession, Gelübden und Leben, so die falschen Geistlichen tun* ([Augsburg: Heinrich Steiner], 1523), B^v–Bii, Köhler 47/131.

[35] Kattelsburger, *Ein Missive*, Aiiii^v.

St. Francis's,[36] or to leave the order, for they were not baptized in the name of Peter or Paul, but in Christ's name.[37]

Furthermore, members of the regular clergy were said not only to have encouraged "divided hearts" through their allegiances to the founders of their orders, but they were also accused of having "multiplied the objects of Christian worship and charity beyond necessity" by creating "new saints daily."[38] In a well-known dialogue, for instance, Franz von Sickingen explains to *Karsthans* (the archetypal German peasant): "First and foremost, the monks want their order to have the most saints." He then goes on to describe how, in his view, the orders were able to create new saints so easily: "When [the monks] have put some old brother in the grave, about whom they can make some claims, they write to the pope, saying [the dead monk] has given a sign. Then the pope exacts his fee for the bull, and when he receives [his money], he makes him a saint."[39]

Finally, because of their devotion to the saints, the regular clergy were frequently chastised for behavior and belief contrary to scriptural injunction. Luther, for example, wrote in a discussion of Mariolatry (1528–29) that "the pope with his monks…lets Christ, the Son, go and clings to the mother."[40] Eberlin, for instance, levels this charge:

> Francis's rule is not the Gospel.
> The rule is contrary to the Gospel.
> It is contrary to all reason.
> It is nothing other than foolishness.
> Francis is either a fool or a knave.[41]

Eberlin's views are particularly interesting not only because of the virulence with which he indicts his former order, but also because of his revealing remarks about the female Franciscans, the Poor Clares. Regarding the nuns, Eberlin warns: "Oh, Francis, how blind you are; do you not know what this poverty will lead to? In time, they will have to become whores."[42] In addition, Eberlin points out one of

---

[36] *Der Barfüßer zu Magdeburg Grund ihres Ordens* (Magdeburg: [Heinrich Öttinger], 1526), Ciii (gloss), Köhler 433–34/1174.

[37] Staygmayer, *Ein schöner Dialogus*, Biᵛ.

[38] *Gesprächbüchlin neu Karsthans* (n.p., n.d.), Eiii, Köhler 172/475.

[39] *Gesprächbüchlin neu Karsthans*, Eiiiʳ⁻ᵛ. The Augsburg weaver Utz Rychsner similarly criticizes the elevation of so many saints, in his *Eine schöne Unterweisung, daß wir in Christo alle Brüder und Schwestern sind* ([Augsburg: Heinrich Steiner], 1524), in *Flugschriften der frühen Reformationsbewegung (1518–1524)*, ed. Adolf Laube (Vaduz, Liechtenstein: Topos, 1983), 1:427.

[40] WA 28:403, Plass 4009/1257.

[41] [Eberlin], *Wider die falsch scheinende[n] Geistlichen*, Bii.

[42] [Eberlin], *Wider die falsch scheinende[n] Geistlichen*, Fiᵛ.

the many ways in which St. Francis's rule, as followed by the sisters, violated Scripture: About the fact "that Francis requires women to sing and read in church, Paul gives this answer: 1 Cor. 14[:34–35]; 1 Tim. 2[:11–12]."[43] Thus, Eberlin furnishes a glimpse at one of the scriptural arguments which served to sustain the narrowing of sanctioned feminine spiritual activity in early modern Germany. At the same time, moreover, he, like Luther, accuses the regular clergy—with their vow to follow a saint's *regula*, of unscriptural belief and unchristianlike piety.

SOLA SCRIPTURA

In any analysis of Reformation literature, the matter of *sola Scriptura*, the authority of Scripture alone, is of overwhelming significance. For this reason, choosing pamphlets and tracts which address the issue is a particularly daunting task. Virtually all reformers make reference to the scriptural basis of their arguments and conversely to the lack of scriptural sanction for—or the outright proscription of—the positions of those whom they oppose. Therefore, this examination has been limited to a sample of those works whose primary, rather than supporting, focus is the matter of biblical instruction, either about the invocation and veneration of the saints or the use of religious images. Several of the pamphlets selected are essentially annotated compendia of topically organized scriptural citations,[44] while others are traditional tracts, sermons, letters, dialogues, and poems which emphasize Scripture over any other point of debate. While the passages invoked as evidence vary widely, the scriptural arguments mustered by the reformers fall into three broad categories.

The first category, which deals specifically with the veneration of saints, can perhaps be summed up most concisely in a line written by the Nuremberg *Meistersinger*

---

[43] [Eberlin], *Wider die falsch scheinende[n] Geistlichen*, Fii. 1 Cor. 14:34–35 reads: "Let your women keep silence in the churches: for it is not permitted unto them to speak; but they are commanded to be under obedience, as also saith the law. And if they will learn any thing, let them ask their husbands at home: for it is a shame for women to speak in the church." 1 Tim. 2:11–12: "Let the woman learn in silence with all subjection. But I suffer not a woman to teach, nor to usurp authority over the man, but to be in silence."

[44] Examples include: [Jörg Berckenmeyer], *Ein Register der heiligen göttlichen Geschrift* (n.p., 1525), Köhler 1655/4269; Benedikt Gretzinger, *Hauptartikel und fürnemlich Punkten der göttlichen Geschrift* ([Wittenberg: Johann Rhau-Grunenberg], 1524), Köhler 1137/2901; Benedikt Gretzinger, *Hauptartikel und fürnehmste Stück unsers Christentums* [Wittenberg: Johann Rhau-Grunenberg, 1525], Köhler 1055–56/2665; Hätzer, *Ein Urteil Gottes*; Seybald Heyden, *Daß der einig Christus unser Mittler und Fürsprech sei bei dem Vater, nicht sein Mutter noch die Heiligen* [Leipzig: Michael Blum, 1526], Köhler 903/2261; Wilhelm, Graf von Isenburg, *Kurzer Bericht und Anzeige aus heiliger, göttlicher Geschrift, wie Gott in seinen Heiligen zu loben ist* (n.p.: Jakob Schmidt, 1526), Köhler 1557/4038; and Clemens Ziegler, *Ein kurz Register und Auszug der Bibel, in welchem man findet was Abgötterei sei* (n.p.,1524), Köhler 1566/4062.

Hans Sachs: "This is totally without foundation in Scripture."[45] In his lengthy encomium of Luther, Sachs charges the pope with having misled the faithful through his advocacy of unsanctioned piety:

> with sacrifices and burning lights,
> with pilgrimages and services to the saints,
> fasting in the evening, celebrating on the day,
> and confession in the old manner;
> with brotherhoods and rosaries,
> with letters of indulgence, church attendance,
> with kisses of peace, sacred spectacle,
> with endowing masses and building churches,
> with altar decorations of great splendor,
> panels in the Italian style,
> velvet chasuble, golden chalice,
> with monstrances and silver images
> in cloisters demanding taxes and fees:
> All of this the pope calls service to God,
> and says people merit heaven through these things
> and are released from their sins.
> This is totally without foundation in Scripture,
> vain fantasy and human trickery
> which God takes no pleasure in.[46]

Similar arguments condemning traditional practices—especially those associated with the cult of the saints—find expression throughout evangelical literature. While Sachs prefaces his denunciation with a long list of abuses, Nikolaus von Amsdorf, Luther's colleague on the Wittenberg theological faculty, argues more simply that "in all of Scripture there is not one letter, not one little stroke about the saints in heaven."[47] Similarly, Johann Eberlin warns against accepting those things which have "no clear expression in Scripture";[48] while Luther notes in his tract against the

---

[45] *"Ist doch als in der schryfft ungrünt"*; Hans Sachs, *Die Wittenbergische Nachtigall* [Bamberg: Georg Erlinger, 1523], in *Flugschriften*, ed. Laube, 1:595.

[46] Sachs, *Die Wittenbergische Nachtigall*, 594–95.

[47] Nikolaus Amsdorf, *Wider die Lügenprediger des hohen Doms zu Magdeburg* (Wittenburg: [Nickel Schirlentz], 1525), Aiii, Köhler 14/61.

[48] Johann Eberlin, *Ein freundlich[e] tröstliche Vermahnung an alle frommen Christen zu Augsburg* [Augsburg: Philipp Ulhart, 1522], Bᵛ, Köhler 233/652.

elevation of Bishop Benno of Meissen: "You cannot demonstrate through Scripture that we should invoke the saints or use them as mediators."[49]

The second type of scriptural attack on the Church of Rome's veneration of the saints involves various charges of misinterpretation. To underscore their conversion from the traditional interpretation—or misinterpretation—of saints as dead paragons, for example, reformers made use of numerous (primarily New Testament) references to saints as living, breathing, believing human beings.[50] Similarly, to support the break with Rome, evangelicals attacked the traditional papal claim to primacy through apostolic succession. In his pamphlet addressed to the Christian nobility, for instance, Luther lashes out at considerable length at the popes' position on this issue. He rejects, for example, the assertion that popes could claim sole authority in the church because of the incident described in Matt. 16:18–19, in which Christ delivers the keys of heaven to St. Peter, who was interpreted traditionally as the first pope.[51] Luther writes: "It is clear enough that the keys were not given to St. Peter alone, but rather to the whole community. Therefore, the keys are not for the purpose of regulating binding and loosing because of teaching or rules, but only because of sin, and it is a vain thing when they write otherwise about the keys."[52]

---

[49]Luther, *Wider den neuen Abgott und alten Teufel der zu Meißen soll erhoben werden*, WA 15(1):197. The following is a list—by no means exhaustive—of works which argue against the veneration and invocation of saints in the same manner: Martin Bucer, *An ein christlichen Rat und Gemein der Stadt Weißenberg: Summari seiner Predigt daselbst getan* [Straßburg: Johann Schott, 1523], Diiii, Köhler 1114–15/2846; Sebastian Goldschmidt, *Ein Unterweisung etlicher Artikel so Bruder Mattheiß öffentlich gepredigt hat* [Worms: Peter Schöffer, 1525], B, Köhler 1476/3879; Heyden, *Daß der einig Christus*, Bv; Michael Sattler, *Brüderlich Vereinigung etzlichen Kinder Gottes sieben Artikel betreffend. Item ein Sendbrief Michael Sattlers an eine Gemeine Gottes samt seinem Martyrium* (n.p., 1527), in *Flugschriften*, ed. Clemen, 2:328; *Ein Sendbrief von einem jungen Studenten zu Wittenberg an seine Eltern in Schwabenland von wegen der Lutherischen Lehre zugeschrieben* (Augsburg: Melchior Ramminger, 1523), in *Flugschriften*, ed. Clemen, 1:14–15; Jörg Vögeli, *Schirmred eines laiischen Bürgers zu Konstanz wider den Pfarrer von Überlingen* (n.p., n.d.), C4ᵛ, Köhler 1556/4035; Eberhard Weidensee and Johannes Fritzhans, *Wie Doctor Cubito, Bonifacius und der Sonntagsprediger im Dom zu Magdeburg Gottes Wort schänden. Dialogus* (n.p., 1526), Ciiᵛ, Köhler 831/1081; Wilhelm, Graf von Isenburg, *Kurzer Bericht*, Biii; Matthias Wurm, *Christenlich kurz Vermahnung zum andern Mal an Jakob Kornkauf, von Fasten, Feiertagen, Beichten* (Straßburg: Johannes Schwan, 1524), Biiiᵛ, Köhler 797/2006; Ulrich Zeuleys, *Daß die Heiligen für Gott nicht anzurufen, ein kurzer Unterricht* (n.p., 1524), Aiiᵛ, Köhler 569/1459.

[50]Such references include: Ps. 30:4, 31:23, 149:1; Rom. 1:7, 12:13, 15:25, 16:2; 1 Cor. 1:2, 6:2; Eph. 2:19; Col. 1:12; 1 Tim. 5:10; Heb. 6:10, 13:24; Jude 1:3; and Rev. 5:8, 13:7, 14:12, 16:6.

[51]"And I say also unto thee, That thou art Peter, and upon this rock I will build my church; and the gates of hell shall not prevail against it. And I will give unto thee the keys of the kingdom of heaven: and whatsoever thou shalt bind on earth shall be bound in heaven: and whatsoever thou shalt loose on earth shall be loosed in heaven."

[52]Luther, *An den christlichen Adel deutscher Nation von des christlichen Standes Besserung*, in *Flugschriften*, ed. Laube, 2:638. Luther refers to Matt. 18:18, in which Christ says to all the disciples, "Verily I say unto you, 'Whatsoever ye shall bind on earth shall be bound in heaven: and whatsoever ye shall loose on earth shall be loosed in heaven,'" WA 6:411–12.

Von einem Schu

macher: vnd Chorherzen: ein vast
kurtzweilig Chrässliche disputation / von der Euan-
gelischen Wittenbergischen Nachtgallen.
M.d.rriiij.   Hans sachs.

Bapst
So dy Nachtgal
auß der schrifft
thut syngen
Mag ich sy doch
wol mit gewalt
vertringen.

COVER OF HANS SACHS'S *DISPUTATION BETWEEN A SHOEMAKER AND A CANON* (1524).
CAPTION READS: "SO THAT THE NIGHTINGALE STILL SINGS FROM SCRIPTURE
I WILL DRIVE YOU OUT WITH FORCE."

Some reformers turned to the metaphor of the rock to undermine what they saw as the popes' co-optation of St. Peter, in their endeavor to shore up their own autonomy. Sebald Heyden is one pamphleteer who brilliantly employs scriptural references to the rock to register his contempt for the popes' claim—although he never actually refers directly to the bishops of Rome. In his pamphlet dealing with Christ as intercessor, Heyden early on makes reference to Eph. 2:20, in which *all* of the apostles are deemed the "foundation," while Christ is proclaimed the "chief cornerstone" of the church. Subsequently, Heyden cites Matt. 16:18 ("Thou art Peter, and upon this rock I will build my church"), the passage upon which popes based much of their claim to primacy. Immediately, however, Heyden counters with, "For it [the church] is built upon a mighty rock," and "the rock is Christ[:] 1 Cor. 10[:4]."[53] In much the same manner, Diepold Peringer, in his pamphlet criticizing the invocation of saints, makes use of a number of biblical passages which refer to God or Christ as "the rock," and he, like Heyden, never explicitly refers to the popes.[54] Perhaps the best example of the argument of misinterpretation has to do with the meaning of Ps. 150. The traditional translation of the first verse of the Psalm is *"Lobet Gott in seinen Heiligen"* ("Praise God in his saints"), a verse used by many orthodox to legitimate invocation of the saints.[55] Reformers' attempts to discredit this passage are prolific, and they include both simple charges of misinterpretation and scholarly arguments about mistranslation. Andreas Karlstadt, for example, claims that the passage had been wholly misunderstood; God works *through* the saints: the saints can do nothing on their own.[56] Kaspar Güttel makes a comparable claim, writing: "The saints are like lanterns that light no one, for the light inside is God himself or his Holy Word."[57] The Nuremberg artist Hans Greifenberger calls attention to the miracles attributed to the saints, but reminds his readers that one should "praise God in his saints" by thanking him for those miracles which were worked by God through the saints. Anything else, he says, is "idolatry."[58]

---

[53] Heyden, *Daß der einig Christus*, Avi^v–Avii.

[54] [Peringer], *Ein Sermon*, iiii^v–v. Peringer cites 2 Sam. 22:2, Ps. 18:2, and Acts 4:11. Other passages cited in this context—although no writer in the sample directly points to the pope—include: Ps. 62:2, 118:22; Is. 51:1; Matt. 21:42; Acts 4:11; 1 Cor. 3:11, 10:4; and Eph. 2:20.

[55] See, for example, Jodocus Clichtoveus, *De veneratione sanctorum libri duo* (Köln: Peter Quentel, 1525), C2, Köhler 209–10/594; Johannes Dietenberger, *Fragstück[e] an alle Christgläubigen* (Köln: [Peter Quentel], 1530), bbii^v, Köhler 802/2016.

[56] Karlstadt, *Von Gelübden*, Aiiii.

[57] Kaspar Güttel, *Von apostolischen Amt und Eigenschaft der Bischof, Pfarrer und Prädikanten* ([Erfurt: Wolfgang Stürmer], 1523), Bi^v, Köhler 270/769. For much the same argument, see *In rechter gründlicher, brüderlicher und christenlicher Liebe Gott recht zu erkennen* [Augsburg: Melchior Ramminger, 1520?], Aiii^r–v, Köhler 215/609; and Brenz, *Ein Sermon von den Heiligen*, Aiii^v.

[58] Hans Greifenberger, *Dies Büchlin zeigt an die falschen Propheten* [Augsburg: Philipp Ulhart, 1523?], Bii, Köhler 255/715.

Other reformers charge different sorts of misinterpretation of the passage. The Swiss author of *A New Disputation between Two Journeymen*, for instance, writes that believers should "praise God in his saints" by praising God for providing such excellent exemplars.[59] Franz von Sickingen, Kaspar Güttel, and the anonymous author of *A Sermon on Worship* point out that one should interpret the passage as an exhortation to believers to praise God for the mercy and grace he has given to the saints, who were, after all, fellow human beings.[60] Unlike most reformers who emphasized misinterpretation of the words *"in seinen Heiligen,"* Diepold Peringer objects to the interpretation of the word *saints* itself, saying that David was not writing about dead saints, but, instead, about the living; furthermore, believers should praise God "through all living creatures."[61] Hans Greifenberger, on the other hand, says simply that the passage itself was a "mistake," one that had misled everyone so that "we use rosaries and psalters, and pray to the saints so many times, and so many times the Our Father; and on this or that day, we stay home; on this or that day, we make pilgrimages; all of this is false, against the Gospel and against the teaching of our Master Christ...."[62]

Scholarly charges of misinterpretation focused on what was said to be a faulty translation of the first verse of Ps. 150. Wilhelm, Graf von Isenburg, for instance, argues that if one reads the "right Hebrew text," one will discover that David never said anything about saints.[63] Johannes Lonicer notes that "according to the Hebrew, the sense of this passage, as David spoke, is 'praise God in his sanctity [*Heiligkeit*].'"[64] More commonly, reformers insisted that the more accurate translation of the passage substituted the word *Heiligtum* (sanctuary) for the traditional *Heiligen* (saints). Benedikt Gretzinger, city clerk of Reutlingen, writes: "Previously, because of misinterpretation, the word *Heiligtum* was translated *Heiligen*."[65]

---

[59] *Ein neues Gespräch von zweien Gesellen, wie sie vom heiligen Wort Gottes geredt haben* ([Augsburg: Heinrich Steiner], 1524), Aiii, Köhler 627/1628. Similar points are made by the author of *In rechter gründlicher, brüderlicher Liebe Gott*, Aiii[v] and by Wilhelm, Graf von Isenburg, *Kurzer Bericht*, Aiii.

[60] Franz von Sickingen, *Ein Sendbrief zu Unterrichtung etlicher Artikel christlichen Glaubens* (Wittenberg: [Johann Rhau-Grunenberg], 1522), Bi[v], Köhler 215/606; Kaspar Güttel, *Dialogus oder Gesprächbüchlein von einem rechtgeschaffen Christenmenschen* (n.p., 1522), Si[v], Köhler 71–72/189; *Ein Sermon von der Anbetung, gepredigt von einem Karmelit* ([Augsburg: Melchior Ramminger], 1522), Aiii[v], Köhler 270/763.

[61] Peringer, *Ein Sermon von der Abgötterei*, Cii[v]–Ciii. Wilhelm, Graf von Isenburg, makes a similar point in *Kurzer Bericht*, Aiii.

[62] [Hans Greifenberger], *Dies Büchel zeigt an, wie wir also weit geführt sind von der Lehre unsers Meisters Christo* ([München: Hans Schobser], 1523), Aiii[v], Köhler 1079/2736.

[63] Wilhelm, Graf von Isenburg, *Kurzer Bericht*, Aii[v]–Aiii.

[64] Lonicer, *Berichtbüchlin*, Iiiii[v].

[65] Gretzinger, *Hauptartikel und fürnehmste Stück*, Gv. Johannes Brenz makes a similar point in *Ein Sermon von den Heiligen*, Aiii[r–v]. Luther's translation of the verse reads: *"Lobet den herrn ynn seynem heyligthum";*

The final type of scriptural attack on the cult of the saints and its trappings virtually clogs evangelical literature. This mode of debate features the quotation of passages from nearly every book in the Old and New Testaments, as well as from some apocryphal books, that the reformer-authors interpret as prohibitions of the invocation of saints and/or the veneration of their images. Despite the wide variety of passages used for this purpose, however, the starting point of such instruction is invariably the same: whether implicitly or explicitly cited, Exod. 20:3–5, or less frequently, Deut. 5:6–9, provides justification for innumerable assaults on the saints and/or on images. These particular passages, portions of the Decalogue, include the pertinent admonitions: "Thou shalt have no other gods before me," and "Thou shalt not make unto thee any graven images."[66]

One example of a preacher who adopted what became a classic pattern of argument is Martin Bucer in his sermon supporting iconoclasm in Strasbourg, entitled *That Images Will No Longer Be Tolerated by the God-Fearing.*[67] Bucer begins by quoting Exod. 20:3–5, identifying these passages as "the first two commandments." He goes on, however, to focus primarily on Exod. 20:4, the proscription of images, noting that while some biblical laws no longer apply to Christians—he lists circumcision and dietary restrictions, among others—the commandment concerning images is still valid: "Thus we are not free from the prohibition of images, as long as they are being exhibited; and no right-believing Christian will deny that images have been venerated or are now in danger of being venerated and that in true faith and love of God they should be destroyed."[68] Andreas Karlstadt makes much the same argument, deeming the faulty notion that Christians need not obey the law forbidding images "heretical."[69]

Both Karlstadt and Ludwig Hätzer point to Is. 44:6–20 as ample documentation in support of their condemnation of both idols and makers of idols.[70] Indeed, the biblical ban on images allowed reformers enormous latitude in their use of Scripture

---

Martin Luther, *Die Deutsche Bibel, D. Martin Luthers Werke: Kritische Gesamtausgabe* (Weimar: H. Böhlau, 1906), 1:563.

[66] It is interesting to note that while most Protestant groups ultimately came to consider these passages the First and Second Commandments respectively, Luther retained the Roman Catholic numbering of the commandments, with the prohibition of images as part of the First Commandment and the prohibition of coveting, Exod. 20:17, broken into two commandments. On this subject, see, for instance, Jaroslav Pelikan, *The Reformation of the Bible: The Bible of the Reformation* (New Haven: Yale University Press, 1996), 51.

[67] Martin Bucer, *Daß einigerlei Bild bei den Gottgläubigen an Orten, da sie verehrt, nit mögen geduldet werden* [Straßburg: Johann Knobloch, 1530], Köhler 1439/3824.

[68] Bucer, *Daß einigerlei Bild*, Aii^{r–v}.

[69] Karlstadt, *Von Abtuhung der Bilder*, Di^{v}.

[70] Karlstadt, *Von Abtuhung der Bilder*, Biii^{v}; Hätzer, *Ein Urteil Gottes*, Aiiii^{v}–Bi^{v}.

to support their position. Nearly every condemnation of pagan idolatry was enlisted in the effort to discredit the use of saints' images, as saints were equated to "other gods," "false gods," "strange gods," "false prophets," "idols," and the like.[71]

The Commandment "Thou shalt have no other gods before me" provided even broader range for interpretation. Once again, construing the saints as "other gods," the reformers mined chapters and verses which emphasized the majesty and the uniqueness of the Judeo-Christian God.[72] Zwingli, for instance, includes Ps. 96:5— "For all the gods of the nations are idols: but the Lord made the heavens"—in his

---

[71]Passages cited by writers examined for this study include:

Gen. 31:33–35

Exod. 20:22–23, 32:4–6, 34:13–17

Lev. 26:1

Num. 23:5–7, 25:1–4

Deut. 4:23–28, 7:5–6, 11:16–17, 12:1–13, 13:1–5, 27:15, 29:17–20, 32:16–19

Josh. 24:19–20

Judg. 10:15–16

1 Sam. 7:3

1 Kings 12:28, 18:21–22

2 Kings 11:17–18, 17:37–39, 18:4, 23:4, 14–15

2 Chron. 33:15

Ps. 97:7, 106:36, 115:1–11

Isa. 19:1–2, 37:38, 40:18–19, 42:8, 17, 43:11–12, 44:9–20, 45:16, 65:3–4, 66:3

Jer. 2:11–13, 28, 8:19, 9:13–15, 10:3–5, 14–15, 13:9–10, 23:13, 27, 51:47

Ezek. 6:3–7, 14:2–8, 18:5–9, 22:4, 44:12–13

Dan. 3:1, 5:22–23

Hos. 9:10, 13:4

Mic. 1:7

Hab. 2:18–19

Mal. 2:11

Matt. 6:24, 15:7–9, 24:24

John 1:18

Acts 13: 44–46, 14:11–15, 15:20, 17:21–23, 21:25

Rom. 1:21–25, 16:17–18

1 Cor. 5:11, 6:9, 8:4, 10:6–7, 12:2

2 Cor. 6:16

Gal. 5:19–21

Phil. 3:2

1 Thess. 1:9

2 Thess. 2:2–4, 8–10

1 Tim. 1:4, 4:1–2

Titus 3:10

1 Pet. 4:3

1 John 5:21.

[72]These include:

Gen. 15:1

Exod. 15:2

Lev. 20:8

Num. 16:5–7, 35:34

Deut. 6:5

2 Sam. 10:19

2 Chron. 6:19–20, 16:7–9, 20:20

Ps. 2:6–8, 4:4, 8, 7:1–2, 9:13–14, 11:4, 15:1–2, 22:3–6, 33:4, 35:3, 36:6, 40:4, 44:1, 46:1–3, 50:15, 60:10–12, 61:7–8, 63:1–4, 65:2, 66:1, 68:5, 72:18, 73:28, 76:8–9, 84:5, 86:1–5, 9–12, 96:5, 101:1, 103:8. 107:6, 118:5–9, 119:1, 120:1, 144:1–2, 14–15, 145:18–20

Prov. 30:5–6

Isa. 1:13–14, 6:3, 9:6, 12:2, 16:5, 29:13–14, 41:10, 43:7, 44:1,

6, 22, 46:9, 48:12, 49:15, 26, 52:6, 55:1, 5, 8, 57:15, 58:13–14, 63:16, 64:5, 8, 66:1, 23

Jer. 9:24, 17:5, 7, 23:1–2, 24:7, 29:12, 33:8

Ezek. 33:18–19, 34:6–7, 36:22–23, 39:7

Hos. 2:19–20, 7:13, 11:3, 13:4

Joel 2:12

Mal. 3:2, 4:6

Matt. 1:21, 3:16–17, 4:10, 6:6–7, 9, 7:19–23, 9:2, 10:8–9, 11:11, 28, 12:46–50, 13:15, 14:28–31, 17:1–2, 5, 18:10, 19–20. 19:17, 20:20–23, 21:22, 22:37, 23:9, 24:14, 25:40, 28:19–20

Mark 6:7–8, 10:18, 12:32–33, 16:20

Luke 5:24, 9:23–24, 10:22, 11:9, 18:19

John 1:6–8, 3:13, 16, 4:21–24, 6:51, 10:1–2, 14:26, 15:4, 5, 16:13–14, 20:26–27, 29

Acts 3:12–13, 12:21–23, 15:7–9, 26:18

Rom. 2:10–11, 3:23–26, 5:6, 15, 17, 19–21, 8:3–4, 12:4–5, 15:16

1 Cor. 1:13, 30–31, 2:9, 11–12, 3:16–17, 7:14, 12:6, 13

2 Cor. 1:3–5, 10:17–18

Gal. 3:28

Eph. 4:4–6

Phil. 2:11, 3:17

Col. 3:11–13

1 Thess. 2:13, 14, 4:3–4

1 Tim. 1:12–13, 15–17, 4:10

continued

list of "places in Scripture.... In which one clearly sees the heathens elevating idols and not God."[73] Benedikt Gretzinger writes: "That one should trust only in God, call only on him, and find refuge only in him is demonstrated clearly by the Master of Truth and the sole Doctor of Holy Scripture, the Holy Ghost."[74] Similarly, Philipp Melhofer, who refers to Jer. 29—"Then shall ye call upon me"—writes, "Our only helper, protector, and savior is God"; thus, we should call only upon him.[75] Several other reformers cite Jer. 17:5—"Cursed be the man that trusteth in man"— arguing, as does Ulrich Zeuleys, that those who call upon others "make idols out of the saints who were, indeed, men like us."[76] The similar sentiment expressed in Ps. 118:8–9—"It is better to trust in the Lord than to put confidence in man... [or] in princes"—was used in much the same way, with reformers implicitly classifying saints with all other humans, thus, unworthy of trust.[77]

When reformers turned to the New Testament, they often looked to anecdotes for object lessons about the impropriety of human arrogance. A favorite incident is the story of Herod in Acts 12, which features the king addressing his people who proclaimed, in awe, that he had spoken in "the voice of a god, and not of a man." Because Herod subsequently failed to give "God the glory," he was "eaten of worms, and gave up the ghost."[78] Similar, if less dire, lessons came from incidents described in Acts 10 and Rev. 22. In the former text, the Apostle Peter was met by the devout centurion Cornelius, who "fell down at [Peter's] feet, and worshipped him." Peter, unlike Herod, responded by saying, "Stand up; I myself also am a man."[79] In the latter text, John "fell down to worship before the feet of the angel

---

| Heb. 2:9–11, 10:9–10 | 1 Pet. 1:18–21, 2:9 | Rev. 19:10. |
| James 1:17 | 1 John 4:9–10 | |

[73] Zwingli, *Ein Antwort, Valentino Compar gegeben*, Iii^v; idem, *Sämtliche Werke*, 4:112.

[74] Gretzinger, *Hauptartikel und fürnehmste Stück*, Fv^v.

[75] Philipp Melhofer, *Offenbarung der allerheimlischsten Heimlichkeit der jetzigen Baalspriester* [Augsburg: Philipp Ulhart, ca. 1529], Bvii, Köhler 1530–31/3982. The same passage is also cited by Wilhelm, Graf von Isenburg, who admonishes his readers to "call only on God"; *Kurzer Bericht*, Ciii. Other passages which use this language include Ps. 18:3, 50:15, 86:5, 145:18; Rom. 10:12–13; and 1 Cor. 1:2.

[76] Zeuleys, *Daß die Heiligen*, Aii^v; others who use the same passage in a similar manner include: Gretzinger, *Hauptartikel und fürnehmste Stück*, Gi^v; Heyden, *Daß der einig Christus*, Bvii^v; Wilhelm, Graf von Isenburg, *Kurzer Bericht*, Fi^v; Zwingli, *Ein Gegenwurf und Widerwehr*, Fi^v; idem, *Sämtliche Werke*, 3:270; idem, *Von wahrem und falschem Glauben*, 210^v; idem, *Sämtliche Werke*, 3:834.

[77] Gretzinger, *Hauptartikel und fürnehmste Stück*, Fviii^v; [Peringer], *Ein Sermon*, V^v.

[78] Acts 12:21–23. See Gretzinger, *Hauptartikel und fürnehmste Stück*, Fiiii; [Peringer], *Ein Sermon*, iiii; Wilhelm, Graf von Isenburg, *Kurzer Bericht*, Ci.

[79] Acts 10:25–26. See Gretzinger, *Hauptartikel und fürnehmste Stück*, Fiii; [Peringer], *Ein Sermon*, iii^v–iiii; Vögeli, *Schirmred*, H2; Wilhelm, Graf von Isenburg, *Kurzer Bericht*, Biiii^v.

which shewed [him] these things." The angel responded, "See thou do it not: for I am thy fellowservant." John was admonished instead to "worship God."[80]

While scriptural references to the mother of Jesus are few, biblical accounts of incidents involving the Virgin Mary provided ideal illustrations of the primacy of God and the lowliness of human beings, regardless of their exalted stature. A favorite example is the passage from Luke regarding the Annunciation. Having been told that she will conceive of the Holy Ghost and bear the Son of God, Mary humbly exclaims: "Behold the handmaid of the Lord; be it unto me according to thy word." Jakob Schenck von Stauffenberg points to this passage as evidence that Mary did not see herself as the Queen of Heaven, worthy of veneration, but rather as a humble, dutiful, unworthy mortal.[81] The implication, of course, is that she and other saints should be treated accordingly. Nuremberger Sebald Heyden, in his effort to discredit the *Salve Regina*, points to two additional scriptural passages which likewise underscore the Virgin's humble status. First he refers to a passage from Luke, in which a woman, echoing the *Ave Maria*, says to Christ: "Blessed is the womb that bare thee and the paps which thou hast sucked." Heyden notes that Christ rejects this praise of his mother, inferring from this that it is imperative not to make Mary into an idol.[82] Further, Heyden points to the curious passage from John in which Christ abruptly dismisses Mary when she expresses her concern that the wedding guests "have no wine." Heyden interprets this passage by saying, "So, indeed, Christ himself cautions us about the misguided veneration of his mother."[83] Perhaps even more interesting are the several verses from John in which Christ is quoted as saying essentially, "The Son can do nothing of himself, but what he seeth the Father do."[84] Reformers frequently used nearly the same language to diminish acts attributed to the saints; for example, Wilhelm, Graf von Isenburg, writes: "The saints have

---

[80]Rev. 22:8–9. See A.S., *Ein Epistel, meinen lieben Brüdern in Christo Jesu zugeschrieben* (n.p., 1523), Aii, Köhler 222/622; Gretzinger, *Hauptartikel und fürnemmste Stück*, Fii^v–Fiii; [Peringer], *Ein Sermon*, iii^v; Wilhelm, Graf von Isenburg, *Kurzer Bericht*, Biiii^v.

[81]Luke 1:38. See Jakob Schenck von Stauffenberg, *Sendbrief an seine Geschweihen* ([Speyer: Jakob Schmidt], 1524), Aii^v, Köhler 139/385. Sebald Heyden uses this passage to explain that the faithful must praise Mary appropriately, but not excessively; Heyden, *Daß der einig Christus*, Biii^v. Similar conclusions are drawn about John the Baptist through John 1:6–8 and Matt. 11:11.

[82]Luke 11:27–28. See Heyden, *Daß der einig Christus*, Bii^v.

[83]John 2:3–5. See Heyden, *Daß der einig Christus*, Bii^v. See also A.S., *Ein Epistel*, Aiii^v.

[84]John 5:19, cited by Heyden, *Daß der einig Christus*, Aviii^v; Zwingli, *Ein Antwort, Valentino Compar gegeben*, Ki^r–v; idem, *Sämtliche Werke*, 4:116. Other, similar passages include: John 7:16 and 8:16, cited by Zwingli, *Ein Antwort, Valentino Compar gegeben*, Ki^v and Ki^r, respectively (Zwingli, *Sämtliche Werke*, 4:177 and 4:118 respectively); John 8:28, cited by Schenck von Stauffenberg, *Sendbrief*, Aiii^r–v; John 12:49 and 15:1, cited by Heyden, *Daß der einig Christus*, Aviii and Bviii, respectively; and John 14:13, cited by Zeuleys, *Daß die Heiligen*, Aiii.

worked no miracles through their own power; therefore, they are undeserving of veneration or glory."[85]

The recurring charge that veneration of the saints encouraged works righteousness led numerous reformers to employ scriptural passages touting the efficacy of faith rather than works in their attacks on the cult.[86] It is particularly important to note the strikingly revised concept of intercessor promulgated by the Protestants in their treatment of this issue. First, it is critical to make clear the intimate association between intercessor and good works in the view of the reformers. A quotation from a sermon by Luther serves this purpose well:

> One says we forbid good works. That, we do not do; rather, we forbid only those hypocritical works. Proper good works, which are appropriate to a Christian, we certainly uphold and preach. Christ speaks about these in Matt. 25[:40]: "Inasmuch as ye have done it unto one of the least of these my brethren, ye have done it unto me." He does not say, "Did you become a monk, a nun, a priest; or did you go on a pilgrimage?" Rather, he says, "Did you reject your needy neighbor? In Matt. [5:42],[87] it is written, "Give to him that asketh thee." First [Matthew] says, "If any man will sue thee at the law, and take away thy coat, let him have thy cloke also [Matt. 5:40]"; second, he says, "One should lend"; third, "Give to him that asketh thee"; and if you do not do this, then you are no Christian. Thus, are you, first and foremost, responsible to defend your neighbor if you hear evil rumors being spread about him; 1 John 2:1: "And if any man sin, we have an advocate with the Father, Jesus Christ the righteous." Similarly, Rom. 1:34: "Who is he that condemneth? It is Christ that died, yea, rather, that is risen again, who is even at the right hand of God, who also maketh intercession for us."[88]

Thus, the evangelicals did not reject good works (except, of course, as the path to heaven); instead, they insisted that "good works depend only on Christ."[89] Significantly, neither did evangelicals reject the concept of intercessor; instead, they repudiated the pantheon of saints in this role, while at the same time embracing Jesus as sole intercessor. Of the numerous passages enlisted to denigrate the saints as

---

[85] Wilhelm, Graf von Isenburg, *Kurzer Bericht*, Biiii[v]. See also, Goldschmidt, *Ein Unterweisung*, Bii[r-v]; [Peringer], *Ein Sermon*, iii[v]; and numerous other examples.

[86] Examples of these include: Rom. 3:23–26, 5:1–2; Gal. 5:6; Eph. 3:16–19; 1 Tim. 4:1–2; Heb. 11:1.

[87] Luther cites Matt. 6:42.

[88] Luther, *Predigt zu Altenburg, Montag nach quasimodogeniti nachmittags.* 28 April 1522, WA 10(3):102.

[89] Luther, *Predigt zu Altenburg,* WA 10(3):101.

intercessors, the three most frequently cited include: John 14:6: "Jesus saith unto him, 'I am the way, the truth, and the life; no man cometh unto the Father, but by me'"; Rom. 8:34: "It is Christ that died, yea rather, that is risen again, who is even at the right hand of God, who also maketh intercession for us"; and 1 Tim. 2:5: "For there is one God, and one mediator between God and men, the man Christ Jesus." The remarkable number of times that one reads the pronouncement, "Christ is the only intercessor," suggests that the reformers recognized that many simple Christians,[90] who embraced much about the Protestant message, were nonetheless confronted with a profoundly difficult intellectual and emotional adjustment when it came to the matter of intercession.[91] Rejection of a pantheon of comforting fully human petitioners in favor of a single, intimidating, divine mediator was clearly no small shift. Indeed, it seems plausible to conclude that the ubiquitous references in early Reformation literature to Christ as mediator reflect the reformers' sensitivity to the magnitude and significance of this change in pious practice. In addition, such references provide insight into the methods Protestants used in their effort to pave a smooth, gradual, and persuasive transition for fledgling members of the evangelical flock—a transition from a medieval piety, which embraced a host of familiar, immanent mediators, to a simplified reformed worship of a thoroughly transcendent deity.

[90] Cf. Luther's concerns about the "weak" who struggled to abandon the saints, WA 10(2):166.
[91] See a list of these works in appendix 2.

ociety

AND

THE SAINTS

CHAPTER 3

THE SAINTS AS AGENTS OF SUPERSTITION AND DISORDER

Another method reformers used in attempts to wean their flocks from reliance on the cult of the saints was to link the veneration of the saints with superstitious belief and practice. Such a connection obviously did not originate with Protestant reformers. One need look no further than Erasmus, to find entreaties to the saints deemed a "sea of superstition."[1] Yet Protestant reformers found the superstition enveloping the saints enormously troubling not only in itself but also because of its close association with what some contemptuously labeled *Totenfresserei* or "feeding on the dead."

In early Reformation literature, condemnations of the people's relationship with the saints are common, but one sermon preached by Johannes Brenz is a model dissertation on the subject. In *A Sermon concerning the Saints*, Brenz outlines a variety of objections to the cult.[2] He focuses, however, upon its pagan origins, raging against the efficacies attributed to a long list of specific saints. Brenz instructs his parishioners: "The pagans had two kinds of gods. Some were venerated because they bestowed favors, some because they warded off evils, such as fever, pestilence, and so forth. We too venerate some saints because they bestow favors, such as Nicholas, and some because they turn away evil, such as Valentine and Sebastian." He concludes this portion of his analysis unequivocally, with a summary "O paganism."[3] Perhaps an even more shocking criticism of the saints is an anonymous pamphlet, constructed as a dialogue between a Christian and a Jew, in which the Jew

---

[1] Erasmus, *The Praise of Folly* in *The Essential Erasmus*, ed. John P. Dolan (New York: New American Library, 1983), 131. Erasmus condemns the superstition associated with the veneration of the saints in many of his other writings as well, most notably, in several of the *Colloquies*. On this subject, Eire writes: "The line between Christian principles and heathen magic was not clearly established in the popular mind, and the clergy who controlled the *cultus* offered little guidance on this point"; *War against the Idols*, 25.

[2] Brenz, *Ein Sermon*. For additional analysis of this sermon, see the preface of this book.

[3] Brenz, *Ein Sermon*, Aii[v].

compares the Christian saints to the gods and goddesses of the pagans, saying, it is "as if the only God were not powerful enough."[4]

References to the invocation of saints as *alter Glaube* (old religion)[5] or *Aberglaube* (superstition)[6] give way at times to a more scrupulously Christian construction: worship of the saints as satanic *(teuffelisch)*.[7] Nonetheless, the satanic and the pagan amounted essentially to the same order of false and dangerous belief.[8] Numerous writers single out pilgrimages—to Einsiedeln, Aachen, Regensburg, Grimmental, Altötting, and many other saints' shrines—as practices of grave concern to the Christian community.[9] "False," "unchristian," and "of the devil" are labels Martin Bucer, for one, likewise applies to the associated belief—clearly of pagan origins—that one site, such as a shrine, is somehow more blessed than any other piece of ground.[10]

In a sermon preached to the congregation of St. Gangolf's in Bamberg on All Saints' Day, 1 November 1523, *custos* Johannes Schwanhauser pursues a similar theme: "We foolish people pervert everything, want to serve the dead and to forget

[4] *Ein Gespräch auf das kürzest zwischen einem Christen und Juden, auch einem Wirte samt seinem Hausknecht, den Eckstein Christum betreffend* ([Erfurt: Michel Buchfürer], 1524), Aiiii^v, Köhler 621/1608.

[5] *Ein Gespräch auf das kürzest zwischen einem Christen und Juden,* Aiiii^v, Köhler 621/1608.

[6] See, for example, Martin Bucer, *Grund und Ursach aus göttlicher Schrift der Neuerungen zu Straßburg vorgenommen* ([Strassburg: Wolfgang Köpfel], 1525), Aii, Köhler 676–77/1770; Eberlin, *Sermon zu den Christen in Erfurt,* Aiiii^v; Heinrich von Kettenbach, *Ein Gespräch mit einem frommen Altmütterlein von Ulm* (Augsburg: Melchior Ramminger, 1523), in *Flugschriften,* ed. Clemen, 2:58; Wenzeslaus Linck, *Ein schöne christliche Sermon von dem Ausgang der Kinder Gottes aus des Antichrists Gefängnis* ([Nuremberg: Hans Hergot], 1524), Diii, Köhler 273/781; *Ein Sendbrief von einem jungen Studenten,* in *Flugschriften,* ed. Clemen, 1:9–18.

[7] See, for example, Amsdorf, *Wider die Lügenprediger,* Aiii; Cronberg, *Ein Christliche Schrift,* Aiii^v; Hausmann, *Unterricht und Warnung,* Bi^v; Thomas Stör, *Von dem christlichen Weingarten* ([Bamberg: Georg Erlinger, 1524]), in *Flugschriften,* ed. Laube, 1:373.

[8] Burke, *Popular Culture,* 209. In his *Answer to Valentin Compar,* Zwingli says as much: "All the gods of the pagans are devils"; *Ein Antwort, Valentino Compar gegeben,* Jii^v in Zwingli, *Sämtliche Werke,* 4:112. Similarly, words such as *spöttlich* (mocking), *kindisch* (childish), and *Affenspiel* (monkey play) put the cult of the saints into its proper place among Christians. See *Christliche Unterrichtung eins Pfarrherrn an seinen Herrn, ein Fürsten des heiligen Reichs, auf vierzig Artikel und Punkten gestellt* (n.p., 1526), Eii; Brenz, *Ein Sermon von den Heiligen,* Aii^v.

[9] Steven D. Sargent points out that, at least in Bavaria, the number of people making pilgrimages declined between 1520 and 1570. Despite this fact, there is no shortage of pejorative references to pilgrimage sites in the pamphlets considered for this study. See Sargent, "Miracle Books and Pilgrimage Shrines," 471. See also Lionel Rothkrug, "German Holiness and Western Sanctity in Medieval and Modern History," *Historical Reflections/Réflexions historiques* 15 (1988): 180 n. 71, 189 n. 99. John Bossy lends a different perspective in *Christianity in the West: 1400–1700* (Oxford: Oxford University Press, 1985; Oxford University Press Paperback, 1992). He writes concerning pilgrimages: "I see no reason to suppose that a practice which has thrived during the nineteenth and twentieth centuries was on its last legs in the fifteenth" (53).

[10] Martin Bucer, *An ein christlichen Rat,* Fiii. See also Melhofer, *Offenbarung,* Biii. On the pagan origins of the *locus sanctus,* see Stephen Wilson, "Introduction," in *Saints and Their Cults,* 39; Robert Hertz, "St. Besse: A Study of an Alpine Cult," in ibid., 55–100. On the special role of the *locus sanctus* in German religious history, see Rothkrug, "German Holiness," 161–90.

the living, carry to the dead gold, silver, gemstones, jewels, cows, pigs, hens, geese, cheese, bread, salt, lard, and so forth.... Are we not fools that we hang such things there on a stone or on wood or set food out, like the pagans?"[11] Schwanhauser, moreover, moves beyond criticism of the pagan-like behavior of those who venerated the saints to a critique of the medieval and early modern *mentalité* which maintained a link between the living and the dead. Citing both Old and New Testament passages dealing with sanctification,[12] Schwanhauser points out that Scripture says very little about dead saints and almost always focuses upon the living.[13] Thus, he warns his flock, "God does not want us to concern ourselves with the dead saints who now live in Christ; rather, we should pay attention to the living."[14]

While "the Lutherans were stricter than Luther"[15] when it came to judgments of traditional piety, Luther himself clearly advocated a revision in the believers' understanding of saints. In the *Large Catechism*, for example, he explains the reference in the Apostles' Creed to the "communion of saints" in this way: "There is *upon earth* a little holy group and congregation of pure saints, under one head, even Christ, called together by the Holy Ghost in one faith...."[16] In a later exposition he writes more bluntly: "Let us...reject the stupid and godless notion about the term 'saints' according to which we imagined that the word was fitting only for the saints in heaven and for hermits and monks on earth who had performed certain extraordinary works. Let us now learn from Holy Scripture that all believers in Christ are saints."[17]

Zwingli, for his part, seems to have viewed references to saints somewhat more analytically than did Luther and the Lutherans in general. True to his humanistic methods, Zwingli assessed scriptural references to the saints from a philological perspective. In article 20 of the *Schlußreden*, for instance, Zwingli demands in reference to Job 5: "When are you going to learn that 'sanctus' means a good person and not a saint."[18] Similarly, referring to Heb. 1:14, he writes: "You would here have to translate 'sanctos' by 'good Christians.'"[19] Thus, despite his more scholarly and less

---

[11]Johannes Schwanhauser, *Ein Sermon, geprediget anno 1523 an dem 22. Sonntag nach Trinitatis, an aller Heiligen Tag* [Bamberg: Georg Erlinger, 1523], Biiii, Köhler 1042/2622.

[12]Lev. 20:7; Num. 16:1–3; Deut. 7:1–6; Rom. 8:30; and Eph. 5:25–27.

[13]Schwanhauser, *Sermon*, Ai^v–Aii. For examples of similar criticisms, see [Eberlin], *Lob der Pfarrer*; Linck, *Ein schöne christliche Sermon; Ein Sermon von der Anbetung; Ein tröstliche Disputation auf Frag und Antwort gestellet, von zweien Handwerksmännern* (n.p., n.d.); Melhofer, *Offenbarung*, Biii;Vögeli, *Schirmred*, H3.

[14]Schwanhauser, *Sermon*, Biiii.

[15]Burke, *Popular Culture*, 218.

[16]Luther, *Large Catechism*, in *Concordia*, 195 (emphasis added);WA 30(1):190.

[17]Luther's exposition of Gal. 5:19 (1531),WA 40(2):104, Plass 3992/1252.

[18]Zwingli, *Writings*, ed. Furcha, 1:161; idem, *Der zwentzgist Artickel*, in idem, *Sämtliche Werke*, 2:202.

[19]Zwingli, *Writings*, ed. Furcha, 1:166; idem, *Der zwentzgist Artickel*, in idem, *Sämtliche Werke*, 2:208.

emotional approach, Zwingli, like Luther, insisted upon the primacy of the sanctified on earth.

As Steven Ozment has written, "Catholic belief that the world of the living could, by almsgiving and prayer, intrude on that of the dead was dismissed as 'feeding on the dead' *(Totenfresserei)*" by many reformers and propagandists.[20] Such critics claimed that Catholic clergy "ate" the dead because many of them derived substantial revenues from gifts and fees given in connection with prayers and vigils for dead souls and with observances connected with the cult of dead saints. The two most well known examples of literature reflecting this theme are plays (both referred to as *Die Totenfresser)* by the dramatists Pamphilus Gengenbach of Basel and Nicolas Manuel of Bern.[21] The practices most often condemned in the literature of *Totenfresserei* are anniversary masses, prayers for the dead, and of course, indulgences; priests and monks are generally seen as merchants engaging in what Wenzeslaus Linck, for one, labels "commerce in death" *(Todtenkramerß).*[22]

In view of these considerations, one might be tempted to ask, just what does all of this have to do with the cult of the saints? Anniversary masses, prayers for the dead, and frequently the purchase of indulgences were, after all, activities on behalf of dead loved ones languishing in purgatory, not ceremonies honoring the saints. When one remembers, however, the mechanism underpinning faith in indulgences—the Treasury of Merits—the significance of the saints' role in "feeding on the dead" can scarcely be overestimated. Furthermore, the saints were *the primary link* between this world and the next.[23]

In addition to breaking the "boundary between heaven and earth,"[24] the cult of the saints served to forge a variety of bonds in medieval and early modern society. Like many other aspects of traditional religion, the saints connected the sacred and the profane;[25] as "invisible companions," they linked the human and the divine[26] and joined the past to the present.[27] Pilgrimages to saints' shrines brought together

[20] Ozment, *Protestants*, 14.

[21] [Pamphilus Gengenbach], *Dies ist ein jämmerliche Klag über die Totenfresser* [Strassburg: Johann Prüss, 1522], Köhler 244/674. The piece attributed to Gengenbach and likely printed in 1521 almost certainly inspired Manuel's play of 1523, *Die Totenfresser.* For useful discussions of this subject, see Rothkrug, "German Holiness," 201–5, and Ozment, *Reformation in the Cities*, 111–16.

[22] Linck, *Ein schöne christliche Sermon*, Diii. See also [Eberlin], *Lob der Pfarrer,* for a blistering condemnation of the death trade.

[23] Indeed, Peter Brown begins his important study of the function of the saints by saying, "This book is about the joining of Heaven and Earth, and the role, in this joining, of dead human beings"; *The Cult of the Saints*, 1.

[24] Brown, *Cult of the Saints*, 21.

[25] On this, see Burke, *Popular Culture*, 218; Scribner, *Popular Culture*, 1–16.

[26] See Brown, *Cult of the Saints*, chap. 3.

[27] Brown, *Cult of the Saints*, 78.

COVER OF PAMPHILUS GENGENBACH'S *DIE TOTENFRESSER* (1522).

town and country, men and women, rich and poor.[28] Traditional piety, of which the cult of the saints was an integral part, was promoted by the medieval Christian church in its effort to "humanize the social universe."[29]

Historians of the early modern period frequently emphasize the many ambiguities inherent in attempting to characterize the emergence of the modern from the medieval. Nonetheless, efforts to reform popular culture feature prominently as one aspect of this transition.[30] Desire to reform popular culture, moreover, reflects a strong concern for order—and a concomitant fear of disorder—which became a pervasive theme during an age in which religious and social change and unrest were widespread and troubling. The cult of the saints was rejected by Protestant reformers (and, indeed, revised by post-Tridentine Catholic reformers) in significant part precisely because it came to be seen as contributing to an undesirable state of disorder.[31]

It is scarcely without irony that the saints became agents of disorder during the early modern era; for the cycle of saints' festivals was one element which had conveyed a sense of "cosmic order" in an earlier age.[32] Devotion to the cult of the saints in the Germanies seems to have been, in fact, on the rise at the beginning of the sixteenth century.[33] Nonetheless, as the Reformation took hold, veneration of the saints came to be characterized as a symptom of a world gone astray. Evidence of this sense that the world was "out of joint" can be found in the prevalent depictions of the Antichrist and of the *verkehrte Welt* (the world turned upside down) in contemporary literature and iconography.[34] Even when one acknowledges the various possible

[28] Brown, *Cult of the Saints*, 41–45. On the subsequent separation of male and female spheres in the sixteenth century, see Merry Wiesner, *Working Women in Renaissance Germany* (New Brunswick: Rutgers University Press, 1986), 7. On the hardening of class lines in the sixteenth century, see Natalie Zemon Davis, *Society and Culture in Early Modern France: Eight Essays* (Stanford: Stanford University Press, 1975), 114.

[29] Bossy, *Christianity*, 95–97. Whether or not one agrees with Bossy's judgment of the Reformation itself, his conclusions regarding the "modern" society that ultimately emerged, in part in the wake of the sixteenth-century religious revolution, attain a certain resonance (35–40). For an interesting critique of Bossy, see Ozment, *Protestants*, 35–40.

[30] Peter Burke refers to the "reform of popular culture" as "the triumph of Lent"; *Popular Culture*, 207–323; quotation is on 207. Burke is, of course, referring to Brueghel's painting, the *Combat of Carnival and Lent*.

[31] Burke, *Popular Culture*, 229–33. On the association of traditional practices with superstition and disorder, see Scribner, "Ritual and Popular Religion," 47–77.

[32] Scribner, *Popular Culture*, 1–16. On the saints and order, see also Michael Baxandall, *The Limewood Sculptors of Renaissance Germany* (New Haven: Yale University Press, 1980), 86–87.

[33] See Moeller, "Religious Life in Germany on the Eve of the Reformation," 16; Otto Clemen, "Zum St. Annenkultus im ausgehenden Mittelalter," *Archiv für Reformationsgeschichte* 21 (1924): 251–53; Sargent, "Miracle Books and Pilgrimage Shrines"; Philip M. Soergel, *Wondrous in His Saints: Counter-Reformation Propaganda in Bavaria* (Berkeley: University of California Press, 1993), esp. chap. 2.

[34] R. W. Scribner, *For the Sake of Simple Folk: Popular Propaganda for the German Reformation* (Cambridge: Cambridge University Press, 1981), 148–89; idem, *Popular Culture*, 97–101. In *For the Sake of*

interpretations of such depictions, the concern for order demonstrated therein seems unmistakable. An equally ubiquitous motif, one which likewise reflects an anxiety over disorder, is the biblical Baal.[35] Significantly literary, rather than iconographic, the Baal motif not only "stresses that the world is disordered and morally *verkehrt*" but also connects this *verkehrte Welt* directly with the cult of the saints.[36]

In some instances the very titles of propaganda pieces bespeak the pointed analogy between the Old Testament regional deities and the saints revered in contemporary society. In the conspiratorial-sounding *Revelation of the Top Secrecy of Today's Baal Priests*, for example, evangelical Philipp Melhofer complains about the manner in which the clergy were misleading the people, particularly concerning the role of the saints: "They have taught that the saints have suffered more harm than they have been encumbered by their sins. Thus, their misfortunes supersede their sin, and, therefore, they have earned their place in heaven through their own works. And, as they have a surplus of merit, they can come to our aid." Melhofer goes on to warn of the dire consequences of those who continue to teach and embrace such blasphemy. In *Refutation of the Prophets of Baal*, Simon Reuter rails against the moneygrubbing idolatrous clerics who promoted the festivals of Mary and the saints for their own gain.[37]

Andreas Karlstadt also energetically condemns the "prophets of Baal": "The prophets of Baal and supposed Christians cry out to our saints and cause the gathered

---

Simple Folk, Scribner notes that the evangelical movement was seen "both as the result of the *verkehrte Welt* and as its corrective" (168). For other works on this topic, see Davis, "Women on Top," in *Society and Culture*, 124–51; Emmanuel Le Roy Ladurie, *Carnival in Romans*, trans. Mary Feeney (New York: George Braziller, 1979, 1980); Lee Palmer Wandel, *Voracious Idols and Violent Hands: Iconoclasm in Reformation Zurich, Strasbourg, and Basel* (Cambridge: Cambridge University Press, 1995), 174–82.

[35] See Güttel, *Dialogus oder Gesprächbüchlein von einem rechtgeschaffen Christenmenschen*; Kaspar Güttel, *Schutzrede wider etliche ungezähmte freche Clamanten* (Wittenberg: [Johann Rhau-Grunenberg, 1522]); Hätzer, *Ein Urteil Gottes*; Andreas Karlstadt, *Ein Frage, ob auch jemand möge selig werden ohn die Fürbit Mariä*, ([Nuremberg: Hieronymus Höltzel], 1524), Köhler 87/238; Karlstadt, *Von Abtuhung*; Linck, *Ein schöne christliche Sermon*; Wenzeslaus Linck, *Ein Sermon von Anrufung der Heiligen* [Augsburg: Heinrich Steiner, 1523], Köhler 107/280; Luther, WA-T 5:5700; Haug Marschalck, *Wer gern wöllt wissen, wie ich hieß, zu lesen mich hät nit verdrieß* (n.p., n.d.), Köhler 42/110; Melhofer, *Offenbarung*; Simon Reuter, *Anntwort wider die Baalspfaffen* [Bamberg: Georg Erlinger, 1523], Köhler 225/633; [Christoph Schappeler], *Verantwortung und Auflösung etlicher vermeinter Argument* (Augsburg: Melchior Ramminger, 1523), in *Flugschriften*, ed. Clemen, 2:362–63; *Von etlichen Klagen, die der allmächtig Gott tut durch seine Knecht* (n.p., 1525), Köhler 411/1122; *Warnung und Ermahnung der christlichen Kirchen zu Germanien ihrer Tochter, daß sie ihre Verführer mit Feuer und Eisen ausrotten wolle* (n.p., n.d.), Köhler 1884/4814; Wurm, *Trost Klostergefangner*; Zurich, Bürgermeister, Rat und Grosser Rat, *Christliche Antwort dem hochwürdigen Herren Hugo, Bischof zu Konstanz, über die Unterricht beider Artikel der Bilder und der Mess* (Zurich: Hans Hager, 1524), Köhler 1437/3816; Zwingli, *Ein Antwort, Valentino Compar gegeben*, Li; idem, *Sämtliche Werke*, 4:124.

[36] See Scribner, *For the Sake of Simple Folk*, 168.

[37] Melhofer, *Offenbarung*, Biii^{r-v}, Cii; Reuter, *Antwort*, Aii^v.

people to chant, 'Saint Peter, Pray for us.'... God reckons such yelling or shouting to the dead saints a mockery and a dishonor." He concludes this tract by reinforcing the image of the *verkehrte Welt*, a world where laypeople must become their own priests and authorities must stand challenged by their underlings. Citing a scriptural passage in which Moses exhorts the Israelites to stone to death prophets who tried to lure them to "other gods," Karlstadt writes: "Now, if the laity should be forbidden to argue with their preachers, how might a layman in the Old Testament lay a hand on a preacher and cast the first stone? He had to know that the preacher was leading the people astray."[38]

A sermon by Luther's friend Wenzeslaus Linck, preached while he was still pastor at Altenburg, is a remarkable example of the use of the Baal, Antichrist, and *verkehrte Welt* motifs all in a single document. In *A Good Christian Sermon about the Exodus of the Children of God from the Antichrist's Prison*, Linck constructs with words a series of contrasting pairs.[39] The church of the Antichrist, Linck charges, labels as heretics those whose beliefs and practices conform more to Scripture than do their own. With its "idolatrous divine service and veneration of saints," the "Antichrist's prison" was ordained not by God, but by men. He continues the diatribe: "Hence, it comes to pass that where one thinks he is revering God, he is revering an idol; where he thinks he is serving the saints, he is serving stocks of wood,...; much as happened to that lover who went into the kitchen and thought he had women and maidens in his arms, but actually they were old rusty kettles and pots."[40]

The cult of the saints thus contributed to disorder because belief in the saints generally led to the embracing of unchristianlike piety as well as false doctrine; but the reformers' objections were not confined to the religious realm. Practices linked to the cult of the saints were also seen as promoting disastrous social behavior, particularly among the popular classes. Zwingli, for example, concerned himself with behavior resulting from a false sense of security generated by faith in the saints: "The intercession of the saints... has made for negligent Christians, indeed. For one could find many a foolish Christian who thought he might not be condemned if he had a patron saint who would intercede without ceasing, thus setting him free to rob, burn, wage wars, gamble, swear, commit adultery."[41] Zwingli was writing in

---

[38] Karlstadt, *Ein Frage*, Aiiii^v. In *Abtuhung*, he refers to those who would retain images as "prophets of Baal" (Di^v). Ibid., Bii; he is referring to Deut. 13:9–10.

[39] Such pairs are reminiscent of those in the Cranach woodcuts entitled *Passional Christi und Antichristi* discussed by Scribner in *For the Sake of Simple Folk*, 149–55.

[40] Linck, *Ein schöne christliche Sermon*, Dii^v.

[41] Zwingli, "The Twentieth Article," in *Writings*, ed. Furcha, 1:151; *Der zwentsgist Artickel*, in idem, *Sämtliche Werke*, 2:187.

a general sense, but by and large, concerns about such sinful behavior focused around two types of occasions centered on the saints: holidays and pilgrimages.

One of the most common complaints about holidays was that there were too many of them: the proliferation of saints' days had simply gotten out of hand, particularly in view of the fact that the only biblically sanctioned holiday is the Sabbath. In a dialogue published in 1522, Kaspar Güttel's "master" instructs his "student": "There are all too many feast days *[feyrtag]* but few holy days *[haylig tag]* among us Christians." He goes on to lament that frequently such feast days led to occasions of the "greatest evil against God," encouraging "all sorts of dark sins." He cites blasphemy, gambling, unchastity, anger, bloodshed, drunkenness, murder, and adultery as the sorts of unsavory activities people engaged in during saints' festivals. The anonymous author of another *Gespräch*, from roughly the same period, labels the holidays the most sinful times of the year, where a person gives himself over to "wine, … dancing, gambling, and going to the brothel, where he loses at gambling and spends more on drink than he has earned in an entire week. …"[42]

Other writers compile similar lists of sins associated with saints' festivals. Luther complains about "drunkenness, gambling, idleness, and a variety of sins"; Sebastian Goldschmidt lists "fornication, mischief, gluttony, drunkenness, and blasphemy"; while Martin Bucer cites "gluttony, haggling *[kauffen]*, gambling, fornication, and all that which the devil teaches."[43] Clearly, the concern is with disruptive, disorderly, and ungodly behavior; a further, if related, concern, however, rests with the effects of such frequent intervals of "mischief" and "idleness" upon productive labor. Kaspar Güttel's "master" tells his "student" that it would be "a hundred times better to work than to celebrate thus"; Andreas Karlstadt too bemoans the idleness of holidays. Indeed, Martin Luther declares that "the holy day is not holy; the work days are holy"; and if one wants truly to honor the saints, then "make a work day out of a holy day."[44] Martin Bucer provides perhaps one of the most aptly stated summaries of the problem of saints' days. He writes:

---

[42] See Güttel, *Dialogus oder Gesprächbüchlein von einem rechtgeschaffen Christenmenschen*, Ri^v; *Ein Gespräch zwischen vier Personen*, in Bentzinger, *Die Wahrheit*, 280. Steven Ozment, *Reformation in the Cities*, 202, notes that "Eberlin is the assumed author" of this pamphlet.

[43] Martin Luther, *An den christlichen Adel*, in *Flugschriften*, ed. Laube, 2:666; WA 6:445–46; Goldschmidt, *Ein Unterweisung*, Biiii^v; Bucer, *Grund und Ursach*, Ni^v. For other similar associations of the saints' days with sin, see, for example, Karlstadt, *Von dem Sabbat*; Linck, *Ein Sermon von Anrufung*; and *Von St. Johanns Trunk ein hübscher neuer Spruch* (n.p., n.d.), Köhler 624/1616.

[44] Güttel, *Dialogus*, Ri^v; Karlstadt, *Von dem Sabbat*, D3; Luther, *An den christlichen Adel*, in *Flugschriften*, ed. Laube, 2:666; WA 6:446. In this context, it is interesting to note Jane Dempsey Douglass's observation that, according to Sister Jeanne de Jussie in *The Leaven of Calvinism, Or the Beginning of the Heresy of Geneva* (1526–35), one behavior attributed to Protestant women was that "they ostentatiously work on feast days"; see Douglass, "Women and the Continental Reformation," in *Religion and Sexism: Images of*

Besides Sunday, there are remarkably many days to honor God, his angels and dead saints, which, through fear of punishment and because of Christian duty, one is obliged to celebrate.... And if, out of necessity, one performs manual labor on such days, one will be severely chastised. But gluttony, haggling, gambling, fornication, and all that which the devil teaches, the holiday has not put a stop to. Thus, the innocent masses are instructed.... No one other than the devil is served: in part, through many superstitious acts, masses, unintelligible songs, the same sort of prayers, salvation by indulgences, and the like; in part, through all sorts of wantonness and fleshly pursuits with which the rude masses never more severely anger God than on holidays.[45]

Like holidays, pilgrimages to saints' shrines were condemned for the behavior they inspired. Bucer condemns pilgrimage cities as "more wicked" than any other, while Luther charges pilgrimages with "increasing drinking and fornication" and providing "countless occasions of sin."[46] Johannes Lonicer, one of Luther's colleagues at Wittenberg, writes:

Is it not a sign of Satan's work: when the youths and maids, stimulated by the devil,... travel with impetuosity and fury to Our Lady in Grimmental, Felbach, Zinsbach, Aachen, Einsiedeln, Regensburg, and countless other shrines to Our Lady in Swabia and other lands? Who is thus the founder of this disgrace but... the devil? What is the result of this journey? They amuse themselves with long-desired love, defiling the virgins, destroying young men, besmirching the temple of God [i.e., their bodies] and their Christian souls.[47]

Finally, it is impossible to ignore one further thread that runs through virtually all of the examples cited above—the negative references to the saints' association with sexuality. "Unchastity," "adultery," "going to the brothel," "fornication," "wantonness," "fleshly pursuits," "long-desired love," "defiling virgins," "besmirching the temple of God": all of these activities are listed disapprovingly among those in which people indulged on holidays and on pilgrimages. In addition, reformers took issue with the sensuality of much religious art of the period.

Women in the Jewish and Christian Traditions, ed. Rosemary Radford Ruether (New York: Simon & Schuster, 1974), 311. Davis, *Society and Culture*, 171, finds a similar behavior in France.

[45] Bucer, *Grund und Ursach*, Ni^v.

[46] Bucer, *An ein christlichen Rat*, Fiiii^v; Luther, *An den christlichen Adel*, in *Flugschriften*, ed. Laube, 2:659, 667; WA 6:337, 447.

[47] Lonicer, *Berichtbüchlein*, Fii^v.

Disapproval of things sensual has frequently been associated most directly with the Swiss. One pre-Reformation propensity in Zurich was marked suspicion of fleshly pursuits: dancing was prohibited by the council around 1519 because of its association with immorality; Zwingli's early love of music and pursuit of worldly pleasures nearly precluded his appointment at the Great Minster in 1518. In addition, evidence suggests a particular antipathy to fleshly or worldly pleasures on the part of authorities in Zurich whose "faithful, in short, had fallen completely captive to the senses." This antipathy to the flesh can be connected to representations of the saints in Zwingli's comments comparing saints' images to those of prostitutes and pimps. Indeed, in article 20 of the *Schlußreden*, Zwingli castigates a depiction of St. Barbara "delicately pictured in the shape of a whore."[48]

Such sentiments, however, were not confined solely to the Swiss. Martin Luther himself expressed concern that the Virgin and the female saints often looked downright whorish.[49] Lutheran Heinrich von Kettenbach's well-known *Altmütterlein* tells Brother Heinrich, "The images make me joyous and devout when they are so beautiful." Brother Heinrich, however, admonishes her that her pleasure is only one of the senses.[50] In a pamphlet by an anonymous Lutheran, "everyman" Karsthans confesses that when he was a boy and heard the organ playing, he wanted to dance; singing moved him bodily but not spiritually. He goes on to reveal that "often I had evil thoughts when I looked at female images on the altar. For no courtesan dresses herself more voluptuously or more shamelessly than they nowadays represent the Mother of God, St. Barbara, or St. Katherine."[51]

To present-day sensibilities, comparisons of images of the Virgin and the female saints to prostitutes may seem odd. It is interesting to note, however, that Catholic reformers also worried about unseemly depictions of holy persons. The twenty-fifth session of the Council of Trent, held 3–4 December 1563, issued a statement on sacred images which read in part: "In the invocation of saints, ... all lasciviousness [shall be] avoided, so that images shall not be painted and adorned with a seductive charm, or the celebration of saints and the visitation of relics be perverted by the

---

[48]Jackson, *Zwingli*, 24, 117–19; Jackson cites chronicler Oswald Myconius and Heinrich Bullinger to this effect; Garside, *Zwingli and the Arts*, 92–93; Baxandall, *Limewood Sculptors*, 89–90; Zwingli, *Writings*, ed. Furcha, 1:151; idem, *Sämtliche Werke*, 2:187–88.

[49]Baxandall, *Limewood Sculptors*, 88.

[50]Kettenbach, *Gespräch*, 61–62. For an interesting discussion of the sensual content of images, see Christopher S. Wood, "In Defense of Images: Two Local Rejoinders to the Zwinglian Iconoclasm," *Sixteenth Century Journal* 19 (1988): 25–44.

[51]*Gesprächbüchlin neu Karsthans*, Ei. For more on this and related matters, see Christine Göttler, "Die Disziplinierung des Heiligenbildes durch altgläubige Theologen nach der Reformation. Ein Beitrag zur Theorie des Sakralbildes im Übergang vom Mittelalter zur Frühen Neuzeit," in *Bilder und Bildersturm im Spätmittelalter und in der frühen Neuzeit*, ed. Bob Scribner (Wiesbaden: Harrassowitz, 1990), 263–95.

people into boisterous festivities and drunkenness, as if the festivals in honor of the saints are to be celebrated with revelry and with no sense of decency."[52] To some extent, these reactions can be attributed to the fact that artwork was, in fact, becoming more "fleshly" by the early sixteenth century.[53] On another level it appears that at least in some quarters a transformation was beginning to take hold, and that, in Lee Palmer Wandel's words, "the images were no longer a place where God's 'presence' might be evoked." If, as Wandel further argues, the images came to be seen as part of a ritual deemed "blasphemous" by the "pious laity," and if they were beginning "to embody so much that opposed God's presence in the world,"[54] then it seems reasonable to suggest that they had become, in effect, "prostitutes," much as the pope had become the "Whore of Babylon."[55]

One final point needs to be raised in this regard. The word prostitute, at least in the parlance of the sixteenth century, is clearly a gender-specific term. The bulk of the references that connect saints, sensuality, and prostitution are specifically references to female saints. One may wonder what importance to attach to this.

Perhaps we can approach an answer by considering the relative significance of a series of developments in the period in question. Sixteenth-century concerns with order often focused around the problem of unmarried (or masterless) women.[56] In such circumstances, powerful women came to be viewed with great suspicion, as

---

[52] *Canons and Decrees of the Council of Trent*, trans. H. J. Schroeder (St. Louis: Herder, 1941), 216–17.

[53] Baxandall, *Limewood Sculptors*, 90. The examples he uses to illustrate are sculptures of Mary Magdalene (91). It is important to point out that defining female sanctity in fleshly terms did not originate in the sixteenth century. Throughout the Middle Ages, men's and women's souls were considered equal in the eyes of the church, but their bodies were not. While men could escape the limits of their physicality, women could not; thus, women's spiritual experiences were always anchored in and defined by their flesh. See Marina Warner, *Alone of All Her Sex: The Myth and Cult of the Virgin Mary* (New York: Knopf, 1976), esp. chap. 5; Elizabeth Robertson, "The Corporeality of Female Sanctity in *The Life of Saint Margaret*," in *Images of Sainthood in Medieval Europe*, ed. Renate Blumenfeld-Kosinski and Timea Szell (Ithaca: Cornell University Press, 1991), 268–87; Rudolph M. Bell, *Holy Anorexia* (Chicago: University of Chicago Press, 1985); Ruth Mazo Karras, "Holy Harlots: Prostitute Saints in Medieval Legend," *Journal of the History of Sexuality* 1 (July 1990): 3–32. Interestingly, while both Robertson and Bell address the misogyny inherent in this emphasis, the former finds its roots in Aristotelianism while the latter finds them in Platonism.

[54] Wandel, *Voracious Idols*, 192. It is important to point out that Wandel emphasizes that "all the objects in churches were 'idols,'" not just depictions of human beings (193).

[55] Merry Wiesner cites Donald Kelley, *The Beginning of Ideology* (Cambridge: Cambridge University Press, 1981), 75, concerning Luther's use of "whore" in a symbolic sense; "Luther and Women: The Death of Two Marys," in *Disciplines of Faith*, 301.

[56] In her groundbreaking article on the Reformation and gender analysis, Merry E. Wiesner argues, "As sixteenth-century men debated women's nature, becoming more obsessed with women's sexuality and controlling unmarried women, gender became increasingly important as a determinant of human experience"; Wiesner, "Beyond Women and the Family: Towards a Gender Analysis of the Reformation," *Sixteenth Century Journal* 18 (1987): 318. See also, Wiesner, *Working Women*, 34, 187.

threats to the natural order of things.[57] To extend this argument, one might ask, If female saints were arguably such powerful (i.e., disorderly) women, what of the prostitutes with whom they were equated?

Throughout the later Middle Ages, prostitution—at least that carried on in municipal brothels—had been officially tolerated as a safety valve of sorts. Indeed, one might argue that much as saints' days had served as an ordering mechanism in medieval society, prostitution functioned to maintain decorum. The annual oath of the Ulm brothel keeper, for example, noted that his function was "to further the interest and piety of the city and its folk, and to warn and keep it from harm."[58] In seeking to close brothels, reformers sought to turn prostitutes into honorable women—or, at least, to drive them to the margins of society.[59] They argued that the *Frauenhaus*—rather than alleviating sexual pressure—actually "caused young men to have impure thoughts about women."[60] Like the pilgrimage house and its saints, the *Frauenhaus* and its prostitutes had become agents of disorder. The reformers had, in effect, "turned [the safety valve] argument on its head."[61] Outcries against female saints as harlots were, in fact, one highly nuanced symptom of the general fear of disorder that engaged a society consumed with its awareness of the Antichrist and the *verkehrte Welt*, as it warily awaited the final days.

THE SAINTS AS ECONOMIC DRAINS

Despite the strength of objections based on scriptural condemnation, rejection of images came about, in large part, because of a growing disgust among the reform-minded with the emphasis upon the material that characterized medieval piety. Lee Palmer Wandel focuses upon this point when she writes: "[The images] had come to embody so much: that place where the wealth of Christians was frozen, kept from

---

[57]Lyndal Roper makes this point in "Luther: Sex, Marriage and Motherhood," *History Today* 33 (December 1983): 34. See also, Margaret L. King, "Book-Lined Cells: Women and Humanism in the Early Italian Renaissance," in *Beyond Their Sex: Learned Women of the European Past*, ed. Patricia H. Labalme (New York: New York University Press, 1980), 76.

[58]"*Der frowen wiert ayd*," cited in Lyndal Roper, "Discipline and Respectability: Prostitution and the Reformation in Augsburg," *History Workshop Journal* 19 (Spring 1985): 4.

[59]Similarly, they sought to turn priests' concubines and nuns into wives.

[60]Wiesner, *Working Women*, 104.

[61]Roper, "Luther: Sex, Marriage and Motherhood," 33. In addition to this work, see Roper, *Holy Household*, chap. 3; Wiesner, *Working Women*, 97–109; and Hans J. Hillerbrand, "The 'Other' in the Age of the Reformation: Reflections on Social Control and Deviance in the Sixteenth Century," in *Infinite Boundaries: Order, Disorder, and Reorder in Early Modern German Culture*, ed. Max Reinhart, Sixteenth Century Essays and Studies (Kirksville, Mo.: Thomas Jefferson University Press, 1998), 260–63, for a discussion of prostitution and the closing of the brothels.

needy human beings; the material links between laity and clergy."[62] In this one sentence, Wandel succinctly summarizes two varieties of economic objections to the cult of the saints.

The latter, "the material links between laity and clergy," is perhaps the more obvious of the two. Humanists and reformers alike had consistently criticized the squandering and ostentation associated with the cult and its trappings. In a pamphlet from 1525, for example, Lutheran Johann von Schwarzenberg condemns "each church" for spending funds glorifying "its Mary" or "its saints." Furthermore, he invokes the prostitute-saint connection when he writes that such expenditures were "much more shameful than prostitutes *[gemeinen Weiber]*[63] selling their chastity."[64] Other writers similarly deplore the wastefulness inherent in building elaborate churches for individual saints and in adorning their images with fine clothing, precious metals, and expensive jewels.[65]

Pilgrimages were common objects of attack because of both the wastefulness and the neglect associated with them. The anonymous writer of a parody of a Catholic vigil mocks the "godless papists, monks, and priests" who encouraged people to "make pilgrimages to the saints in order to buy themselves false indulgences."[66] Sebastian Lotzer, friend of Christoph Schappeler,[67] also warns of the abuses involved in invoking the saints, making pilgrimages, buying indulgences, and the like.[68] In his inventory of accusations against the *Baalspriester*, Philip Melhofer indicts such priests for teaching that "he who makes a pilgrimage to Saint James [of Compostela] does a better work than he who stays home working faithfully to support wife and child."[69] Caspar Adler speaks out similarly against pilgrimages to St. Wolfgang, St. Leonard, Regensburg, and Aachen,[70] while the anonymous author of

---

[62] Wandel, *Voracious Idols*, 192.

[63] For a fascinating analysis of this term, see Lyndal Roper, "'The Common Man,' 'the Common Good,' 'Common Women': Gender and Meaning in the German Reformation Commune" *Social History* 12 (January 1987): 1–21.

[64] [Johann von Schwarzenberg], *Beschwörung der alten teufelischen Schlangen mit dem göttlichen Wort* (Nürnberg: Hans Hergot, 1525), Fiii.

[65] See, for example, *Beklagung eines Laien genannt Hans Schwalb, über viel Missbräuche christlichen Lebens* (Augsburg: Melchior Ramminger, 1521), in *Flugschriften*, ed. Laube, 1:68; Güttel, *Schutzrede*, Ci[v]; [Pamphilus Gengenbach], *Der evangelisch Bürger* (Zwickau: Jörg Gastel, 1524), Biii[r–v]; Bucer, *An einen christlichen Rat*, Fi[v].

[66] *Die deutsche Vigile*, 141–43.

[67] Lotzer, a furrier's apprentice, and Schappeler, a Zwinglian pastor in Memmingen—purported coauthors of the *Twelve Articles*—played active roles in the Peasants' War.

[68] Sebastian Lotzer, *Eine heilsame Ermahnung an die Einwohner von Horb* ([Augsburg: Jörg Nadler], 1523), in *Flugschriften*, ed. Laube, 1:253.

[69] Melhofer, *Offenbarung*, Ci.

[70] Adler, *Sermon*, bbii.

a pamphlet entitled *Christian Instruction* singles out Jerusalem, Rome, St. James, and Aachen, saying, much like Melhofer and Adler, that it would be better for a man "to stay at home to tend to his vocation and to support his wife and child."[71]

In addition to expressing concerns about waste and neglect, pamphleteers who addressed economic abuses surrounding the cult of the saints frequently harshly condemned the clergy for their greedy moneygrubbing. Simon Reuter, for instance, points out that "if the festivals of Mary, All Saints, and even All Souls fail to produce money and other profit, you [i.e., the priests] make a point of not even saying, 'Good morning. How are you? What are you doing?'"[72] Most such criticisms of the clergy similarly accuse them of worldliness and failure to attend to the cure of souls. One interesting anonymous, but obviously Lutheran, pamphlet sounds an even more cynical note. In a mock discussion between Lutheran and "papist" priests, one of the articles debated concerns the abolition of the veneration of saints, of holidays, and of pilgrimages. The "papists," of course, clamor for retaining the practices involving the cult of the saints on the grounds that abolition would result in loss of income. They conclude their argument by saying that without such economic opportunities, "Oh, God, who will want to be a priest anymore?"[73]

Like so many other reformers, Zwinglian Ambrosius Blarer criticized the economic waste that frequently accompanied veneration of the saints. In a pamphlet from 1523, he goes on to suggest that the saints themselves would have been uncomfortable with such displays: "Is it not reprehensible that we encase the blessed saints after their death—doubtless against their will and pleasure—in gold, silver, and precious stones that they never possessed in life, but rather were only righteous poor people?" In the same work, moreover, Blarer voices a second type of economic objection, one which Wandel addresses in the first part of the sentence quoted above: "[The images] had come to embody . . . that place where the wealth of Christians was frozen, kept from needy human beings. . . ." Blarer's indictment continues: "And we now are willing to ordain hunger and cold for the poor rather than demolish the golden bodies and heads of the saints for the use of needy poor people to whom all this surplus indeed belongs."[74]

Several other pamphleteers writing in the 1520s issue much the same admonition. Philipp Melhofer condemns the *Baalspriester* for teaching that "it is much better to provide a silver image on an altar or a gold piece on a vestment than to help poor people."[75] In *Christian Instruction* (cited above), the author advises the impor-

---

[71] *Christliche Unterrichtung*, Ei^v.

[72] Reuter, *Antwort*, Aii^v.

[73] *Klag und Antwort von lutherischen und päpstischen Pfaffen über die Reformation, zu Regensburg ausgangen* ("Lumbitsch auff dem Federmarck" [Nuremberg: Hieronymus Höltzel, n.d.]), Di, Köhler 342/964.

[74] Blarer, *Wahrhaft Verantwortung*, Ciiii^v.

[75] Melhofer, *Offenbarung*, Ci^v.

tance not only of staying home to support one's family but also of helping "the poor as God has commanded."[76] Another anonymous pamphleteer contrasts Christ's teachings with the pope's: "Christ teaches that charity should be extended to the poor.... The pope teaches the buying of indulgences; the building of churches, cloisters, and cells; chapels, altars, vigils, masses, anniversary masses; pilgrimages to the wooden saints...."[77]

In a sermon preached upon his departure from Ulm in 1522, Heinrich von Kettenbach raises the same issue in two separate items. In item 35, he says: "It is anathema to encourage people to burn many candles in the churches and to deny such money to the poor; for God has commanded alms to be given rather than burning candles to the idols." In item 36, he goes on to condemn those who promote "pilgrimages and bringing sacrifices to the wooden Mary and the saints in Grimmental, the Schwarzwald, Aachen, Einsiedeln, etc.," calling it "anathema" to urge people to spend money on the saints and other such things and "leave poor Christians to suffer hunger, want, cold, and poverty."[78] Brother Heinrich, furthermore, indicts not only the clergy for their inattention to Christian charity; he similarly chastises his *Altmütterlein*: "You burn many candles before the saints' statues, St. Ann, St. Helfferin, St. Rutzkolben, etc., and they see nothing. Why don't you burn such light for the poor women here in Ulm who try to spin in winter by moonlight?"[79]

Thomas Stör of Dresden, for his part, invokes Matt. 25 on the same subject, saying that instead of wasting money on the saints and other trappings, Christians should "feed the hungry, give water to the thirsty, clothe the naked, visit the sick, console the prisoners."[80] Johannes Brenz also turns to Matt. 25 while arguing that "it is...no honor to the dead [saints] to consecrate large churches in their name while those here on earth must settle for small huts."[81] He furthermore contrasts the dead saints with the living saints, a term he uses to designate the poor.[82]

---

[76] *Christliche Unterrichtung*, Ei[v].

[77] *Ein klärliche Anzeigung*, Bi[v]–Bii.

[78] Heinrich von Kettenbach, *Ein Sermon zu der löblichen Stadt Ulm zu einem Valete* (Bamberg: Georg Erlinger, [1523]), in *Flugschriften*, ed. Clemen: 2:116. See a similar admonition in *Ein schöner Dialogus und Strafred von dem Schultheiß von Geißdorf mit seinem Schüler wider den Pfarrer daselbst* (n.p., n.d.), Bii, Köhler 264/744.

[79] Kettenbach, *Gespräch*, 59.

[80] Stör, *Von dem christlichen Weingarten*, 365.

[81] Brenz, *Ein Sermon von den Heiligen*, Bii[v].

[82] Cf. *Eine tröstliche Disputation*, Giiii, in which the "living saints" are defined as "the poor, forsaken, sick handworkers; widows; and orphans whom one must help." In a similar manner, Zwingli often refers to the poor as the "living images of God," a concept that is integrally related to his objections to saints' images, as Lee Palmer Wandel demonstrates in *Always among Us: Images of the Poor in Zwingli's Zurich* (Cambridge: Cambridge University Press, 1990).

According to these and other reformers,[83] therefore, the saints were draining resources that God had stipulated should be used to help the poor. With such emphasis placed upon God's commandment, these exhortations bear striking resemblance to the demands of the peasants during the Peasants' War for adherence to what Peter Blickle has labeled "godly law."[84] Using the same terms—and often the same scriptural citations—with which peasants objected to the abuse of tithes by lords, reformers objected to the abuse of saints by clerics. Article 2 of the Twelve Articles is especially illustrative of this point:

> We will gladly pay the large tithe on grain—but only in just measure. Since the tithe should be given to God and distributed among his servants, so the pastor who clearly preaches the word of God deserves to receive it.... *The remainder should be distributed to the village's own poor....* But wherever the tithe holder... did not buy the tithe from the whole village but has it from ancestors who simply seized it from the village, we will not, ought not, and do not intend to pay it any longer, except... to support our elected pastor. And we will reserve the rest or *distribute it to the poor, as the Bible commands.*[85]

[83] See, among others, *Ein Dialogus das ist ein Gespräch zweier Personen, Christus und Christianus* [Nuremberg: Hieronymus Höltzel, 1524], C, Köhler 268/754; [Greifenberger], *Dies Büchel*, Bi^v; Caspar Hedio, *In die erst Epistel S. Joannis des Evangelisten ettliche christenlich Predigt* ([Strassburg: Johann Knobloch], 1524), Aav^v, in *Städtische Predigt in der Frühzeit der Reformation: Eine Untersuchung deutscher Flugschriften der Jahre 1522 bis 1529*, ed. Bernd Moeller and Karl Stackmann (Göttingen: Vandenhoeck & Ruprecht, 1996), 92; Peringer, *Ein Sermon von der Abgötterei*, Bi^v; Wolfgang Russ, *Ein Sermon, in welcher der Mensch gereizt und ermahnt wird zu Lieb der evangelischen Lehre* [Nuremberg: Hieronymus Höltzel, 1523], Ci, Köhler 1084/2745.

[84] See Peter Blickle, *The Revolution of 1525: The German Peasants' War from a New Perspective*, trans. Thomas A. Brady, Jr., and H. C. Erik Midelfort (Baltimore: Johns Hopkins University Press, 1981), esp. chap. 5. Interestingly, in at least two instances saints were used as models of obedience to godly law. Hans Schwalb notes: "Such money that the priests have they should use to feed the poor as St. Nicholas did"; *Beklagung eines Laien*, 352. Hans Staygmayer writes: "We read that St. Lawrence distributed the church's treasure to the poor, and we want to enclose them [i.e., saints] and their bones in silver and gold"; *Ein schöner Dialogus*, Bii^v.

[85] *The Twelve Articles: The Just and Fundamental Articles of All the Peasantry and Tenants of Spiritual and Temporal Powers by Whom They Think Themselves Oppressed*, "The Second Article," in Blickle, *Revolution*, 196–97; *Die gründlichen und rechten Hauptartikel aller Bauerschaft und Hintersassen der geistlichen und weltlichen Oberkeiten* (Regensburg: Paul Kohl, n.d.), Aii^{r–v}, Köhler 1363/3599; emphasis added.

Reformers
AND
THE SAINTS

While Luther and Zwingli are certainly the best-known reformers—as well as the most prolific writers—of the early Reformation era, to consider them the undisputed standard-bearers of contemporary Protestant viewpoints would be at best misleading. In the generally inchoate, unformed situation that existed even at the very end of the period under consideration here, attitudes concerning such issues as the cult of the saints varied from reformer to reformer and over time. Early evangelicals frequently fell outside any clearly defined Lutheran or Zwinglian camp, often exhibiting an eclectic sort of piety that likely reflected influences from among such divergent movements as medieval Catholicism, medieval heresies, lay piety, the *Devotio Moderna*, Erasmian humanism, Lutheranism, and/or Zwinglianism.[1]

A prime example of an evangelical who resists categorization is the Basel reformer Johannes Oecolampadius, one of numerous humanists who early on sympathized with Martin Luther's criticisms of the church. Between 1515 and 1518, Oecolampadius served as a preacher at the cathedral in Basel, associating with Erasmus's humanist circle. In December 1518, he left Basel for a pulpit in Augsburg where he became acquainted with a group of humanist supporters of Luther. In 1519 he published an anonymous pamphlet backing Luther against Johann Eck at the Leipzig Debate.[2] Oecolampadius, however, was no Lutheran.[3] In April 1520, he left Augsburg and entered the Brigittine Cloister at Altomünster for reasons that

---

[1] Paul Russell makes this point about the pamphleteers in his study, *Lay Theology in the Reformation: Popular Pamphleteers in Southwest Germany 1521–1525* (Cambridge: Cambridge University Press, 1986), 1. Similar examples are Domenico Scandella (called Menocchio), in Carlo Ginzburg's *The Cheese and the Worms: The Cosmos of a Sixteenth-Century Miller*, trans. John Tedeschi and Anne Tedeschi (Baltimore: Johns Hopkins University Press, 1980); and Bartolomé Sánchez, in Sara Tilghman Nalle's *Mad for God: Bartolomé Sánchez, the Secret Messiah of Cardenete* (Charlottesville: University Press of Virginia, 2001).

[2] [Johannes Oekolampad], *Canonici indocti Lutherani* [Augsburg, 1519], Köhler 145/401.

[3] Even after Oecolampadius planted his feet firmly in the reformers' camp, he continued to defy categorization. Despite his admiration for Luther, he supported what was essentially Zwingli's view in the Sacramentarian Controversy.

seem unclear. During the nearly two years that he spent in the monastery, he continued to find common ground with much that Luther and other reformers were saying, and his beliefs became increasingly heterodox. In 1521, for example, he wrote a highly positive evaluation of Martin Luther, which was published that same year in Basel.[4] He left Altomünster in February 1522, later aligning with Zwingli at Marburg.

Oecolampadius, whom Bainton calls "the most implacable reformer,"[5] seems to have emerged from the cloister with ambivalent views on the intercessory powers of the saints—particularly of the Virgin Mary. In *In Praise of God through Mary*, a sermon written and published while he was at Altomünster, he is clearly struggling with the issue. On the one hand, he notes that some people occupy themselves too much with devotion to Mary, comparing such people to the astronomer who marvels at the stars but who does not acknowledge their creator. He observes that "Christ taught us to direct our prayers to his Father," and if we should need an advocate, "we should direct our petitions to him [i.e., Christ]." Further on, however, he poses the question, "Are we not to invoke the saints?" In his answer, he walks a fine line: "By all means, but when we implore them, we must turn along with them to Christ...." Oecolampadius closes his sermon on an unequivocally orthodox note: "She [Mary] is most worthy, who is praised above all creatures, and, indeed, God is to be praised through her, in whom such great gifts of God are so clearly visible.... With her interceding again and again on our behalf, may God be both praised and glorified by us...." Oecolampadius eventually did reject the cult of the saints, and by 1529 he was voicing his approval of the iconoclasm that had occurred as the Reformation in Basel was completed.[6]

Numerous others who became Protestant, Martin Luther among them, likewise turned away from the veneration and invocation of the saints only gradually, even reluctantly. In his *Lamentation of a Layman*, reform-minded Hans Schwalb, for example, praises Luther, saying: "Therefore, let us pray to Jesus Christ / That he keeps the pious Martin safe." Further on, however, he writes: "Pray to Mary and her son / That he leads us to his heavenly throne." At least as late as 1521 when the *Lamentation*

---

[4] Johannes Oekolampad, *Iudicium de doctore Martino Luthero* ([Basel], 1521), Köhler 692/1521.

[5] Roland Bainton, *Erasmus of Christendom* (New York: Charles Scribner's Sons, 1969), 223.

[6] Johannes Oekolampad, *De laudando in Maria Deo Sermo* (Basel: Andreas Cratander, 1521), 7, Köhler 627/1628; idem, *Ein Sermon, wie wir Gott in Maria loben sollen* [Augsburg: Sigmund Grimm and Marx Wirsung, 1521], Köhler 530/1351; idem, *De laundando in Maria Deo*, 8, 9, 15 (translation of Latin text is by Kevin Kile). In a sermon on the Magnificat, also written while he was at Altomünster, Oecolampadius concludes in a similar manner: We must "call upon her to protect us like a true mother and...to pray to her son to pardon our sins"; idem, *Ein Sermon von dem Vers im Magnificat* "Exultavit spiritus meus" [Augsburg: Sigmund Grimm and Marx Wirsung, 1520?], Aiiii, Köhler 1100/2800. See Eire, *War against the Idols*, 118.

was published, therefore, this champion of evangelical theology continued to have faith in the intercessory power of Mary, praising Luther for being a "follower of the Virgin" as well. In a comparable manner, Johannes Römer, pastor from Worms and defender of Luther, was also reluctant to abandon the holy intercessors. In one dialogue he writes: "God has rewarded the saints (such as St. James) with eternal bliss; thus God will listen to the dear saints when they pray for us." As the editor of this dialogue, Wilhelm Lucke, points out, Römer, although a defender of Luther, had broken with Rome only with difficulty and had continued to hold "fast to the veneration of the saints, especially Mary."[7]

Indeed, special reverence for certain saints—the Virgin Mary most frequently, but not exclusively—may have been responsible for the gradual manner in which some reformers relinquished their reliance on the cult. Pamphleteer Johann Eberlin is an interesting case in point. While Eberlin seems to have lambasted the veneration and invocation of the saints at nearly every opportunity and for a variety of reasons, in his *Bundsgenossen*, he appears more selective in his condemnation than in his other writings. He cautions, for example: "If you praise Christ and Mary, you will not praise them too much, but with other saints, you will perhaps go too far. If you want to praise the saints, however, praise Peter, Augustine, Jerome, John the Baptist, etc.... Leave your Francis alone...."[8]

For both Zwingli and Luther, the most frequently cited objection to the veneration and invocation of the saints is the lack of scriptural authority. Nonetheless, these reformers, much as did others discussed throughout this study, took exception to practices surrounding the cult on a number of other grounds. For example, they both complained about the propensity of most Christians to use the term "saint" to designate only the venerable dead. Zwingli and many of his closest followers often insisted that saints were more importantly God's living images on earth—specifically, the poor. Luther stressed that the concept of saint included all believers—the dead, but most especially the living—noting St. Paul's frequent usage of the term to this effect.[9] While Zwingli and Luther each focused primarily on different concerns, one point remains clear: both early modern reformers deemed the Christian

---

[7] *Beklagung eines Laien*, in *Flugschriften*, ed. Clemen, 1:347, 357; Johannes Römer, *Ein schöner Dialogus von den vier größten Beschwernissen eines jeglichen Pfarrers* ([Schlettstadt: Lazarus Schürer?], 1521), in *Flugschriften*, ed. Clemen, 3:69; Wilhelm Lucke, introduction to *Ein schöner Dialogus*, in *Flugschriften*, ed. Clemen, 3:30.

[8] See chap. 5 below for a discussion of the "problem" the Virgin Mary presented to reformers. See Eberlin's attacks on the saints because of their connection with monastics, because of their ties to superstition, because of proscriptions in Scripture, and because of their relationship to disorder, chap. 2 above; Eberlin, *Ein klägliche Klag*, "Der vi Bundtsgnos." Once again Eberlin's antipathy toward the Franciscans is apparent.

[9] Cf. Zwingli, "Twentieth Article," *Writings*, ed. Furcha, 1:139; idem, *Sämtliche Werke*, 2:171.

saint a vital human being rather than simply a dead ideal. In addition, both embraced and promoted the concept of godly law.

Zwingli first referred to the poor as the "images of God" in *The Shepherd*, published in 1523/24. In this work, he admonishes "that one should clothe the living images of God, the poor Christians, not the wooden and stone idols, for the honor of God." In contrasting the poor to the idols, Zwingli generates a twofold dichotomy. First, in his choice of words, he differentiates sharply between "*living* images," the poor, and "wooden and stone" images of *dead* saints. Second, he distinguishes the *true* images of God, the Christian poor, from their *false* counterparts, the idols. This distinction is even more clearly drawn in Zwingli's *Answer to Valentin Compar*: "That which we should give to the needy images of God, to poor people, we use to adorn the images of people; for the idols are images of people, but a person is an image of God."[10]

The nexus between deprived poor and indulged idols is a recurring theme in Zwingli's writing. In his influential *Commentary on True and False Religion* (1525), for example, he writes: "Human reason says: 'Set up images to honor God and the saints.' Religion cries out against that: 'No. No. Bestow upon the poor that which you wish to use to honor God.'"[11]

In a similar vein, Zwingli writes to his fellow Toggenbürger, citing the First Commandment against the making of images: "We make them to the detriment of the poor." He goes on to say: "We should have given to them [the poor] that which we used for ornamentation of the idols."[12] In the *Schlußreden*, Zwingli invokes the same connection, while moving beyond insinuations of neglect, failure, or ignorance to accusations of downright malevolence. In addressing the error of those he labels "anti-Christians"—papist clerics, most especially the mendicants—he hurls the following charges:

> The anti-Christians...have persuaded the simple people that Christ should have riches and that these are his honor and ornament....
>
> Thus they are not content with lying to God as if he desires riches but vaunt themselves to be gods. For if the riches which they acquire

[10] See Wandel, *Always among Us*, 43; Huldrich Zwingli, *Der Hirt* (Zurich: C. Froschauer, n.d.), Fiiii, Köhler 340/959; idem, *Sämtliche Werke*, 3:51, 4:108; idem, *Ein Antwort, Valentino Compar gegeben*, Hiiii^v.

[11] Zwingli, *Von wahrem und falschem Glauben*, 277–78; idem, *Sämtliche Werke*, 3:900.

[12] Zwingli to the Toggenbürger, 18 July 1524, in Zwingli, *Sämtliche Werke*, vol. 8, *Briefwechsel 2: 1523–1526*, Corpus Reformatorum (Zurich: Theologischer, 1982), 209. At least until 1526, Zwingli continued to refer to the prohibition of images as part of the First Commandment, despite the fact that the Reformed tradition, in general, considered the prohibition to be the Second Commandment. See idem, *Ein Antwort, Valentino Compar gegeben*, Eiiii^v–Eiiii^v; idem, *Sämtliche Werke*, 4:85, 5:192; idem, *Die erst kurze Antwort*, Aiii^v–Aiiii.

through begging and their false pretenses are God's, why then do they themselves use what is God's? If it is God's, he shall divide it among the poor rather than stuff such lazy bellies with it....

You say it is just in the sight of the saints, thus turning the saints into accomplices of robbers, thieves and usurers.[13]

Zwingli's influential assessment of the appropriate way to honor the dear ones in heaven—by caring for the poor rather than by ornamenting saints' images—is further reflected in a number of mandates proclaimed by the Zurich Council. In 1523, for example, the council began to look into the economic activities of the Great Minster, ordering the cessation of a number of fees and expenditures, including those involving the images. In essence, the council decreed that the church's economic focus should shift from monies spent on securing the afterlife to those spent on worthwhile affairs in this life. Aside from the concern over expenditures on the dead saints, the council objected to the collection of fees for baptisms, dispensations, and the use of candles at burials. Instead, it stressed the education of the ministry, the education of children, and the distribution of money to the poor.[14]

In the following year, the council issued a response to Hugo, bishop of Constance, concerning images and the mass. In addressing the bishop's traditional view that the ornamentation honored "the dear saints who are in heaven" and not the idols, the council responded: "Then if one wants to honor them [the saints] with abundant goods, one will give these goods, as God has commanded and as the dear saints also have done: To the poor."[15]

By the year 1530, the council found it necessary to reiterate—and indeed strengthen—its position vis-à-vis a variety of undesirable social behaviors. In the same document in which the council expressed distress over clandestine episodes of saint worship, it enumerated a long list of related ills that were plaguing a backsliding community.[16] Its initial concern was to abolish "overflowing pubs" and "drinking sprees" by strengthening mandates regarding holidays, church accounts, idols, drinking, gaming, adornment, dancing, Anabaptists, and "innumerable other things."[17] In one section, the council undertook to inform city officials "that church goods will no longer be mishandled, squandered, adjusted, concealed, wasted, or used on anything other than to relieve the poor or afflicted."[18] Hence, the Zwinglian

---

[13] Zwingli, "Twenty-Third Article," *Writings*, ed. Furcha, 1:194–95; idem, *Sämtliche Werke*, 2:240–44.

[14] Jackson, *Zwingli*, 200–25.

[15] Zurich, Bürgermeister, Rat und Grosser Rat, *Christliche Antwort*, Di^v. See also Diii^v.

[16] In this document, the council implicitly expresses its concern with the *verkehrte Welt* discussed in chap. 3 of this book.

[17] Zurich, Bürgermeister, Rat und Grosser Rat, *Christenlich Ansehung*, Ai.

[18] Zurich, Bürgermeister, Rat und Grosser Rat, *Christenlich Ansehung*, Aiiii^v.

connection between true saint and living poor became etched in official policy despite the fact that evidence suggests that exhibitions of popular piety may have continued for some time to cling to the association of saints with dead paragons.

Luther's objections to the veneration of saints and their images generally revolved around rather different issues from Zwingli's. Nonetheless, common ground does exist. For instance, in a Lenten homily from 1525, Luther strikes a familiar Zwinglian chord: "Now when St. Paul mentions the needs of saints, he does that to make us more eager to do Christian good works. We are anxious to serve the saints and pay great attention to what we put on the saints: how true that also is. But he shows us the real saints, namely those stuck in poverty...they look like nothing less than they do like saints, but are poor, abandoned, hungry, naked, imprisoned, dying people, whom everyone must help and who cannot help themselves...."[19] More typically, however, Luther reacted to the cult of the saints from one of two perspectives: the saints, living or dead, are all part of the communion of believing Christians; or the dead saints serve the living as models.

Zwingli's rejection of the cult of the saints was unequivocal, at least as early as 1522, more likely earlier.[20] By 1523 Zwingli claimed that "I am the first [reformer] who has dared dismiss [the intercession of the saints]." He went on to write: "When [the simpleminded] fought in an ugly manner, I said, 'So be it. If you wish to take your concerns to the saints, I shall take mine to God alone. Let us see which of us is on the better road.' Thus I nurtured them with milk so that several of them who once were dead set against me, now cling the firmer to God alone." Comparing this with Luther's empathy with the "weak" who still clung to the saints, one finds Luther's viewpoint considerably gentler. Indeed, Luther's relationship with the cult of the saints remained far more ambivalent than did Zwingli's.[21]

Many biographers have noted young man Luther's strong devotion to the saints, pointing to the Stotternheim incident as early evidence. On 2 July 1505, while a law student at Erfurt, Luther made his well-known pledge to St. Anne, patron of thunderstorms and miners, that if she saved him from the storm, he would become a monk.[22] While Anne and her daughter the Virgin Mary were two of Luther's

---

[19] "Die Epistel auff den andern Sontag nach Epiphanie," WA 17(2):50.

[20] See Garside, Zwingli and the Arts, 94–95.

[21] See Zwingli, "Twentieth Article," Writings, ed. Furcha, 1:137–38; Auslegen und Gründe der Schluss-reden, in idem, Sämtliche Werke, 2:1–457; Luther, Epistel oder Unterricht von den Heiligen an die Kirche zu Erfurt, WA 10(2):166; cf. Karlstadt's viewpoint that "dangerous things should be removed from the weak"; Eire, War against the Idols, 65. On Luther's somewhat "contradictory" views concerning the saints, see Elmer Carl Kiessling, The Early Sermons of Luther and Their Relation to the Pre-Reformation Sermon (Grand Rapids: Zondervan, 1935), 118–19.

[22] WA-T 4:4707.

In Antwurt Huldrychen Zuinglis Valentino Compar alten Landt schrybern zů Ure ggeben über die. iiij. artickel. Die er jm vß sinen schlußreden angetastet hatt.

Vom Euangelio was es sye.

Von den lereren wie vil inen ze glouben sye.

Von den bilden vnnd wie an denen die schirmer vnd stürmer mißlerend.

Vom Fägfhür/ Das gheins sin mag.

Christus Mathei. xj.
Kůmend zů mir alle die arbeytend vnd bladen sind/ vnd ich wil üch rüw geben.

COVER OF ZWINGLI'S *ANSWER TO VALENTIN COMPAR* (1519).

favorite saints, he held a total of twenty-one (three for each day of the week) in particular reverence as his special patrons. Despite anxiety and depression, his devotion
to the saints remained intact as he set off on his pilgrimage to Rome in 1510. As
Roland Bainton comments: "Neither the Rome of the Renaissance nor the Rome
of antiquity interested Luther so much as the Rome of the saints."[23]

In the years following his return from Rome in 1511, Luther began to show
reservations about certain practices connected to the cult of the saints. For example,
in his sermons on the Decalogue, preached in 1516–17 and published in 1518, he
attacked abuses, such as the attribution of special powers to a long list of saints.[24]
Nonetheless, at least until 1519, Luther, while critical, was almost certainly orthodox.[25] Thus it seems likely that prior to 1519, Luther remained traditional in his
views on articles of faith, including veneration of images and the saints.[26] Furthermore, "only on the subject of indulgences and certain excesses in the worship of
saints is there clear evidence that he spoke his mind frankly from the pulpit at this
time."[27]

The cult of the saints stirred concern within both Luther and Zwingli in part
because of the abuses associated with its trappings—images, pilgrimages, and indulgences. While the two reformers responded somewhat similarly to the issues of pilgrimages and indulgences, they reacted in fundamentally different ways when it
came to the matter of religious images. Zwingli, for example, held images to be
invariably idolatrous: "You are a worshiper of strange gods and an idolater that you,
against God's word, have set up your own intercessor and made an image of that
same intercessor. That is outright idolatry with worship of strange gods. For had
you not earlier made a god, you would have neither made an image nor venerated
it later. Thus idolatry follows immediately after the strange god is fixed in your
heart."[28] To Zwingli, therefore, abuse was an inevitable concomitant of the use of
religious images. Luther, on the other hand, acknowledged potentially legitimate

---

[23] See Roland H. Bainton, *Here I Stand: A Life of Martin Luther* (New York: Abingdon-Cokesbury,
1950), 49, 58; one pamphleteer and supporter of Luther referred to him as a "follower of the Virgin and
St. Katherine"; *Beklagung eines Laien*, in *Flugschriften*, ed. Clemen, 1:357.

[24] See WA 1:412–17, cited in Bainton, *Here I Stand*, 71, and Kolb, *For All the Saints*, 12.

[25] In a sermon preached in 1537, Luther says that he himself invoked the saints "for over thirty
years." WA 46:663, Plass 3996/1253.

[26] Heinrich Boehmer, *Martin Luther: Road to Reformation*, trans. John W. Doberstein and Theodore
G. Tappert, A Living Age Book (Meridian) (Cleveland: World, 1957, 1965), 155. For a similar perspective, see Margarete Stirm, *Die Bilderfrage in der Reformation*, Quellen und Forschungen zur Reformationsgeschichte (Gütersloh: Mohn, 1977), 36–37. See, for example, Luther's fairly traditional viewpoint on
the invocation of saints in a writing from 1519: "Luthers Unterricht auf etliche Artikel, die ihm von seinen Abgönnern aufgelegt und zugemessen werden," WA 2(1):69–70.

[27] Boehmer, *Martin Luther*, 155.

[28] Zwingli, *Ein Antwort, Valentino Compar gegeben*, Hiii; idem, *Sämtliche Werke*, 4:105.

use of such representations.[29] Thus while Zwingli adopted a root and branch attitude toward religious art, Luther's stance was far less radical. Luther, for example, wrote to the moderate Zwickau pastor Nikolaus Hausmann: "[The images] will fall on their own when people learn that they are nothing in the presence of God."[30]

Luther's gradual withdrawal from devotion to the saints themselves parallels his attitude toward images.[31] By the late 1520s and the 1530s, his criticisms of the saints were becoming considerably more pronounced.[32] In a homily preached on St. Anne's Day, 1527, he notes, "I should also say about St. Anne, whose feast we celebrate today, that I cannot find a word about her in Scripture."[33] In 1531, he once again rejects his beloved St. Anne, saying, "If you invoke Anne, you will soon be helping the devil."[34] He follows in 1533 with the comment that he considers Gregory the "most harmful pope" because during his papacy so many condemned practices, including the cult of the saints, became entrenched in the church.[35]

Unlike Zwingli, Luther worried far less about possible idolatry associated with images than he did about the connection between the trappings of the cult and works righteousness:

> To me the absurd business of the images is extremely unpleasant. And if [images] are evil, [the iconoclasts] are doing things the wrong way. One, indeed, finds people who misuse wine and bread, gold and silver, and

[29] Luther, *Acht Sermone* in *Ausgewählte Schriften*, 1:188–90. See Carl C. Christensen, "Iconoclasm and the Preservation of Ecclesiastical Art in Reformation Nuernberg," *Archiv für Reformationsgeschichte* 61 (1970): 205–20, for an interesting discussion of the more moderate Lutheran attitude toward religious art.

[30] Luther to Nikolaus Hausmann, 15 March 1522, WA Br. 2:474–75.

[31] Heinrich Bornkamm writes: "In retrospect he could not tell when he had ceased calling on the saints.... The change one day simply happens by itself"; Bornkamm, *Luther at Mid-Career*, 99.

[32] In 1524 the canonization of St. Benno, twelfth-century bishop of Meissen, by Adrian VI undoubtedly moved Luther to a more negative assessment of the cult of the saints. In his view, the canonization of a Saxon bishop, whose major contribution had been support of the pope during the Investiture Controversy, seemed overtly political. See *Wider den neuen Abgott*, WA 15(1):170–98. On St. Benno, see also Paul Bachman, *Ein Sermon des Abts zu Cellen in Aufnehmung der Reliquien Sancti Bennois* (Dresden: Wolfgang Stöckel, 1527), Köhler 1183/2966; J. N., *Von der rechten Erhebung Bennos* ([Wittenberg: Hans Lufft], 1524), in *Flugschriften*, ed. Laube, 2:1343–47; Johannes Groner, *Zu Trost allen armen Gewissen: Ein klein Büchlin* (Wittenberg: Hans Lufft, 1524), Fiii^v–Fiiii; "Ein Lied von dem heiligen Benno, Bischof zu Meißen," in *Die historischen Volkslieder der Deutschen vom 13. bis 16. Jahrhundert*, ed. Rochus, Freiherr von Liliencron (Leipzig: F. C. W. Vogel, 1867), 3: 419–20; Bagchi, *Luther's Earliest Opponents*, 153; Brecht, *Martin Luther*, 2: 89–90; Soergel, *Wondrous in His Saints*, 182–91.

[33] Stephen Roth's *Festpostille*, 1527, WA 17(2):475.

[34] WA-T 2:1289.

[35] WA-T 2:1873. *"Ich halt Gregorius sey der aller schedlichst bapst gewesen. Is invexit in ecclesiam missam privatam, purgatorium, votum religionis, cultum sanctorum."* Although Luther does not specify which Pope Gregory, he is presumably referring to Gregory I (ca. 540–604) who was a strong promoter of monasticism, the veneration of the early saints, the primacy of the Bishop of Rome, and the doctrine of Purgatory.

who treat them as strange gods.... Should one, therefore, destroy all bellies, gold and wine?...

It's true I wish [the images] were out of the church, not because of
the danger of praying to them—for I fear people pray to the saints themselves more than to the images—but because of people's false belief that
they can do good works for God through them....[36]

For Luther, works righteousness was a danger associated even more strongly with
pilgrimages and indulgences. On the subject of pilgrimages, he was especially ada-
mant, condemning them as devilish practices.[37] In 1523, for instance, he wrote to
the mayor and council of Regensburg about one of the most popular pilgrimage
sites of the period, the Shrine of the Beautiful Maria. He warned that now that the
Jews had been expelled from the city, the devil, using Mary's name, had installed
himself in their stead: "For [the devil] has the power to appropriate the name of
God, Christ, and the Holy Ghost; why then should he not start up with the name
of Mary?"[38] Indeed, Luther even seems to downplay his objections to violent iconoclasm in the case of pilgrimage sites: "The destruction and demolishing of images
at Eichen, in Grimmental, and Birnbaum, or places to which pilgrimages are made
for the adoration of images (for such are truly idolatrous images and the devil's hos-
pices), is praiseworthy and good."[39] This is ironic, especially when one considers
that Luther had criticized overly zealous iconoclasts as being guilty themselves of
works righteousness.[40]

The issue of indulgences was, of course, manifestly central to Luther's posting of
his *Ninety-Five Theses*, 31 October 1517. Three of the theses—56, 57, and 58—tar-
geted indulgences explicitly; and of the three, the last spoke directly to the issue of
the saints: "Nor are [indulgences] the merits of Christ and the saints, for, even without the pope, the latter always work grace for the inner man, and the cross, death,
and hell for the outer man."[41]

[36] Luther to Graf Ludwig zu Stolberg, 25 April 1522, WA Br. 2:513–14.

[37] See Luther, *An den christlichen Adel*, WA 6:381–469; De captivitate Babylonica ecclesiae praeludium,
WA 6:484–573; WA-T 4:4779.

[38] Luther to the mayor and council of Regensburg, 26 August 1523, *Ausgewälte Schriften*, 6: 65–66;
WA Br. 3:141–42.

[39] Luther, *Against the Heavenly Prophets, LW,* 40:91–92; WA 18:37–214.

[40] Letter to the Princes of Saxony, *LW,* 40:69. See also Eire, *War against the Idols*, 69.

[41] Martin Luther, *Ninety-Five Theses or Disputation on the Power and Efficacy of Indulgences*, in Lewis W.
Spitz, ed., *The Protestant Reformation*, Sources of Civilization in the West (Englewood Cliffs, N.J.: Prentice
Hall, 1966), 47–48; Martin Luther, *Disputation zur Erläuterung der Kraft des Ablasses*, WA 1:233–38. Cf.
Zwingli's critique of the Treasury of Merits, "Twentieth Article," *Writings*, ed. Furcha, 1:139–50; idem,
Sämtliche Werke, 2:172–85.

Zwingli likewise spoke out against traditional practices such as pilgrimages and indulgences: "To run up and down streets to shrines...to purchase indulgences, to pray for pay, chant, walk in processions, decorate temple walls and such like innumerable goldmines, invented by humans, is not of God and therefore utter hypocrisy."[42] Yet Zwingli reserved his most venomous language for human creations: religious images; while Luther's most vociferous criticism was for human behaviors: undertaking pilgrimages and peddling and purchasing indulgences.

If, for Zwingli, the term saint implied primarily the "living images of God"—the poor—for Luther, the term extended to the entire Christian community, living and dead, with emphasis upon the living. Indeed, in a sermon preached in 1523, Luther speaks of being compelled to "reclaim the noble name" for living believers.[43] Throughout his career, Luther continued to deplore the fact that "we have been led by our seducers into the blasphemous humility of calling only the dead holy and of regarding it as the highest presumption if any one of us were to call himself holy." Luther blames these circumstances on "the shameful abomination called the canonizing of saints."[44] Instead, he preaches that the "true saints" are "people graced and gifted with an understanding of Holy Scripture and with many fine, splendid endowments of the Holy Spirit," but who do not claim "they are able to redeem people from sins and justify them before God."[45] Luther rejoices that he has known "numberless true saints" of "the kind Christ and the apostles depict and describe." In fact, he asserts: "I am one of them."[46] In a sermon from 1527, he goes on to point out that "I should not look upon the lowliest Christian with less regard than I do upon St. Peter and all the saints in heaven"; for "it cost Christ as much to redeem me as to redeem St. Peter."[47]

For Luther, the "false humility" that compelled people to hesitate to proclaim themselves saints was yet another instance of the trappings of the cult which promoted works righteousness. He preaches in an Advent homily from 1522, for example: "You must not consider it presumption that by faith you place yourself on a level with the saints.... God wants such presumption on his proffered grace and threatens the loss of eternal salvation if it is lacking.... It would be presumption if you wanted to become saintly and to be saved through yourself and your works, as they, the apostate papists, are now teaching...."[48] In a sermon from 1528, he refers

---

[42] Zwingli, "Fifth Article," *Writings*, ed. Furcha, 1:33; idem, *Sämtliche Werke*, 2:48.

[43] WA 12:262, Plass 3980/1247.

[44] *Fastenpostille* from 1525, WA 17(2):50, Plass 3993/1252.

[45] Sermon from 1537, WA 46:592, Plass 3988/1250.

[46] Exposition of Gal. 5:19, 1531, WA 40(2):104, Plass 3992/1251.

[47] WA 24:484–85, Plass 3982/1248.

[48] WA 10, pt. 1 (2):25, Plass 3981/1248.

specifically to works righteousness: "The false humility of our work-righteous folk says: Why, God preserve me! How could anyone be so arrogant as to let himself be called holy?" He goes on to preach, moreover, that this attitude is attributable to the old belief that saintliness means the performance of "splendid works" and the attainment of reward in heaven. He notes, however, that "real saints ... must be good, stout sinners...." They are saints not "because they are without sin or have become saintly through works...but...through [the holiness] of the Lord Christ, which is given them by faith and thus becomes their own."[49]

In addition to his insistence that "real saints" are believing Christians, Luther also acknowledges the significance of the dead saints in heaven, whose lives, he instructs, should serve as models for all believing Christians. The idea of using dead saints' lives as archetypes was, in fact, a departure from the traditional medieval model of sainthood in which saints' lives were not "to be emulated but rather to be admired. They glorify God; they do not provide models for mortals." The medieval worldview deemed saints perfect and thus incapable of being emulated. Indeed, the saints in heaven were considered not so much "dead," as they were "members of a separate but still important segment of society," who, in their relics, continued "to live among their people."[50]

Luther turned this medieval model on its head. He clearly saw the dear ones in heaven as most assuredly dead, separated from the earthly community, although part of the greater Christian communion. While they were dead in a conventional sense, however, they had at one time lived decidedly human lives; for the great saints had been not only saintly, but sinful as well: "It is a great comfort to us to hear that great saints, who have the Spirit of God, also sin. Of this comfort those would deprive us who say that saints do not sin."[51] While Luther does preserve a distinction between dead "great saints" and living Christians, whom he often calls "true saints," he continually emphasizes their common ground, thus portraying both groups either as formerly or currently flesh and blood mortals. In a sermon from 1527, for example, Luther explains that it is important to acknowledge and remember the sins of the great saints "to illustrate that no man is so holy or stands so firmly that he cannot fall again. If [the biblical saints] could fall so deeply, is it surprising that we stumble?"[52] In another sermon from the same year, he says: "One should not turn the saints into

[49] WA 28:177–78, Plass 3978/1246–47.

[50] Patrick J. Geary, *Living with the Dead in the Middle Ages* (Ithaca: Cornell University Press, 1994), 22, 118. See also Brown, *Cult of the Saints*, esp. chap. 3, "The Invisible Companion."

[51] Exposition of Gal. 2:11, 1531, WA 40(1):196–97, Plass 3985/1249.

[52] WA 24:355, Plass 3984/1249. On the subject of saints and sin, see also WA 19:197–98, Plass 3983/1249; WA 43:604, Plass 3986/1250.

sticks; one should let men and nature remain what they are."[53] Even into his final years, Luther continued to insist upon the importance of acknowledging the sinfulness of saints and the saintliness of sinners: "True saints are all believers...who...each in his own vocation does what God orders and refrains from sins of the flesh. That they are not all equally strong, but many will trespass and show weakness, does not detract from their holiness, as long as they sin not from evil intentions but from weakness."[54]

In arguing for the fallibility and humanity of all saints, Luther revised the medieval Christian view in two ways: first, he erased the foundation of the Treasury of Merits; second, he proclaimed the propriety of emulating the great saints as Christian, albeit human, exemplars: "Next to Holy Scripture there certainly is no more useful book for Christendom than that of the lives of the saints, especially when unadulterated and authentic....[55] Although the Spirit performs his work abundantly within, it nonetheless helps very much to see or to hear the examples of others without."[56]

---

[53] WA 24:631, Plass 3987/1250.

[54] WA-T 6:6729.

[55] Luther frequently expressed his concern about the authenticity of the saints' legends, complaining that most of them were full of lies. See, for example, WA 17(2):251, Plass 3990; WA-T 5:5674, Plass 3991. See also Melanchthon's concern about "the fabulous stories concerning the saints" expressed in his *Apology of the Augsburg Confession* (1531), article 21(9), in *Concordia*, 107; *CT* 353.

[56] WA 46:592, Plass 3989. See Robert Kolb, "Festivals of the Saints in Late Reformation Lutheran Preaching," *Historian* 52 (1990): 613–26, on saints as models. See also Kolb, *For All the Saints*, 1–20. Cf. Melanchthon in *Augsburg Confession*, article 21, in *Concordia*, 16; *CT* 57.

$\mathcal{V}$irgin $\mathcal{M}$ary
AMONG THE SAINTS

CHAPTER 5

The theme of saints as models appears frequently in evangelical literature. Konrad Schmid, who died at the Battle of Kappel with Zwingli, for instance, writes that "the saints are presented to us as examples to follow. But Christ is given to us as an example and also a helper and intercessor and savior. . . ." In a sermon addressed to the Christian community of Zwickau, Luther's friend Wenzeslaus Linck preached that "the saints will be well honored if our faith in God is increased by their example," while fellow Lutheran Johann Diepolt told his congregation at Ulm of the model "attributes" of Mary Magdalene: "her faith and trust in God's mercy" and her "remorse over her sins."[1]

Similar instances abound throughout the work of both lay and clerical writers;[2] and by the late sixteenth century, Protestants were producing martyrologies, many

---

[1] Konrad Schmid, *Antwort auf etlich Widerred derer, so die Predigt, durch ihn getan, geschmät* ([Zurich: C. Froschauer], 1522), Cii, Köhler 1955/4988. Wenzeslaus Linck, *Artikel und Positiones, so durch Wenzeslaum Linck zu Altenburg geprediget* (Grimma: [Wolfgang Stöckel], 1523), Aii^v, Köhler 980/2470. Johann Diepolt, *Ein Sermon, an Sankt Mariae Magdalenae Tag geprediget zu Ulm* [Augsburg: Philipp Ulhart, 1523], Ai^v, Aiii, Köhler 456/1233. Other examples of saints' being cited as positive models can be seen in [Gengenbach], *Der evangelisch Bürger*, Bi^v; *Ein guter grober Dialogus deutsch, zwischen zweien guten Gesellen* [Augsburg: Melchior Ramminger, ca. 1521], Aii^v–Aiii, Köhler 264/743.

[2] The following examples are representative: Wilhelm, Graf von Isenburg, writes, "We [should] walk in the footsteps of the dear saints and praise God in whom we believe"; *Kurzer Bericht*, Aiii. An anonymous (likely Swiss) author writes that saints' lives should be "an example for you to follow. That is the proper way to honor the saints"; *Ein neues Gespräch*, Aiii. Benedikt Gretzinger, *Stadtschreiber* of Reutlingen, writes, "We should use the saints as models and examples; that is, we should imitate the saints..."; *Hauptartikel und fürnehmlich Punkten*, Evii. Heinrich von Kettenbach writes that a Christian should preach the word of God everywhere. He gives examples such as St. Katherine of Alexandria and St. Affra of Augsburg; *Ein Sermon zu der löblichen Stadt Ulm*, in *Flugschriften*, ed. Clemen, 2:107. Zwingli writes: "If they [saints, prophets, or holy men] adorned religious devotion by sanctity of life, we should follow in their footsteps and be pious, holy, and innocent as they were"; *Exposition of the Christian Faith*, in *On Providence and Other Essays*, ed. William John Hinke (Philadelphia: 1922; repr., Durham, N.C.: Labyrinth, 1983), 240; *Christianae fidei brevis et clara expositio ad regem Christianum*, in Zwingli, *Sämtliche Werke*, vol. 6, pt. 5, *Werke von Sommer bis Herbst 1531, Nachträge und Briefen*, 59.

of which were aimed at teaching children Christian virtues.[3] One of the best-known of these is *Jungfrawenspiegel (The Maiden's Mirror)* by Conrad Porta, Lutheran pastor of Saints Peter and Paul Church in Eisleben. Porta's guidebook contains, among other things, profiles of forty female virgin martyrs, which, the author assures his readers, are historically (although not biblically) based rather than rooted in papist legends.[4] In the foreword to this section of the book, Porta justifies his use of *virgin* exemplars—before a Protestant audience who presumably had abandoned belief in the superiority of the celibate life—by quoting a piece on marriage from Luther's *Tischreden*. According to Porta, Luther cautions that rushing into "passion" or "courting" at an early age will lead to an "unstable marriage." "But," Luther notes, "when [young people] have reached their adulthood and then want to court, [they may do so] with God's advice and the direction and approval of their parents, in an orderly manner, as is proper; or else there comes the dog Remorse who bites many people."[5] Furthermore, Luther justifies using virgin martyrs as examples by arguing that they were able to remain celibate only because of their early deaths: "God has not allowed virgins to live long, but hurried them out of this world...."[6] It seems that Porta chose virgin models not in an effort to induce his young readers, themselves *Jungfrauen*, to opt for lifelong celibacy, but simply to continue to practice celibacy until they had reached a suitable age for marriage.

In addition to focusing on the virgin martyrs, Porta directs his readers' attention to the most celebrated virgin in Christendom, "the highly praiseworthy and regally born Virgin Mary."[7] Porta gives an account of the Virgin's life, supported by biblical citations, disavowing nonscriptural traditions such as the Immaculate Conception[8] and the *Salve Regina*.[9] Drawing from the portraits and vocabulary of numerous earlier commentaries on the Virgin Mary, Porta provides a summary of the mainstream Lutheran—and by and large Protestant—perspective.

---

[3] See Cornelia Niekus Moore, *The Maiden's Mirror: Reading Material for German Girls in the Sixteenth and Seventeenth Centuries* (Wiesbaden: Harrassowitz, 1987).

[4] Conrad Porta, *Jungfrawenspiegel: Faksimiledruck der Ausgabe von 1580*, ed. Cornelia Niekus Moore, with an introduction by Cornelia Niekus Moore (Bern: Peter Lang, 1990), 113^v.

[5] Porta, *Jungfrawenspiegel*, 112^v.

[6] Wiesner, "Luther and Women," 301, citing WA 10(2):708.

[7] Porta, *Jungfrawenspiegel*, 34^v.

[8] It is generally conceded that Luther rejected the Immaculate Conception; see Plass, 1257 n. 13, e.g., Horst Dietrich Preuß, however, argues that Luther was extremely ambivalent on the issue; *Maria bei Luther* (Gütersloh: Bertelsmann, 1954), 14. See also *Flugschriften*, ed. Laube, 1:71. Zwingli's position is equally ambiguous although many feel his rejection of the Immaculate Conception can be derived from his theology; Emidio Campi, "Die unbefleckte Empfängnis," chap. 7 in *Zwingli und Maria: Eine reformationsgeschichtliche Studie* (Zurich: Theologischer, 1997).

[9] Porta, *Jungfrawenspiegel*, 34^v–47. On the Immaculate Conception, see 35; on the *Salve Regina*, see 46^v.

This viewpoint holds, first and foremost, that the honor due Mary stems only from her role as the Mother of God or the Mother of Christ. She is neither Christ's equal nor an intercessor with him: "Her unique place in the whole of mankind," Luther writes, is "that she had a child by the Father in heaven."[10] Emphasis upon Mary's motherhood is nearly universal in any Protestant writings that deal with the role of the Virgin.[11] The reformers' concerns revolved around their belief that for too long the mother had been considered perhaps even more laudable than the child. Luther writes: "Mary is praiseworthy and can never be lauded and extolled enough.... Yet we should laud and praise the mother in such a way that we do not let the Infant she has born [sic] be torn from our eyes and hearts."[12] Indeed, the cult of the Virgin had thrived in the High Middle Ages, with Mary holding sway as the Queen of Heaven.[13] However, as Lyndal Roper points out, a shift occurred in the sixteenth century which demoted the Queen of Heaven to Humble Handmaid.[14] Evidence of this appears, for example, in a letter Jakob Schenck von Stauffenberg wrote to his sister-in-law defending his wife's conversion to Lutheranism. Von Stauffenberg criticizes the designation Queen of Heaven, noting that Mary has often been credited with abilities that belong only to God.[15] In his exposition of the *Magnificat*, Luther too refers to Mary's regal title: "It is necessary also to keep within bounds and not make too much of calling her 'Queen of Heaven,' which is a true-enough name and yet does not make her a goddess...."[16] While it is interesting that Luther does not dismiss the title Queen of Heaven out of hand, it is perhaps of greater significance that his lengthiest section in this work deals with Mary's humility.[17]

Humility, credulity grounded in faith, and modesty are, in fact, three of the most important characteristics attributed to Mary in sixteenth-century evangelical

---

[10] *Das Magnificat Vorteutschet und außgelegt*, 1521, WA 7:572; translation is from Plass 4006/1256.

[11] Some representative examples include: Porta, *Jungfrawenspiegel*, 40ᵛ; Amsdorf, *Wider die Lügenprediger*, Aiiiᵛ; Martin Bucer, *Verantwortung M. Bucers auf das ihm seine Widerwärtigen zum ärgsten zumessen*, ([Strassburg: Johann Schott], 1523), Diᵛ; Kaspar Güttel, *Ein selig neu Jahr von neuen und alten Gezeiten* (Erfurt: [Matthes Maler], 1522), Giiiiᵛ, Köhler 1189–90/2985; Karlstadt, *Ein Frage*, Bii; Luther, Exposition on John 19:25–27, WA 28:402–3; Urbanus Rhegius, *Die neu Lehr samt ihrer Verlegung* ([Strassburg: Johann Knobloch], 1527), Ciiᵛ; Hans Staygmayer, *Eine kurze Unterrichtung von der wahren christlichen Bruderschaft* ([Augsburg: Philipp Ulhart], 1524), Aii, Köhler 142/391; Zwingli, *Eine Predigt*, in Campi, *Zwingli und Maria*, 144, idem, *Sämtliche Werke*, 1:400; Sattler, *Brüderlich Vereinigung*, in *Flugschriften*, ed. Clemen, 2:328.

[12] Sermon from 1531, Plass 4007/1256; WA 34(2):500.

[13] See Warner, *Alone of All Her Sex*, chap. 7, "Maria Regina." Traditional for centuries, the doctrine that declared Mary Queen of Heaven was not proclaimed until 1954 (116).

[14] Roper, "Luther: Sex, Marriage and Motherhood," 34–35.

[15] Schenck von Stauffenberg, *Sendbrief*, Aiiᵛ.

[16] WA 7:573, Plass 4006/1256.

[17] WA 7:559–70. The passage from the *Magnificat* under consideration is "For He has looked with favor on His lowly servant. From this day all generations shall call me blessed."

Die wunderbarlichen zaichen be-
schehen zu der schönen Maria zu Regenspurg / Jn.xix.jar.

Qui totam tete pulchram veneratur amicam
Ac semper puram te fine labe colit
Hoic adfis Maria noceat nec peftis apeila.
Aut fubilae montes nec aconyta piceot.

COVER OF A *MIRACLE BOOK* FROM THE SHRINE OF THE BEAUTIFUL MARIA, REGENSBURG (1519).

◆

literature. In particular, Mary's response to the angel Gabriel at the Annunciation is a frequently cited example of her humility and faith. According to Porta, for instance, her ready acceptance of the angel's "unnatural" pronouncement that she, a virgin, would bear God's son, is an admirable example of her "great and totally irrational faith."[18] Zwingli also sees Mary's behavior as a model when he tells his congregation that they, like the Virgin, should not doubt, but should give themselves as servants to God.[19] Sebastian Goldschmidt uses the designation "tool of God" to describe Mary's humble role,[20] while a pamphlet from 1524 underscores the significance of humility by praising the Virgin in this way: "Even the most beloved mother Mary makes herself humble and small, for it is God's will that honor be given only to God."[21] For reformers in the sixteenth century, the Queen of Heaven had, indeed, become "the pure, humble Mary."[22]

The emphasis upon Mary's humility can be seen as well in an examination of the way in which the reformers dealt with customary prayers and songs connected with the Virgin. They could not discard the traditional prayer to Mary, the *Ave Maria* for example, because of its foundation in Scripture. Instead, they insisted that it was not a prayer at all, but rather a greeting. Andreas Karlstadt, for instance, writes: "That the *Ave Maria* is related in part in the Bible, [and is] in part a greeting, makes the *Ave Maria* not a prayer, while further on the *Ave Maria* is an account of how good and how full of grace God has rendered Maria."[23] Zwingli argues in a similar manner: "The *Ave Maria* is not a prayer but a greeting and a commendation." He goes on to point out that the *Ave Maria* is not a request for anything, but a greeting, just as if one had said, *"Gott grüsse dich, Anna oder Grete."*[24] A pamphlet published in 1526 goes one step further by actually changing the title of the *Ave Maria* to *Gegruszt bist du Maria.*[25] As for the Virgin's song known as the *Magnificat*, clearly Protestant reformers retained

---

[18] Porta, *Jungfrawenspiegel*, 35ᵛ.

[19] Zwingli, *Eine Predigt*, in Campi, *Zwingli und Maria*, 131; idem, *Sämtliche Werke*, 1:397. Other examples include Johan Diepolt, *Zwo nützlich Sermon, gepredigt zu Ulm* ([Nuremberg: Johann Stuchs], 1523), Biʳ⁻ᵛ, Köhler 394/1072; Andreas Keller, *Ein Sermon auf den Tag der Verkündung Mariae, gepredigt zu Rottenburg* ([Augsburg: Heinrich Steiner], 1524), Biiʳ⁻ᵛ, Köhler 393/1069; Zeuleys, *Daß die Heiligen für Gott nicht anzurufen*, Biᵛ.

[20] Goldschmidt, *Ein Unterweisung*, Biiʳ⁻ᵛ.

[21] *Ein tröstliche Disputation*, Giiii.

[22] Schenck von Stauffenberg, *Sendbrief*, Aiiᵛ.

[23] Karlstadt, *Ein Frage*, Biᵛ. See also Luther, WA 10(2):407–9; Johannes Lange, *Ein Sermon von menschlicher Schwachheit* (Erfurt: [Wolfgang Stürmer, 1523]), Aiiii, Köhler 1849/4727.

[24] Zwingli, *Eine Predigt*, in Campi, *Zwingli und Maria*, 124; idem, *Sämtliche Werke*, 1:408. See also Johann Locher [Johann Rott], *Vom Ave-Maria-Läuten den Gläubigen fast fürderlich* ([Zwickau: Jörg Gastel], 1524), Aiiiᵛ, Köhler 248/689.

[25] *Ein fast schöne Unterweisung, aus der Heiligen Geschrift gegründet* ([Augsburg: Heinrich Steiner], 1526), Diii, Köhler 1579/4086.

this traditional work, as they did the *Ave Maria*, primarily because of its scriptural basis (Luke 1:46–55); however, the fact that it is, in itself, a proclamation of Mary's "lowliness" undoubtedly made it additionally palatable.

By contrast, the traditional—and nonscriptural—*Salve Regina* provoked a predictably different reaction. Andreas Karlstadt, in his typical, blunt manner, simply dismisses the *Salve Regina* as nothing more than a "heretical song."[26] In 1524, by contrast, Andreas Osiander, Lutheran reformer in Nuremberg, preached a sermon on the errors of the mass, in which he also took great pains to outline the "basis and reason to put aside the *Salve Regina*." Osiander's reasons include the fact that the prayer at the time was only about four hundred years old,[27] certainly not grounded in Scripture. In addition, Osiander objects to the reference to the Virgin as intercessor, a role reserved only for Christ. Further, he claims the prayer is "slanderous" because it refers to the Virgin Mary, Mother of Mercy, as "our life, our sweetness, and our hope"; only God deserves these designations.[28] Finally, he notes that while some would recommend changing the words, he believes that, despite any such alterations, the meaning itself would remain, and most people would fail to notice any changes. Therefore, he advocates abandoning the "godless" *Salve Regina* entirely.[29]

Johannes Freisleben, founder of the Reformation in Weiden (Oberpfalz), adopts the opposite view. After railing against the *Salve Regina* for more than four pages in his short pamphlet, Freisleben presents a revised version of the prayer—the *Salve Regina*, "Considered and Put Right"—which he begins by substituting *"Salve Jesu Christe / misericordierer"* for the traditional *"Salve Regina, mater misericordiae."*[30] While

---

[26]Karlstadt, *Ein Frage*, Aiii, Bii.

[27]It is said to have originated at Cluny around 1100.

[28]Countless pamphlets confront this image of the Virgin with biblical passages which attribute mercy (*Barmherzigkeit*), life (*Leben*), sweetness (*Süßigkeit*), and hope (*Hoffnung*) to God alone.

[29][Andreas Osiander], *Grund und Ursach aus der heiligen Schrift, wie und warum die Pröpst zu Nürnberg die Mißbrauch bei der heiligen Meß geändert haben*, ([Zwickau: Jörg Gastel, 1525]), Li. Kaspar Güttel raises similar objections in *Von merklichen Mißbräuchen*, Aiiii^v, as do Johannes Oekolampad, *Von Anrufung der Heiligen* (Basel: Adam Petri, 1526), Aii^v–Aiii, and Johannes Lonicer, *Berichtbüchlin*, Aiiii^v.

[30]Johannes Freisleben, *Das "Salve regina" nach dem Richtscheid, das da heißt Graphitheopneustos, ermessen und abgericht* [Regensburg: Paul Kohl, 1523], Köhler 1282/3300. The discussion is on pages Aiiii–Avi. The revised prayer is on page Avi. See also Heyden's revised version of the *Salve Regina* in *Daß der einig Christus*, Aiiii. Other pamphlets which contain songs with altered lyrics include: Michael Stifel, *Wider Doktor Murnars falsch erdict Lied von dem Untergang christlichs Glaubens* ([Strassburg: Reinhard Beck Erben, 1522?]), Köhler 249/695; Hans Sachs, *Etliche geistliche, in der Schrift gegründte Lieder, für die Laien zu singen* ([Augsburg: Philipp Ulhart], 1526), Köhler 1587/4096. Sachs "corrects" the songs "O Gentle Mary," which becomes "O Gentle Jesus," and "The Heavenly Lady," which becomes "The Heavenly Jesus" (A1^v–A2^v). In addition, he alters the lyrics of several traditional songs devoted to other saints. The *Salve Regina* was defended in any number of orthodox pamphlets in the 1520s. See, for example, Hieronymus Gebwiler, *Beschirmung des Lobs und Ehren der hochgelobten himmlischen Königin Mariä* ([Strassburg: Johann Grüninger, 1523]), Köhler 1475/3876; Georg Hauer, *Drei christlich Predigt vom "Salve Regina"* ([Ingolstadt: andreas Lutz, 1523]), Köhler 1026/2586; Georg Hauer, *Ander zwo Predigt vom "Salve Regina"* (Landshut:

it is undeniably true that the *Salve Regina* lacks scriptural authority, and was clearly rejected for this reason, it is interesting to note that, in addition, its vocabulary flies in the face of the model of the humble mother and handmaid Protestants preferred.

Such domestication of the former Queen of Heaven fits well with the Protestant view of the centrality of marriage and family and of housewife as the proper vocation for women. In an early sermon on marriage, Luther remarks: "Married people should know that they might do nothing better for God, Christendom, the entire world, themselves and their children than that they raise their children well. Pilgrimages to Rome, to Jerusalem, to St. James mean nothing. Building churches, endowing masses, or having holy water sprinkled means nothing compared to this single work: that married people raise their children; for this is their legitimate path to heaven...."[31]

This particular passage illustrates well the shift in worldview that was under way in the early modern period. In some ways, it might be said that life was becoming more simplified—certainly more orderly. In Protestant areas, no longer were there multiple paths to heaven, but only one.[32] No longer could a man or a woman, with full approval, choose celibacy or marriage, but only marriage. No longer could some females choose cloister or household, but only the home.[33] No longer was there a pantheon of helpers, male and female, but only one male intercessor with God the Father.

Johann Weißenburger, 1526), Köhler 69/182; Kaspar Schatzger [Schatzgeyer], *Von der lieben Heiligen Ehrung und Anrufung das erst deutsch Büchlin* (Munich: Hans Schobser, 1523), Köhler 706–7/1811; Johannes Dietenberger, *Grund und Ursach aus der heiligen Schrift wie unbillig und unredlich das "Salve Regina" wird unterlassen* ([Cologne: Peter Quentel], 1526), Köhler, 802/2016; Augustin von Alveldt, *Ein Vorklärung aus heller Warheit, ob das "Salve regina misericordiae" ein christlicher Lobesang sei oder nicht* ([Leipzig: Nickel Schmidt], 1527), Köhler 780/1961; Johannes Fabri (von Leutkirch), *Epistola... de invocatione et intercessione Mariae* (Vienna: Johann Singriener, 1529), Köhler 607/1565.

[31] "Ein Sermon von dem ehelichen Stand" (1519), WA 2(1):169–70.

[32] Eire notes that the cult of the saints "was inextricably bound in myriad ways to the salvational system of the Roman Catholic Church"; *War against the Idols*, 27.

[33] The question of whether the Reformation enhanced or diminished the status of women is hotly debated. Steven Ozment, on the one hand, writes: Protestants "exalted the patriarchal nuclear family as the liberation of men, women, and children from religious, sexual, and vocational bondage"; Ozment, *When Fathers Ruled: Family Life in Reformation Europe* (Cambridge: Harvard University Press, 1983), 6. Lyndal Roper argues, on the other hand: "The Reformation narrowed women's choice by removing the option of an independent religious vocation in which a woman might develop her own talents: it also limited the range of acceptable feminine identities"; Roper, "Luther: Sex, Marriage and Motherhood," 35. See also Albrecht Classen, "Footnotes to the German Canon: Maria von Wolkenstein and Argula von Grumbach," in *The Politics of Gender in Early Modern Europe*, Sixteenth Century Essays and Studies, vol. 12 (Kirksville, Mo.: Sixteenth Century Journal Publishers, 1989), 131–47. For a discussion of the debate concerning women's status in the early modern period, see Wiesner, "Luther and Women."

This Christocentric focus of Protestantism produced at least three consequences of particular significance to women. For one thing, in demoting the Virgin from quasi deity to humble wife and mother, Protestant reformers did away—at least for the moment—with Christianity's feminine element.[34] Furthermore, by desanctifying female saints, they effectively obliterated nearly all festivals which honored women and in which ordinary women played a public role.[35] Finally, after banning the cults of the Virgin, St. Anne, and St. Margaret, they instructed women, in Merry Wiesner's words, "to pray during labor and childbirth to Christ, a celibate male, rather than to a woman who had also been a mother."[36] For all these reasons, some historians have suggested that women may have been more reluctant than men to abandon entirely the invocation of the Virgin Mary and the other saints.[37]

Reformers were likely attempting to appeal to women by placing great emphasis upon Mary's having been a very ordinary woman herself, one with whom other ordinary women ought to be able to identify and fashion themselves after. Porta, for one, quotes Luther to this effect:

> Luther says in his *Hauspostille* about [Mary's] docility: "Shouldn't a god-fearing and pious housemaid, who cooks and must perform other chores, take consolation and joy in such an example as the Mother of God and say: "That I must cook and do other chores, even the Virgin Mary had duties at the wedding [in Cana]. She had to make sure everything was carried out correctly. And so, even if it is only a small chore, I will do it to honor the one who ordered it so that it pleases him well."[38]

[34] The "feminization" of Christianity was a product of the High Middle Ages. On this topic, see Caroline Walker Bynum, *Jesus as Mother*, esp. the introduction and chap. 4. The relationship between the cult of the Virgin and the actual position of women in society is, however, problematic. See Wiesner, "Luther and Women," 303; Warner, *Alone of All Her Sex*. Warner sees Mary's role as beginning to erode by the fourteenth century—long before the birth of Protestantism. She points to the rise of Joseph in importance as evidence (188).

[35] Merry E. Wiesner, "Nuns, Wives and Mothers: Women and the Reformation in Germany," in *Women in Reformation and Counter-Reformation Europe*, 14.

[36] Wiesner, "Nuns, Wives and Mothers," 14. See Luther, "Vom ehelichen Leben" (1522), in *Ausgewählte Schriften*, 3:190. Steven Ozment finds evidence of one woman who acquiesced, apparently willingly, and surely many others did as well. See his account of Anna Platter's labor in *When Fathers Ruled*, 110; also in *Protestants*, 178–79. Interestingly, Platter named her newborn daughter Margaret. Ulrich Zeuleys begins his pamphlet condemning the invocation of the saints with an anecdote about his mother's attending a woman giving birth. Being in pain, the woman called upon the Virgin for alleviation. His mother told the woman, "Dear daughter, the Mother of God will not give birth to the child for you. Cry out to God. He will make you more cheerful." Zeuleys, *Daß die Heiligen für Gott nicht anzurufen*, Aii.

[37] See Kiessling, *Early Sermons*, 118; Jeffrey R. Watt, "Women and the Consistory in Calvin's Geneva," *Sixteenth Century Journal* 24 (1993): 429–39.

[38] Porta, *Jungfrawenspiegel*, 40ᵛ. Other writers refer to Luther's comparing the Virgin Mary to "other pretty virgins," to "a poor housemaid," to "ordinary wives," or to "washerwomen." For the former two,

The admiration of the Virgin Mary's irreproachable life had been, at best, a mixed message during the Middle Ages. Although a number of medieval women had been free to opt for Mary's path of lifelong virginity, obviously, none could or would have aspired to become the Mother of God. For Protestant women, the Virgin Mary as exemplar was utterly incongruous. Virtually all reformers condemned the celibate life as unworthy, while professing belief not only in the Virgin Birth, but also in Mary's perpetual virginity and, at the same time, pronouncing the Virgin Mary an ordinary, humble woman—an example to emulate.[39] It is largely because of this discrepancy that the resultant marginalization of Mary in Protestant circles has been termed "the death" of the Virgin Mary.[40]

Concerning the demise of the feminine element in Christian spirituality that accompanied the "death" of the Virgin and the female saints, Lyndal Roper writes: "By the second half of the century, Protestant women may have been able to develop a female-centered piety. ..." She notes, however, that "this subject lies beyond the scope of this book."[41] The subject lies beyond the scope of the present study as well, but the discussion should not be closed without reference to a tantalizing passage in Porta's work. Porta is discussing Mary's Visitation to Elizabeth shortly after the Annunciation. He refers to a homily Luther had preached on the subject and quotes Luther extensively: "St. Luke says [Mary] went quickly into the hill country. That is splendidly modest. ... Girls and women should stay home, go quickly from their place, not stay out two hours. ..." For this reason St. Luke has applied the word quickly, so that girls and women will not say: 'Why should I always stay home, like a nun in a cloister, and not go walking about? Didn't the Virgin Mary do this? If it was not a sin for her, it's not a sin for me either.' "[42] This passage suggests that speculations concerning the Virgin's "death" may be somewhat exaggerated. It also suggests that the use of the Virgin as an exemplar may have occasionally produced unanticipated—and undesired—results.

---

see *Ein Dialogus oder Gespräch zwischen einem Vater und Sohn die Lehre Martini Luthers und sonst andere Sachen des christlichen Glaubens belangend* (Erfurt: Michael Buchführer, 1523), in *Flugschriften*, ed. Clemen, 1:36. For the latter two, see Jörg Vögeli, *Schirmred*, H1ᵛ–H2. Steven Ozment discusses this pamphlet in detail in *Reformation in the Cities*, 79–83.

[39] See Preuß, *Maria bei Luther*, 14. Preuß provides numerous citations from Luther's works to illustrate his belief in Mary's virginity. Examples from representative works of other reformers include: Porta, *Jungfrawenspiegel*, 39 and 41ᵛ–42; Zwingli, *Eine Predigt*, in Campi, *Zwingli und Maria*, 115–16; idem, *Sämtliche Werke*, 1:426–27; Weidensee and Fritzhans, *Wie Doctor Cubito*, Ciiᵛ; Blarer, *Wahrhaft Antwortung*, D. Curiously, Blarer refers to Mary as the "immaculate, eternally pure Virgin Mary."

[40] Wiesner, "Luther and Women," 295–308.

[41] Roper, *Holy Household*, 265–66. An English example is discussed by Ellen Macek, "The Emergence of a Feminine Spirituality in *The Book of Martyrs*," *Sixteenth Century Journal* 19 (1988): 63–80.

[42] Porta, *Jungfrawenspiegel*, 42ᵛ–43.

$\mathcal{U}$biquity of the SAINTS

DISPUTATIONS, DIETS, AND COLLOQUIES

If it is an exaggeration to proclaim the "death" of the Virgin Mary, clearly dismissal of the cult of the saints by some historians and by some reformers—Zwingli and Luther, most notably—is likewise an exaggeration. While not usually occupying center stage, the cult of the saints and its associated trappings remained topics of debate or discussion between 1517 and 1531—a contentious era of frequent disputations, diets, and colloquies. A sampling of these events illustrates this point well.

The first such incident occurred only months after Luther's posting of his *Ninety-Five Theses*. As discomfort mounted over the unusually wide dissemination of and interest in the *Theses*, the first reaction of the Roman Curia was to deal with the impudent monk through his own Augustinian Order. Luther was requested to appear at the General Chapter meeting in Heidelberg in April–May 1518. He and his colleague Brother Leonhard Beier were given the task of introducing the University of Wittenberg's new theology to the order by means of a disputation. In the resulting Heidelberg Disputation, Luther and Beier defended forty theses, both theological and philosophical. While the issue of indulgences was almost certainly of foremost concern in the wake of the *Ninety-Five Theses*, it was nonetheless addressed only tangentially in the May disputation—through reference to the Treasury of Merits and thus to the contributions of Christ, Mary, and the saints. Thesis 6 reads: "The works of God (we speak of those which he does through man) are...not merits, as though they were sinless."[1]

The Treasury of Merits became far more of a focal point a few months later when Luther arrived in Augsburg for his "fatherly" interviews with Cardinal

[1] For a discussion of the Heidelberg Disputation, see Brecht, *Martin Luther*, vol. 1, *His Road to Reformation 1483–1521*, 235; Schwiebert, *Luther and His Times*, 326–30. Schwiebert contends that the theses were selected by Vicar Johannes von Staupitz "to have Luther appear in a favorable light" (328); hence the failure to emphasize indulgences and the focus on the anti-Scholastic philosophical theses. See also, Thomas Fuchs, *Konfession und Gespräch: Typologie und Funktion der Religionsgespräche in der Reformationszeit*

Cajetan. Denied the right of a disputation and urged to recant his error, Luther asked the cardinal to specify how he had erred. Cajetan, in preparation for the discussion, had carefully studied Luther's recently published works, the *Sermon on Penance* and *Explanations of the Ninety-Five Theses*. In the first interview, Cajetan declared their subjects—the sacrament of penance and the matter of indulgences—to be the two major issues of contention between them. Moreover, according to one observer Cajetan advised Luther to "recant the two points. We can solve the rest by applying distinctions."[2] Concerning indulgences, Cajetan cited as proof of Luther's erroneous position the papal bull *Unigenitus*, issued by Clement VI in 1343. The bull had plainly established, Cajetan argued, not only that the foundation of the Treasury was Christ's suffering and death, but also that the Treasury had increased over the ages because of the contributions made by the sinless Virgin Mary and the other saints: "Christ entrusted this treasury for distribution to the faithful by St. Peter…for the remission in whole or in part of the temporal punishment due for sin.… The aggregate of this treasury is known to be increased by the merits of the Mother of God and of all the elect."[3] The issue at Augsburg was, of course, not so much discord over the saints or penance, but rather disagreement over where ultimate authority rested: with the pope or with the word. Nonetheless, as in other instances, the cult of the saints and its trappings provided a mechanism for the airing of these and similar disagreements and, largely because of such usefulness, it remained a topic of debate.

In June and July of 1519, one of the most significant debates of the early Reformation era occurred in the city of Leipzig. Sanctioned by Duke George of Saxony, the Leipzig Disputation pitted Luther and Karlstadt against Johann Eck, the erudite professor of theology from the University of Ingolstadt who had become one of the most outspoken critics of Luther's theology. The focus of the debate turned on disputes over the authority of the pope and the primacy of Rome. Nonetheless, in the

---

(Cologne: Böhlau, 1995), 116–20. For an English translation of the theses, see Heidelberg Disputation, May 1518, <http://www.augustana.edu/religion/lutherproject/HEIDELBU/Heidelbergdisputation.htm> (28 February 2003). The original Latin text is critically edited in WA 1:350–74.

[2] Jared Wicks, ed. and trans., *Cajetan Responds: A Reader in Reformation Controversy* (Washington: Catholic University of America Press, 1978), 21, quoting Christoph Scheurl, "a jurist of Nuremberg, formerly of Wittenberg" (260 n. 47). For Cajetan's response on thesis 58 (indulgences), see 68–85. For his response on thesis 7 (penance), see 49–55. For more on the Diet of Augsburg (September 1518) and its aftermath (Luther's interviews were on 12–14 October 1518), see Gerhard Hennig, *Cajetan und Luther: Ein historischer Beitrag zur Begegnung von Thomismus und Reformation* (Stuttgart: Calwer, 1966), 61–97; Brecht, *Martin Luther*, 1:246–73; Bainton, *Here I Stand*, 90–97; Schwiebert, *Luther and His Times*, 346–54.

[3] Cajetan, quoting *Unigenitus*, in *Augsburg Treatises*; see Wicks, *Cajetan Responds*, 71–72.

discussions between Eck and Karlstadt, issues involving the cult of the saints came to the fore.[4] Johannes Rubius, formerly a student at Wittenberg, published a satirical rhymed pamphlet about the disputation only three months after it had adjourned.[5] In an entire section devoted to the topic "On the Veneration of All the Dear Saints," he tended to make fun of both sides, but in his section on the saints, he clearly leaned to Rome:

> A fellow came to the Leipzig Disputation
> And cruelly took away prayers.
> O, God, what an evil heart this fellow has,
> Truly, it must hurt him body and soul.
> He has desecrated all the dear saints.
> Oh, God, he has not learned such lessons from a Christian teacher.[6]

Luther's appearance at the Diet of Worms nearly two years after the Leipzig debate resulted in his refusal both to repudiate his written works and to recant his heretical beliefs. Placed under imperial ban, but allowed safe conduct for forty days, Luther went into exile at the Wartburg. The Edict of Worms stressed Luther's civil offenses more than his religious errors because it was issued by civil authority.[7] Yet the Edict certainly did not overlook Luther's religious heresies; and while its reference to the cult is admittedly veiled, the saints maintain a presence in the item dealing with indulgences:

> He has written, in Latin and German, several books full of heresy and blasphemy which have been condemned by the sacred councils of the Catholic Church....

[4]On the Leipzig Disputation, see Otto Seitz, ed., *Der authentische Text der Leipziger Disputation (1519)* (Berlin: Schwetschke u. Sohn, 1903). The issue of indulgences may, indeed, have held more than a theological interest for Eck. Schwiebert points out that Eck was "financed during the period of the Leipzig debate by the Fuggers, whose financial interest in restoring the indulgence trade has been noted." Schwiebert, *Luther and His Times*, 385, citing E. Reinhardt, *Jacob Fugger der Reiche aus Ausburg* (Berlin, 1926), 143. On the Leipzig Disputation in general, see Brecht, *Martin Luther*, 1:299–330; Schwiebert, *Luther and His Times*, 384–437; Fuchs, *Konfession und Gespräch*, 144–87; Bainton, *Here I Stand*, 111–20; Kurt-Victor Selge, "Die Leipziger Disputation zwischen Luther und Eck," *Zeitschrift für Kirchengeschichte* 86 (1975): 26–40. Luther's account is in WA 2:254–383; his comments on indulgences are on 344–50.

[5]Johannes Rubius, *Ein neues Büchlein von der löblichen Disputation in Leipzig* ([Leipzig: Valentin Schumann], 1519), in *Flugschriften*, ed. Laube, 2:1275–77. Rubius had written an earlier Latin work on the debate which provoked a sharp retort from the Lutheran side.

[6]Rubius, *Ein neues Büchlein*, in *Flugschriften*, ed. Laube, 2:1276.

[7]Roland H. Bainton, *The Reformation of the Sixteenth Century* (Boston: Beacon Press, 1952), 61. On the Diet of Worms, see Brecht, *Martin Luther*, 1:433–76.

Item. Regarding purgatory and the masses and prayers said for the souls of our dead, *and also the suffrages and forgivings of our Holy Mother Church*: he agrees, not with our church opinion, but with that of the Waldensian and Wycliffite heresies.[8]

The period following the issuance of the Edict of Worms in May 1521 was one of exceptional religious ferment in the Germanies. Despite Luther's exile, the evangelical movement was growing, a circumstance which caused concern among both civil and religious authorities and which generated doubt that the edict could ever be effectively enforced. Luther's moderate position during the radical eruptions at Wittenberg, however, created a certain amount of goodwill with civil authorities, while the new pope, Adrian VI (1522–23), acknowledged the existence of corruption within the Curia and vowed to take steps to end the problem. Adrian, on the other hand, had no intention of compromising with heretics over matters of faith, despite common ground on the issue of abuses. It is within this atmosphere that the first and second diets of Nuremberg became entangled in the ongoing religious struggle.[9]

The emperor's representative at the first Diet of Nuremberg was his brother, Ferdinand of Austria; the papal nuncio was Bishop Chieregati of Tiramo. Adrian's goal at the diet was, in essence, to effect a bargain: reform of the Curia in exchange for extirpation of heresy. If the heretics refused to recant, however, he urged immediate enforcement of the Edict of Worms. The pope's difficulty in achieving his end lay in the positive attitude many in the diet had come to hold for Luther as well as in the popularity Luther was enjoying among the public; his movement clearly had the force of momentum on its side. In addition, Adrian's acknowledgment of abuse and corruption validated many of Luther's claims about the church. Ultimately, the diet concluded that it could not comply with Adrian's directive to enforce the Edict of Worms. On 6 March 1523, the session came to a close with an agreement to call a Christian Council within one year and in the interim to persuade the heretics to refrain from publishing controversial works or from preaching heretical views. In January 1524 the new pope, Clement VII, sent his representative, Archbishop (later Cardinal) Lorenzo Campeggio, to the second Diet of Nuremberg. Clement hoped, as had Adrian, to secure enforcement of the Edict of Worms, but he failed as completely as had his predecessor.

---

[8] *Edict of Worms*, in *Confrontation at Worms: Martin Luther and the Diet of Worms*, ed. and trans. De Lemar Jensen (Provo: Brigham Young University Press, 1973), 83–87; emphasis added.

[9] The first Diet of Nuremberg met from November 1522 to March 1523; the second, from January to April 1524. On the two diets, see Brecht, *Martin Luther*, 2:109–15; MacKinnon, *Luther and the Reformation*, 3:149–58; Günter Vogler, *Nürnberg: 1524/25*, Studien zur Geschichte der reformatorischen und sozialen Bewegung in der Reichsstadt (Berlin: VEB Deutscher Verlag der Wissenschaften, 1982), 46–64.

Attempts to silence evangelical preachers and writers in the early to mid-1520s were equally futile. As if in defiance of efforts to enforce the Edict of Worms, writers—especially ones with connections to Nuremberg—were tremendously productive in the period. Among the many topics addressed, denunciation of the cult of the saints was prominent. One of the most controversial pieces of the era appeared in August 1523, a work by the popular preacher and pamphleteer Heinrich von Kettenbach. In the pamphlet—a fierce denunciation of both pope and emperor—Brother Heinrich refers early on to the Edict: "Listen, you poor empire, laughing stock of Rome and all the world! Your sages have given foolish advice at the Diet of Worms before that poor child Charles, called the Roman Emperor."[10]

In addition to attacking pope and emperor, Brother Heinrich lashes out at the sacraments, the holidays, and other traditional practices, while writing in glowing terms about Luther and his teachings. He also composes a section entitled "On the Invocation of Saints," in which he argues: "All saints pray to God, place their solace, hope, trust, heart, and soul in God, even the Virgin Mary, even St. Michael and all the good angels. Therefore, we should do likewise...."[11]

Diepold Peringer, "the peasant from Wöhrd-by-Nuremberg," preached in a similar vein. A defrocked priest turned popular preacher, Peringer focused a portion of a 1524 sermon on the invocation of saints. In this sermon, he admonishes his listeners that "the saints have not worked miracles through their own powers, but God through them as through a tool."[12] He closes by saying: "[The Lord] says: 'Come to me; I will attend to you and make you free from your sins.' He does not say, 'Go to St. Peter or Paul.'"[13]

One of the best-known residents of Nuremberg in the period was the shoemaker and *Meistersinger* Hans Sachs, who wrote numerous popular works supporting the evangelical cause, many of them in the form of mock disputations.[14] Sachs touched on all of the contentious issues, supporting Luther wholeheartedly. In one of his best-known works, *A Disputation between a Shoemaker and a Canon*, his characters too address the persistent and intricate issue of the cult of the saints:

Canon: I want Luther to be burned with his books. I have never
            read any and don't want to.

---

[10] Heinrich von Kettenbach, *Ein Practica practiciert aus der heiligen Bibel auf viel zukünftig Jahr* (Bamberg: Georg Erlinger, 1523), in *Flugschriften*, ed. Clemen, 2:185.

[11] Kettenbach, *Ein Practica*, 198–99.

[12] [Peringer], *Ein Sermon, geprediget vom Bauern zu Wöhrd bei Nürnberg*, iii[v].

[13] [Peringer], *Ein Sermon*, v[v].

[14] For an interesting analysis of popular dialogue literature during the Reformation, see Bentzinger, ed., *Die Wahrheit muss ans Licht!* 8–40.

Shoemaker:	Christ says ... you should pray to God your Lord and serve only him.
Canon:	Yes, but we have to have intercessors with God.
Shoemaker:	St. John says if anyone sins, we have an intercessor, Jesus Christ....
Canon:	Sure, sure, but necessity breaks iron. If your hand were broken, you would quickly call on St. Wolfgang.
Shoemaker:	No, Christ says ... come to me all who labor and are heavy laden. I will unburden you. Where would we look for better help? You have made idols out of the saints and thus have led us from Christ.[15]

One final example should serve to illustrate that the questions involving the cult of the saints were still provoking serious controversy in 1523—and that the evangelicals certainly did not easily prevail over the Old Believers. Much as had Johannes Freisleben, Sebald Heyden "corrected" the lyrics of the *Salve Regina: "Salve Jesu Christi / eyn kunig der barmhertzigkeyt...."*[16] The reaction to this new rendition was not altogether positive; indeed, some parishioners aired their objection by painting Heyden as an ass on the wall of Nuremberg's cathedral, while proclaiming that he deserved to be run out of town.[17]

Old Believers and reformers had similarly squared off in June 1522 in Riga, as Lutheran Andreas Knopken engaged in a disputation with members of the city's clergy. In the preceding year, the city had undergone an episode of iconoclasm.[18] Perhaps because the ensuing Riga Disputation lacked the stars of some earlier or subsequent events, however, little else is known about it, including who prevailed. Nonetheless, a list of twenty-four theses, drafted by Knopken, does survive. Among these are issues pertaining to the pope and church hierarchy; to works righteousness, including ceremonies; and to old church practices, such as indulgences, pilgrimages, and the veneration of saints and images.[19] Knopken, who bolsters his objections to the veneration of saints and images with references to the First Commandment, also

---

[15] Hans Sachs, *Von einem Schuhmacher und Chorherren eine Disputation* ([Strassburg: Wolfgang Köpfel, 1524), Biii^{r-v}, Köhler 1820/4666.

[16] Heyden, *Daß der einig Christus unser Mittler und Fürsprech sei*, Aiiii.

[17] Vogler, *Nürnberg*, 53.

[18] Stirm, *Bilderfrage*, 130 n. 1.

[19] Fuchs, *Konfessionen und Gespräch*, 231–34. On Riga, see also, Leonid Arbusow, *Die Einführung der Reformation in Liv-, Est- und Kurland*. Quellen und Forschungen zur Reformationsgeschichte (Leipzig: Heinsius, 1921), 208–15.

effectively conveys the foolhardiness of revering the "lifeless": "A great madness has affected some people today who invoke little gods in different locations and who are under the illusion that lifeless little pictures are full of God's grace."[20]

In Zwingli's Zurich, issues involving such "lifeless little pictures" and the veneration of the saints featured prominently in the four disputations called by the council between January 1523 and January 1524. Shortly before the beginning of the first Zurich Disputation (19 January 1523), Zwingli published in German his sixty-seven *Schlußreden*, essentially a summary of his teachings.[21] The articles included among other items: assertion of the primacy of the Gospel; rejection of the church hierarchy; rejection of belief in the mass as a sacrifice; assertion that food restrictions are unscriptural; approval of clerical marriage and rejection of the vow of chastity; rejection of purgatory; and assertion that Christ is the sole mediator and rejection of belief in the intercession of saints. Article 20, Zwingli's longest, begins: "That God wants to give us all things in his name. It follows from this that we need no other mediator but him beyond the present time."[22] What ensues is a long discourse—backed with multiple scriptural citations—on the fallacies of belief in the intercession of saints. Summing up one section of the article, Zwingli writes: "Finally, reliance upon intercession of the saints obscures, denies and rejects the wholesome suffering of Christ and is an offence to the saints. The first and foremost commandment is as follows, … 'The Lord your God is one God. You shall love the Lord your God with all your heart and with all you [*sic*] soul and with all your might and with all your mind.'"[23]

The disputation took place in Zurich's city hall, with approximately six hundred people, both clergy and laity, in attendance. The chief contestants were Johannes Fabri, representing the bishop of Constance, and of course, Zwingli himself. After heated discussion over the source of ultimate authority (Scripture or church tradition), the question of the intercession of the saints became the topic. Zwingli demanded that Fabri show him where in Scripture the intercession of the saints is sanctioned. When he could not do so, Fabri turned to church tradition—a solution totally unsatisfactory to Zwingli and his followers.[24]

While the Council pronounced the disputation a victory for Zwingli, many issues remained unresolved. A second Zurich Disputation was summoned in October

---

[20] Knopken, quoted in Arbusow, *Die Einführung der Reformation*, 211–12.

[21] Huldrich Zwingli, *Auslegen und Gründ der Schlußreden oder Artikeln* (Zurich: C. Froschauer, [1523]), Köhler 58–63/162; idem, *Sämtliche Werke*, 2:1–457.

[22] Zwingli, "Twentieth Article," in *Writings*, ed. Furcha, 1:135; idem, *Sämtliche Werke*, 2:166.

[23] Zwingli, "Twentieth Article," in *Writings*, ed. Furcha, 1:153; idem, *Sämtliche Werke*, 2:190.

[24] On the first Zurich Disputation, see Potter, *Zwingli*, 97–103; Jackson, *Huldreich Zwingli*, 179–98; Garside, *Zwingli and the Arts*, 96–98.

1523, in part to address the problem of the iconoclasm that had erupted in Zurich in the months following the first debate. Despite the fact that two of the three days during which the disputation took place were devoted to the issue of the nature of the mass, the question of images commanded nearly equal attention.[25] Disagreements arose not only between Old Believers and reformers, but among the reformers themselves. While Zwingli was not a proponent of violent iconoclasm, he nonetheless was unequivocal in his view of the ultimate fate of the images: "It is clear that the images and other representations which we have in the houses of worship have caused the risk of idolatry. Therefore they should not be allowed to remain there, nor in your chambers, nor in the marketplace, nor anywhere else where one does them honour. Chiefly they are not to be tolerated in the churches...."[26]

A more moderate position was offered by Konrad Schmid, son of a wealthy peasant from Küssnacht, canton of Zurich, and friend of Zwingli. Schmid, adopting a position similar to Luther's, urged a gradual approach to the removal of images: "If a weak man clings to a reed that wavers with him, one should leave that in his hand, and at the same time show him a stronger staff, so that he will then of his own accord let the reed fall, and grasp the stronger staff."[27]

The Second Zurich Disputation closed with a resolution in place against the mass and images. Actual removal of the images was another matter. Not until 20 June 1524 did a committee, headed by the city architect and the three *Leutpriester*, or people's priests (Zwingli, Leo Jud, and Heinrich Engelhard), begin a systematic removal—this only after the briefly held Third and Fourth Zurich Disputations reinforced the decisions of the Second.[28]

The outcome of the Zurich disputations greatly strengthened Zwingli's following in certain Swiss regions, while shoring up the resolve of the Church of Rome to resist his incursions in others. In July 1524, for example, the canton of Appenzell planned a disputation directly inspired by the Zurich experience. Indeed, both Zwingli and Jud were invited to take part, with Jud accepting (along with Sebastian Hofmeister) and Zwingli declining the invitation. The debate articles began with the question of the efficacy of works, including specifically masses for the dead, the seven sacraments, indulgences, and the veneration of saints. Although the author of the seven articles to be debated at Appenzell is unknown, he surely was evangelical. The disputation broke down over procedural questions, however, and while one

---

[25] See Potter, *Zwingli*, 130–33; Jackson, *Huldreich Zwingli*, 199–210; Ozment, *Reformation in the Cities*, 146; Garside, *Zwingli and the Arts*, 129–45.

[26] Jackson, *Huldreich Zwingli*, 208, quoting Zwingli.

[27] Garside, *Zwingli and the Arts*, 139, quoting Schmid.

[28] Eire, *War against the Idols*, 82.

chronicler notes that a second debate was planned in Appenzell, there is no evidence that it ever took place.[29]

Throughout the 1520s the Swiss continued to experience religious controversy, with images and intercessors in the forefront. In late April 1524, for instance, Balthasar Hubmaier, a supporter of Zwingli at the Second Zurich Disputation, convened a colloquy in Waldshut, where he had been pastor since 1521. Echoing Zwingli in most points, Hubmaier—who later became one of the first Anabaptists and was martyred in Vienna—composed a list of eighteen theses to be debated. Two of these eighteen address issues involved the cult of the saints:

vii: Images are good for nothing; therefore, no more should be spent on wood and stone, but on the living, needy images of God.

ix: As Christ alone died for our sins, and as we are baptized in his name, he alone should be called upon as an intercessor. Thus we do away with all pilgrimages.[30]

While it is unclear whether the debate actually took place, by June 1524, the Waldshut church had been purged of paintings and statues.[31] As controversy continued to spread among the Swiss, theses nearly identical to the two cited above were among those debated—with ambiguous results—in Ilanz, canton of Gräubunden (Grisons), in January 1526.[32]

The two most important Swiss disputations of the late 1520s took place in Baden-Aargau in 1526 and in Bern in 1528.[33] These two disputations were "astonishingly symmetrical," both in the issues debated and in the fact that in the former, the Roman Catholic delegation dominated; in the latter, the Zwinglian party did so.[34]

---

[29] Fuchs points out that "the suggestion of the scriptural standard in the sixth article reflects a new-belief origin of the articles"; *Konfession und Gespräch*, 306. On the Appenzell Disputation, see ibid., 305–9.

[30] Nikolaus Prugner and Balthasar Hubmaier, *Achtunddreißig Schlußreden, so betreffende ein ganz christlich Leben* ([Strassburg: Johannes Schwan], 1524), Biiii, Köhler 144/393. This short pamphlet contains two sets of articles: twenty by Nikolaus Prugner of Mühlhausen and eighteen by Hubmaier.

[31] Garside, *Zwingli and the Arts*, 144.

[32] [Johannes Comander] *Überdiese nachkommenden Schlußreden wollen wir, der Pfarrer zu Sankt Martin zu Chur samt anderen, einem jeden Antwort und Bericht geben* [Augsburg: Melchior Ramminger, 1526], Köhler 360/1006. See theses 7 and 12. On the Ilanz Disputation, see Fuchs, *Konfession und Gespräch*, 309–19.

[33] On the Baden Disputation, see esp., Potter, *Zwingli*, 228–38; Jackson, *Huldreich Zwingli*, 270–75; and Irena Backus, *The Disputations of Baden, 1526, and Berne, 1528: Neutralizing the Early Church*, Studies in Reformed Theology and History (Princeton: Princeton Theological Seminary, 1993), 1–78. On the Bern Disputation, see Jackson, *Huldreich Zwingli*, 281–86; Potter, *Zwingli*, 246–63; and Backus, *Disputations*, 79–119.

[34] Backus, *Disputations*, 121.

The Baden Disputation, held from 21 May to 18 June 1526, pitted representatives of the bishop of Constance, Johann Eck and Johannes Fabri, against Reformed preachers, including Johannes Oecolampadius of Basel and Berchthold Haller of Bern. Prior to the convening of the debate, a pamphlet war of sorts promoted arguments over the location of the disputation (the Zwinglians unsuccessfully pushed for Zurich); over the principles to be followed (the Zwinglians urged *Schriftprinzip*, to no avail); and over the topics to be discussed. In some respects a Roman Catholic response to earlier Zwinglian successes, the disputation ultimately took place in Baden, a Catholic center, but only fourteen miles from the Protestant stronghold of Zurich.[35] The Catholic advantage over the Protestants was clear, not only when it came to the matter of its respective participants—most notably, the presence of Eck and the absence of Zwingli[36]—but also in terms of sheer numbers. One estimate is that of the 118 priests in attendance, some eighty-seven supported Eck.[37]

On 19 May, two days before the debate began, Eck posted seven theses on the Baden church and town council doors. The issues included were "transubstantiation, the mass as a sacrifice, mediation of the Virgin Mary and the saints, images, purgatory, original sin and the efficacy of infant baptism, the regular stock-in-trade of the hardened controversialist." The number of theses actually debated appears somewhat in question. While scholars seem to agree on the seven posted, Backus, for example, fails to discuss the last two—original sin and the efficacy of infant baptism—and refers somewhat unclearly to "the five main subjects of the Baden Disputation." Potter may explain some of this lack of clarity when he notes that "there never was...an agreed account or minutes of this colloquy."[38]

In any case, the cult of the saints was one issue that stirred controversy in Baden before, during, and after the disputation. In preparation for the debate with Zwingli, Johannes Fabri had written a lengthy attack on six of the reformer's major doctrines, including his proscription both of images and of the veneration of saints. Fabri had planned to deliver the condemnation in person at Baden, but the opportunity never materialized because Zwingli refused to attend. Nonetheless, Fabri quickly published the treatise in the form of a pamphlet, in which, among other things, he argues: "[Zwingli] not only destroys the invocation of saints, he also

---

[35] Potter, *Zwingli*, 235.

[36] Zwingli was absent in part because of the refusal of the participants to adopt the *Schriftprinzip* and in part because, despite assurance of safe conduct, he and the Zurich Council feared for his life. As Potter points out, Jan Hus's fate as well as more recent fears for Luther's safety at Worms underlined the opinion that "faith need not be kept with heretics." Potter, *Zwingli*, 230–32, quotation on 230; Backus, *Disputations*, 8.

[37] Potter, *Zwingli*, 234.

[38] See Potter, *Zwingli*, 236–37; Backus, *Disputations*, 63, 79.

rejects the mass and the sacrament. And, indeed, just as the beast with its mouth open wants to defile God, so he [Zwingli] rejects God's tabernacle, that is, the chosen, immaculate Virgin Mary, whom God has sanctified, and also those who live in heaven, the dear saints."[39]

During the disputation, the capable Eck successfully debated with four Reformed opponents in the struggle over thesis 4: "The Images of the Lord Jesus and the Saints Must Not Be Removed." Thesis 3—"Mary and the Saints Should Be Called upon as Intercessors"—paired Eck with Oecolampadius. In the course of this debate, Eck reminded Oecolampadius that the living can and do pray for us; why not the dead? While Oecolampadius acknowledged the scriptural support for prayers by the living, he noted that in no place does Scripture render accounts of prayers by the dead.[40] At work in this confrontation was an ever-widening difference in perspective. First of all, Eck had adopted the attitude that whatever Scripture does *not prohibit* is potentially acceptable doctrine: the Bible does not say dead saints *do not* intercede; therefore, we can say they do. The reformers, by contrast, required explicit sanction. In addition, once again the issue of the living versus the dead came into play. Eck evidently recognized no distinction between saints on earth and saints in heaven—if one group prays for us, the other must too. Oecolampadius, on the other hand, clearly distinguished between the living and the dead, much in the manner of other reformers, including Luther and Zwingli. In attempting to support his assertions, however, Oecolampadius was at a distinct disadvantage. Bumping up against the medieval *mentalité* which blurred the line between living and dead, he was challenged to "prove" a negative; plainly, he failed. While both sides claimed victory in the Baden Disputation, it is clear that "the Catholic party triumphed."[41]

Although Zwingli did not attend the Baden Disputation, his voice was not entirely silent. On 21 May 1526, he issued his first written response to the seven theses Eck had posted on 19 May.[42] Zwingli's second written reply, which dealt only with theses 1 through 3, was issued on 3 June, one day after the participants had begun to debate thesis 3.[43] In the *First Reply*, Zwingli argues, concerning thesis

---

[39]Johannes Fabri (von Leutkirch), *Christenliche Beweisung über sechs Artikel des unchristenlichen Ulrich Zwinglins* (Tübingen: Ulrich Morhart, 1526), Bbii, Köhler 668–72/1766. See also Backus, *Disputations*, 111–12.

[40]The four Reformed participants were Heinrich Linck, Johannes Hess, Dominik Zili, and Oecolampadius; see Backus, *Disputations*, 48–58.

[41]Kurt Aland, *Four Reformers: Luther-Melanchthon-Calvin-Zwingli*, trans. James L. Schaaf (Minneapolis: Augsburg, 1979), 82.

[42]Zwingli, *Die erst kurze Antwort*. For a discussion of the first reply, see Backus, *Disputations*, 63–66.

[43]Huldrich Zwingli, *Die ander Antwort über etlich unwahrhaft Antworten, die Eck gegeben hat* (Zurich: Hans Hager, 1526), Köhler 304/880; idem, *Sämtliche Werke*, 5:207–36. For a discussion of the second reply, see Backus, *Disputations*, 67–69.

4, that images are contrary to God's law, citing several scriptural passages, including the First Commandment. While he addresses thesis 3 on the invocation of saints in both replies, his response in the *First Reply* is longer and more detailed than that in the second. Citing Scripture to differentiate between prayers of the living and intercession by dead saints, Zwingli also underlines the importance of recognizing Christ as sole mediator: "Christ teaches us to go to the heavenly father and say the 'Our Father,' not [to go] to St. Clare.... He says to us... 'Come to me all who labor and are burdened.' He will give us peace. He means to come to him, not to St. Christopher."[44]

Zwingli's replies were made available to those debating at Baden, and also were published in short order. In addition, partisans on both sides put forth several publications dealing with issues discussed in the disputation—a common enough practice in the era.[45] One of the most interesting of these was originally a sermon preached by Oecolampadius—presumably in Basel—on All Saints' Day 1526, only a few months after the Baden Disputation had adjourned. Smarting from his defeat at Baden by Eck, Oecolampadius devotes the bulk of the sermon, *Concerning the Invocation of Saints*, to attacks on orthodox beliefs about the saints. In the sermon, Oecolampadius takes the opportunity to assail arguments for the invocation of saints, particularly those presented in "a thick book against Ulrich Zwingli (who, as far as I am concerned, is a true preacher of Christ's word)...put together by Fabri." Prominent among the points Oecolampadius makes is once again the differentiation between living and dead: "They [Fabri and his followers] say, indeed, Moses and Abraham, the prophets and the apostles have prayed [for others]. Therefore, the dead also pray for us, the masses, so that we should have them for intercessors. They could not justify this even if they collected all of Scripture together. For the quarrel is not about those who are living, but those who are dead."[46]

If the Baden Disputation was a Catholic victory, the disputation in Bern in January 1528 was a matching triumph for the evangelical party. Unlike in Baden, Zwingli participated directly at Bern along with such notable supporters as Martin Bucer and Wolfgang Capito (Köpfel) from Strasbourg and Berchthold Haller from Bern. Haller and his colleague Franz Kolb drew up ten *Schlußreden*, of which two pertain to the cult of the saints: number 6 declares Christ the only intercessor; number 8 proclaims

---

[44] Zwingli, *Die erst kurze Antwort*, Aiii^v–Aiiii; idem, *Sämtliche Werke*, 5:192.

[45] See Backus, *Disputations*, 71–78, for the post-Baden publications; see ibid., 111–19, for the post-Bern publications.

[46] Oekolampad, *Von Anrufung der Heiligen*. The response to Fabri begins on Av^v and continues to the end of the pamphlet, Bvi^v, for a total of nineteen pages. The "thick book" referred to is Fabri's *Christenliche Beweisung*, discussed above. Zwinglian Sebastian Mayer makes a similar argument in his pamphlet, *Widerrufung an ein löbliche Freistadt Straßburg*, Biiii^v–Ciiii^v.

the veneration of images to be against God's word.[47] On the Catholic side, only some lesser-known theologians participated; for Catholics "had...no more desire than Zwingli [at Baden] to talk to deaf ears or to expose themselves to insult and possible physical violence."[48]

During the course of the disputation, which ran from 6 to 26 January, evangelical preachers delivered a total of nine sermons. Ultimately, these sermons were published in a pamphlet edited by Konrad Schmid, but as the debate proceeded, they effectively served to punctuate the disputed subjects with additional detailed argument. For example, in the midst of the debate over the veneration of the saints (on 22 January 1528) Martin Bucer delivered a sermon in which he sounded several of what had become familiar evangelical themes on the issue of the saints. In particular, Bucer denounces those who had "encased [the dear saints'] bones in silver, in order to turn them into idols; sung the same old idolatrous songs to them; played the organ; rung bells; burned candles for those who cannot see; anointed them, while they cannot smell; clothed them, while they cannot feel cold; given money and other things for nourishment, while they cannot eat; built expensive houses, while they are sensitive neither to the sun nor to thunderstorms."[49] The Bern Disputation, which adjourned on 26 January 1528, completed the introduction of the Reformation into the city, with the abolition of the mass and images coming on the very next day. By April, Christoph Froschauer of Zurich had published in pamphlet form the ten *Acts of the Disputation*, which included, among others, two articles addressing the sin of fornication and two others condemning the cult of the saints.[50]

The unfinished business of the Diet of Worms and the two Nuremberg diets resurfaced in 1526. Convening 25 June of that year, the Diet of Speyer took up once again the question of enforcement of the Edict of Worms. Primarily a meeting of moderates, the First Diet of Speyer focused as well on the abuses that had been an issue in Nuremberg. Indeed, the participants agreed upon a compromise—one which in many ways favored the Lutheran party: permission of clerical marriage, curtailment of the mendicant orders, and abolition of private masses were among

---

[47] *Berner Synodus mit den Schlussreden der Berner Disputation und dem Reformationsamt*, Dokumente der Berner Reformation (Bern: Paul Haupt, 1978), 8–9.

[48] Jackson, *Huldreich Zwingli*, 281.

[49] Bern, Disputation (1528), *Die Predigten so von den fremden Prädikanten, die zu Bern auf dem Gespräch gewesen, beschehen sind* (Zurich: C. Froschauer, 1528), esp. Gv^v, Köhler 772–74/1948. For more on the sermons, see Backus, *Disputations*, 99–109.

[50] See Bern, Disputation, *Ratschlag*, Bi^v–Bii. Article 9 promotes marriage as desirable for all and condemns fornication and unchastity. Article 10 condemns priests for their scandalous behavior. Article 6 proclaims Christ the sole intercessor. For a discussion of the links between fornication and the cult of the saints, see chap. 3 above.

the points of consensus.[51] Concerning the cult of the saints specifically, the participants advocated the revision of many traditional practices. For example, no longer would pilgrimages be imposed as penance for sinners; the number of festivals and fast days was greatly curtailed, and the festivals remaining (in honor of Christ, the Virgin, the Apostles, the martyrs, and other saints) would become far more decorous; finally, indulgences were recognized as abusive.[52] Georg Spalatin commented on the proposal: "Never before in any diet was there such free and independent and outspoken criticism of the pope, the bishops, the clergy, as in this one."[53]

Such amicable compromise, however, was not to be. Acting upon a directive issued by the emperor in March, imperial commissioners demanded revocation of the agreement and immediate implementation of the Edict of Worms. Evangelicals continued to call for settlement by a Christian Council. Ultimately, the diet acted on its own, proclaiming a recess *(Reichstagsabschied)* and authorizing each state to use its own good judgment vis-à-vis the Edict of Worms.[54]

The first prince to take advantage of this policy was Landgrave Philip of Hesse. In calling the Synod of Homberg for 21–22 October 1526, Philip set out to organize one of the first Protestant territorial churches. At the Landgrave's request, Franz Lambert of Avignon, a French Franciscan who had been converted to Protestantism in part by Zwingli and in part by Luther, drew up 158 theses *(Paradoxa)* for debate with Old Believers led by Nikolaus Ferber. Lambert's theses—and thus Philip's Hessian Reformation—reflect the influence of both Lutheran and Reformed Protestantism. Specifically, in the matter of church polity, Lambert's Zwinglian connections are apparent; and while these features are perhaps the most interesting and most significant aspects of the Homberg disputation, the traditional questions—including those surrounding the cult of the saints—played a role as well. In particular, the veneration of images, the observation of ceremonies, and the proper role of the *Ave Maria* were among the issues debated.[55]

In the following year in Düsseldorf, the Franciscan Johann Heller von Korbach prepared ten theses for debate with Friedrich Myconius, former Franciscan turned Lutheran. Heller's seventh thesis reads: "One should call upon the Virgin Mary and

---

[51] On the First Diet of Speyer, see Brecht, *Martin Luther*, 2:358; MacKinnon, *Luther and the Reformation*, 3:274–80. See also, Walter Friedensburg, *Der Reichstag zu Speier 1526* in *Zusammenhang der politischen und kirchlichen Entwicklung Deutschlands im Reformationszeitalter*, Historische Untersuchungen (Berlin: R. Gaertner, 1887).

[52] Friedensburg, *Der Reichstag*, 355–57. On the saints as agents of disorder, see chap. 3 above.

[53] Quoted in MacKinnon, *Luther and the Reformation*, 3:277.

[54] As MacKinnon points out, this decision promoted German particularism, extending it from the political to the religious sphere; MacKinnon, *Luther and the Reformation*, 3:279.

[55] On the Synod of Homberg, see Fuchs, *Konfession und Gespräch*, 319–31. On Franz Lambert of Avignon, see chap. 1 above.

was he content with a mere rebuttal of the arguments made in the *Confutatio.* ...ead, Melanchthon proceeded with a full-scale condemnation, revisiting every ...or evangelical objection to the cult of the saints.[68]

...Permeating the *Apology,* assertions of the fundamental tenet of *sola Scriptura* ...olve around two loci: "No testimony concerning the praying of the dead is ...nt in the Scriptures...," and "neither a command, nor a promise, nor an exam- ...can be produced from the Scriptures concerning the invocation of saints...." ...anchthon acknowledges that in the *Apology* he focuses almost exclusively upon ...ses on the part of the educated elite: "Here we do not as yet recite the abuses of ...common people [how manifest idolatry is practiced at pilgrimages]. We are still ...king of the opinions of the doctors." He, nonetheless, does attribute much of ...disorder among the popular classes to the failures of the elite. Because of their ...e teachings, for example, "in public opinion the blessed Virgin has succeeded ...gether to the place of Christ." The elite are also heavily responsible for the ...ad of superstition: "With the learned this error also prevails, namely, that to each ...t a particular administration has been committed, that Anna bestows riches..., ...astian keeps off pestilence, Valentine heals epilepsy, George protects horsemen. ...se opinions have clearly sprung from heathen examples." Furthermore, these ...ulous stories concerning the saints" were the product of "certain triflers" who ...e invented stories...in which there are nothing but superstitious examples con- ...ing certain prayers, certain fastings, and certain additions of service for bringing ...ain." Indeed, "the bishops, theologians, and monks applaud these monstrous and ...ed stories."[69]

...In particular, Melanchthon faults the cloistered—"foolish monks"—for teach- ...people superstitions about the saints. He writes: "Some of us have seen a doctor ...heology dying, for consoling whom a certain theologian, a monk, was ...loyed. He pressed on the dying man nothing but this prayer: 'Mother of grace, ...ct us from the enemy; receive us in the hour of death.'" He continues with ...her example: "In a certain monastery we...have seen a statue of the blessed ...in, which moved automatically by a trick...so as to seem either to turn away ...[those who did not make a large offering] or nod to those making request." In ...as in additional instances, he attributes to monks—and to others in the ...ch—motivations of economic greed: "Many learned and excellent men long ...re these times deplored the abuses of the Mass, confidence in monastic obser- ...es, services to the saints intended to yield a revenue...." Finally, he associates

---

...[68] These objections are identified in chap. 1 above as revolving around *sola Scriptura,* saints' associa- ...with the cloister, socioeconomic abuses, superstition, and disorder.
...[69] "Article 21," *Apology,* 104–7; CT 345, 347, 351, 353–55.

the dear saints to pray to God for us."[56] Heller went on to cite biblical examples to justify this, including Job's praying for others (Job 42:8) and Isaac's praying for Rebekah to become fruitful (Gen. 25:21). The Handlung records an interesting exchange over such support for thesis seven. Myconius asked Heller to show him where Scripture says that we should invoke dead saints as well as where it says that dead saints are intercessors for us before God. The *Handlung* continues: "Then [Heller] takes his Bible and says that it's in there but that he can't find it right now." When Heller goes on, however, to cite further examples of the living praying for one another, Myconius demands, "Does that mean to call on *dead* saints?" Ulti- mately, Heller was unable to find appropriate scriptural passages and was forced to concede the point to Myconius.[57]

Despite Protestant gains, the issue of the Edict of Worms came to the fore once again in March 1529 with the repeal of the recess and the convening of the Second Diet of Speyer.[58] While the recess had led to persecution of evangelicals in predom- inantly Roman Catholic areas, it had also promoted consolidation of the evangelical movement in areas—Hesse, for example—receptive to the Protestant message.[59] The decree issued at the Second Diet of Speyer sought once again to enforce the Edict of Worms; in addition, it set out to limit or undo evangelical gains by obliging Lutherans to tolerate Roman Catholic beliefs and practices in their territories with- out requiring a reciprocal toleration of Lutherans by Roman Catholics.[60] These decisions led to the famous *Protestation* signed by Elector John of Saxony; the mar- grave of Brandenburg; Philip, the landgrave of Hesse; the dukes of Brunswick and Luneburg; Wolfgang, the prince of Anhalt; and the imperial cities of Strasbourg, Nuremberg, Ulm, Constance, Lindau, Memmingen, Kempten, Nördlingen, Heil- bronn, Reutlingen, Issna, St. Gall, Weissenburg, and Windsheim.[61]

---

[56] *Handlung und Disputation,* Aiᵛ.

[57] *Handlung und Disputation,* Biiᵛ–Biii; emphasis added. On this exchange, see also C[ajetan] Schmitz, *Der Observant: Joh. Heller von Korbach: Mit besonderer Berücksichtigung des Düsseldorfer Religionsge- sprächs vom Jahre 1527,* ed. Joseph Gering, Reformationsgeschichtliche Studien und Texte (Münster: Aschendorff, 1913), 89–119.

[58] On the Second Diet of Speyer, see Brecht, *Martin Luther,* 2:362–63; MacKinnon, *Luther and the Reformation,* 3:297–305.

[59] It also may have exacerbated growing dissension between Lutherans and Zwinglians, as the blos- soming Sacramentarian Controversy led to the Marburg Colloquy in October 1529. Additional fissures among the evangelicals are reflected in the agreement among most of the participants at Speyer to repress the Anabaptists.

[60] Lutheranism was the only evangelical form permitted. As MacKinnon points out, "The differen- tiation between Lutherans and Zwinglians was a skilful device for playing off the one against the other and thus paralysing the evangelical opposition." MacKinnon, *Luther and the Reformation,* 3:301.

[61] *Die Appellation und Protestation der evangelischen Stände auf dem Reichstage zu Speier 1529,* ed. Julius Ney, Quellenschriften zur Geschichte des Protestantismus (Darmstadt: Wissenschaftliche Buchgesell- schaft, 1967).

The thread connecting the Second Diet of Speyer to debates over the cult of the saints is decidedly thin. Neither the pronouncements of the diet nor the *Protestation* itself mentions the saints directly or even obliquely. Yet the diet's affirmation of the Edict of Worms—with its plank condemning Luther's position on indulgences—and the *Protestation*'s objections to outdated liturgy and practices constitute a flimsy, but not wholly insignificant, tether. With the convening of the subsequent Diet of Augsburg in June 1530, however, the link binding the Reichstag to the question of the saints gained considerable substance. Both Catholics and Lutherans took heart at Charles V's announcement that he would preside over the Reichstag himself. Catholics hoped that the heretics would be summarily crushed, while Lutherans hoped at long last for a resolution to convene a church council.

For a variety of reasons, the diet's April opening was delayed until June. Luther, still under the ban of the Edict of Worms, dared not attend the diet; but a delegation led by Philipp Melanchthon represented Wittenberg's interests at Augsburg. Melanchthon's focus was upon the preparation and revision of a profession of faith that would make the Lutheran case at Augsburg. The resulting document, the *Augsburg Confession*—written in both German and Latin—was read in German on 25 June 1530, by Christian Beyer, chancellor of Electoral Saxony, before the assembled Reichstag. [62] Consisting of twenty-nine articles, the *Confession* failed to reconcile Catholics and Lutherans; the emperor, issuing a response in August and perceiving no progress in mending the schism, declared the Reichstag in recess as of 23 September.

What is important to this study is not so much the relative success or failure of the *Augsburg Confession*, but rather certain aspects of its content. Namely, articles 20 and 21—added in one of the final revisions[63]—both focused part of the continuing debate once again explicitly upon the "childish matter" or the "superfluous concerns" surrounding the cult of the saints. In article 20, "Of Good Works," for instance, Melanchthon condemns "our adversaries" for having promoted "needless works," such as "services in honor of saints," and for having overlooked the necessity of faith while preaching such "unprofitable works."[64] In article 21, "Of the Worship of the Saints," moreover, he reiterates the Lutheran position on the issue: the saints may be used as models, but they must not be invoked because Christ is the only mediator. Furthermore, he writes: "This is about the Sum of our Doctrine, in which, as can be seen, there is nothing that varies from the Scripture, or from the Church Catholic, or

from the Church of Rome as known from its writers. This being th[...] harshly who insist that our teachers be regarded as heretics."[65]

Advising Charles V in the response, analysis, and ultimate refuta[...] *burg Confession* were such luminaries as Campeggio, Usingen, [...] Cochlaeus, and Konrad Wimpina. The *Confutatio,* read aloud on[...] turned once again to church tradition: not only did the universal c[...] invocation of the saints, but so had many church fathers, such as A[...] Cyprian, Chrysostom, Basil, and Bernard. Furthermore, Cathol[...] their refusal to acknowledge the distinctions between living and d[...] Lutherans insisted upon making. Once again Catholics supported [...] the saints by pointing to examples such as Job's praying for his [...] praying for the people of Israel. Finally, the *Confutatio* draws a dis[...] types of mediators *(Mittler):* "As the whole church confesses, there [...] *[mittler der erlösung],* but for intercession, many other mediators."[66]

Almost immediately after the *Confutatio* was read, Melanchtho[...] his *Apology of the Augsburg Confession*, a document considerably lon[...] inal *Confession.* When the diet recessed in September, he had not [...] opportunity to have this work read before the assembly. Revised [...] the spring of 1531 and published together with the *Augsburg Conf[...] was far more critical of the Catholic position than the original Co[...] Melanchthon's initial point of attack in the article dealing with th[...] the issue of living versus dead: "They do not effect anything else t[...] should be honored; likewise, that the saints who live pray for o[...] indeed, the invocation of dead saints were on that account ne[...] Cyprian, because he asked Cornelius while yet alive to pray for [...] departing. By this example they prove the invocation of the dead[...] note that "even supposing that the saints pray for the Church ev[...] does not follow that they are to be invoked." Melanchthon further[...] tinction the Catholics had drawn between types of mediators: "Al[...] a distinction between mediators of *intercession* and mediators ... [...] they plainly make the saints mediators of redemption."[67]

What is most interesting about the *Apology*, however, is that [...] not stop with a reiteration and amplification of the points made [...]

---

[62] For a concise, yet detailed account of the Diet of Augsburg, see *Appellation und Protestation der evangelischen Stände*, ed. Ney, 714–35. See also, Brecht, *Martin Luther*, 2:369–410.

[63] *Appellation und Protestation der evangelischen Stände*, 727.

[64] Article 20: "Of Good Works," *Augsburg Confession*, in *Concordia*, 15; *CT*, 53.

[65] Article 21: "Of the Worship of the Saints," *Augsburg Confession*, in *Concordia* [...]

[66] "Vom Dienst der Heiligen" / "De Cultu Sanctorum," in *Die Confutatio* [...] *vom 3. August 1530,* ed. Herbert Immenkötter, Corpus Catholicorum, vol. 33 (I[...] 1979), 124–26, 128.

[67] Article 21(9): "Of the Invocation of Saints," *Apology of the Augsburg Confessi[...] *CT* 343, 345, 347.

such unsavory practices as indulgence peddling with abuses involving the cult of the saints, particularly those practices undertaken out of economic greed. Citing 1 Cor. 3:8, he writes: "'Every man shall receive his own reward according to his own labor,' i.e., they cannot mutually bestow their own merits, the one upon the other, as the monks sell the merits of their orders." Melanchthon ends this section on the saints by beseeching Emperor Charles "not to assent to the violent counsels of our adversaries, but to seek other honorable ways of so establishing harmony that godly consciences are not burdened, that no cruelty is exercised against innocent men, as we have hitherto seen, and that sound doctrine is not suppressed in the Church."[70]

In reviewing the problems addressed at the disputations, diets, and colloquies discussed above, one notes that the cult of the saints was rarely the primary subject of debate. Except among the Swiss, where the topic of images carried so much weight, the saints were almost always relegated to an ancillary position, overshadowed by the mass, authority, or other more ponderous issues. Nonetheless, the saints clearly did not fade away over the years in question. If anything, Melanchthon, in the *Apology*, allots them considerably more space than many earlier evangelical writers had done. In analyzing the activities of these meetings, one can hardly ignore the resilience of the cult of the saints as a minor, yet tenacious matter. Perhaps it is largely because the cult of the saints remained a convenient vehicle for the airing of a variety of confessional disagreements that it not only endured, but also maintained a vital presence in sixteenth-century German society, popular piety, and religious discourse.

THE ERFURT INCIDENT

As if to underscore the utility of the cult in religious disputes, the *Pfaffensturm* (parson storm or riot) that disturbed the peace of Erfurt between 1521 and 1525 coalesced in large part around the issue of the saints.[71] One of Thuringia's leading cities—center of trade, producer of woad, home to a prestigious university—Erfurt, by the end of the fifteenth century, enjoyed and endured a complex political status, one reflective of that of the empire itself. The city, located within Electoral Saxony after the division of the territory in 1485, continued from time to time to attract the interest of Albertine Saxony. To make matters even more complicated, Erfurt's nominal overlord

---

[70] "Article 21," *Apology*, 106–8; *CT* 349, 351, 353, 355, 357. Regarding economic greed, he writes that adversaries "invent these things, not in order to treat the saints with honor, but to defend lucrative services"; ibid., 105; *CT* 351.

[71] This reconstruction of the chronology of the Erfurt incident relies heavily upon Scribner, "Civic Unity and the Reformation in Erfurt," in *Popular Culture*, 185–216; Weiss, *Ein fruchtbar Bethlehem*, 68–81; Kleineidam, *Universitas*, 3:2–35.

was the archbishop of Mainz. By the beginning of the sixteenth century, however, the city had become nearly autonomous, an enviable—albeit precarious—status.[72]

During the years 1509 through 1516, for instance, Erfurt came close to losing its jealously guarded autonomy because of a series of political upheavals brought on primarily by social and economic strains. While these events had settled down in 1516, by 1520 tensions began mounting again. Initially, the issue was economic. Trade was declining steadily in the city, largely because of increased customs tariffs imposed by the archbishop of Mainz. While the resulting protests began by targeting the tariff issue, old concerns soon blended with new, and the clergy became a handy target. In difficult economic times, the clerics—with their immunity from taxation, not to mention their frequently cited greed—understandably came under harsh criticism. Such criticism was exacerbated by the fact that by 1520, Martin Luther had acquired a following among students and humanists in the university. Two of the more prominent Martinists were Luther's friend and fellow Augustinian Johannes Lang, and Justus Jonas, who began preaching the new theology in late 1520.[73] Clearly, the two interest groups fed on one another: those feeling the economic pinch whose resentment led to anticlericalism and those embracing evangelical tenets whose revised theology produced anti-Romanism. The common denominator was, of course, hostility to the Roman Catholic clergy and its supporters.

The discord neared a peak on 6–7 April 1521, when Luther stopped in Erfurt en route to the Diet of Worms. Welcomed by the council, the university, and many townspeople, Luther preached a rousing sermon to an overflowing crowd at the Augustinerkirche. The subject was justification by faith alone and the futility of seeking salvation through works. Among other points, he warned against relying on the efficacy of such things as pilgrimages "to St. James or St. Peter's." He furthermore lashed out once again at the Treasury of Merits: "I say that none of the saints, no matter how holy they were, attained salvation by their works. Even the holy mother of God did not become good, was not saved, by her virginity or her motherhood, but rather by the will of faith and the works of God, and not by her purity, or her own works."[74]

In addition to his warm reception at the church, Luther was honored with a feast by the university.[75] After he had proceeded to Weimar, however, he learned—

---

[72] Scribner, "Civic Unity," 186–87.

[73] Scribner, "Civic Unity," 194–95.

[74] *Sermon Preached at Erfurt on the Journey to Worms*, in *LW,* 51:60–66; WA 7:808–13.

[75] Weiss, *Ein fruchtbar Bethlehem*, 68. Weiss notes that the University's *Rechnungsbuch* records: "Thirty-one *Schneeberger Groschen* is what the reception for the honorable Doctor Martin Luther cost." Weiss adds, "That was about as much as a journeyman earned in twenty-one days" (68).

the dear saints to pray to God for us."[56] Heller went on to cite biblical examples to justify this, including Job's praying for others (Job 42:8) and Isaac's praying for Rebekah to become fruitful (Gen. 25:21). The Handlung records an interesting exchange over such support for thesis seven. Myconius asked Heller to show him where Scripture says that we should invoke dead saints as well as where it says that dead saints are intercessors for us before God. The *Handlung* continues: "Then [Heller] takes his Bible and says that it's in there but that he can't find it right now." When Heller goes on, however, to cite further examples of the living praying for one another, Myconius demands, "Does that mean to call on *dead* saints?" Ultimately, Heller was unable to find appropriate scriptural passages and was forced to concede the point to Myconius.[57]

Despite Protestant gains, the issue of the Edict of Worms came to the fore once again in March 1529 with the repeal of the recess and the convening of the Second Diet of Speyer.[58] While the recess had led to persecution of evangelicals in predominantly Roman Catholic areas, it had also promoted consolidation of the evangelical movement in areas—Hesse, for example—receptive to the Protestant message.[59] The decree issued at the Second Diet of Speyer sought once again to enforce the Edict of Worms; in addition, it set out to limit or undo evangelical gains by obliging Lutherans to tolerate Roman Catholic beliefs and practices in their territories without requiring a reciprocal toleration of Lutherans by Roman Catholics.[60] These decisions led to the famous *Protestation* signed by Elector John of Saxony; the margrave of Brandenburg; Philip, the landgrave of Hesse; the dukes of Brunswick and Luneburg; Wolfgang, the prince of Anhalt; and the imperial cities of Strasbourg, Nuremberg, Ulm, Constance, Lindau, Memmingen, Kempten, Nördlingen, Heilbronn, Reutlingen, Issna, St. Gall, Weissenburg, and Windsheim.[61]

---

[56] *Handlung und Disputation*, Ai[v].

[57] *Handlung und Disputation*, Bii[v]–Biii; emphasis added. On this exchange, see also C[ajetan] Schmitz, *Der Observant: Joh. Heller von Korbach: Mit besonderer Berücksichtigung des Düsseldorfer Religionsgesprächs vom Jahre 1527*, ed. Joseph Gering, Reformationsgeschichtliche Studien und Texte (Münster: Aschendorff, 1913), 89–119.

[58] On the Second Diet of Speyer, see Brecht, *Martin Luther*, 2:362–63; MacKinnon, *Luther and the Reformation*, 3:297–305.

[59] It also may have exacerbated growing dissension between Lutherans and Zwinglians, as the blossoming Sacramentarian Controversy led to the Marburg Colloquy in October 1529. Additional fissures among the evangelicals are reflected in the agreement among most of the participants at Speyer to repress the Anabaptists.

[60] Lutheranism was the only evangelical form permitted. As MacKinnon points out, "The differentiation between Lutherans and Zwinglians was a skilful device for playing off the one against the other and thus paralysing the evangelical opposition." MacKinnon, *Luther and the Reformation*, 3:301.

[61] *Die Appellation und Protestation der evangelischen Stände auf dem Reichstage zu Speier 1529*, ed. Julius Ney, Quellenschriften zur Geschichte des Protestantismus (Darmstadt: Wissenschaftliche Buchgesellschaft, 1967).

The thread connecting the Second Diet of Speyer to debates over the cult of the saints is decidedly thin. Neither the pronouncements of the diet nor the *Protestation* itself mentions the saints directly or even obliquely. Yet the diet's affirmation of the Edict of Worms—with its plank condemning Luther's position on indulgences—and the *Protestation*'s objections to outdated liturgy and practices constitute a flimsy, but not wholly insignificant, tether. With the convening of the subsequent Diet of Augsburg in June 1530, however, the link binding the Reichstag to the question of the saints gained considerable substance. Both Catholics and Lutherans took heart at Charles V's announcement that he would preside over the Reichstag himself. Catholics hoped that the heretics would be summarily crushed, while Lutherans hoped at long last for a resolution to convene a church council.

For a variety of reasons, the diet's April opening was delayed until June. Luther, still under the ban of the Edict of Worms, dared not attend the diet; but a delegation led by Philipp Melanchthon represented Wittenberg's interests at Augsburg. Melanchthon's focus was upon the preparation and revision of a profession of faith that would make the Lutheran case at Augsburg. The resulting document, the *Augsburg Confession*—written in both German and Latin—was read in German on 25 June 1530, by Christian Beyer, chancellor of Electoral Saxony, before the assembled Reichstag. [62] Consisting of twenty-nine articles, the *Confession* failed to reconcile Catholics and Lutherans; the emperor, issuing a response in August and perceiving no progress in mending the schism, declared the Reichstag in recess as of 23 September.

What is important to this study is not so much the relative success or failure of the *Augsburg Confession*, but rather certain aspects of its content. Namely, articles 20 and 21—added in one of the final revisions[63]—both focused part of the continuing debate once again explicitly upon the "childish matter" or the "superfluous concerns" surrounding the cult of the saints. In article 20, "Of Good Works," for instance, Melanchthon condemns "our adversaries" for having promoted "needless works," such as "services in honor of saints," and for having overlooked the necessity of faith while preaching such "unprofitable works."[64] In article 21, "Of the Worship of the Saints," moreover, he reiterates the Lutheran position on the issue: the saints may be used as models, but they must not be invoked because Christ is the only mediator. Furthermore, he writes: "This is about the Sum of our Doctrine, in which, as can be seen, there is nothing that varies from the Scripture, or from the Church Catholic, or

[62] For a concise, yet detailed account of the Diet of Augsburg, see *Appellation und Protestation der evangelischen Stände*, ed. Ney, 714–35. See also, Brecht, *Martin Luther*, 2:369–410.

[63] *Appellation und Protestation der evangelischen Stände*, 727.

[64] Article 20: "Of Good Works," *Augsburg Confession*, in *Concordia*, 15; *CT*, 53.

from the Church of Rome as known from its writers. This being the case, they judge harshly who insist that our teachers be regarded as heretics."[65]

Advising Charles V in the response, analysis, and ultimate refutation of the *Augsburg Confession* were such luminaries as Campeggio, Usingen, Fabri, Johannes Cochlaeus, and Konrad Wimpina. The *Confutatio,* read aloud on 3 August 1530, turned once again to church tradition: not only did the universal church uphold the invocation of the saints, but so had many church fathers, such as Augustine, Jerome, Cyprian, Chrysostom, Basil, and Bernard. Furthermore, Catholics continued in their refusal to acknowledge the distinctions between living and dead saints that the Lutherans insisted upon making. Once again Catholics supported the invocation of the saints by pointing to examples such as Job's praying for his friends or Moses' praying for the people of Israel. Finally, the *Confutatio* draws a distinction between types of mediators *(Mittler):* "As the whole church confesses, there is only one savior *[mittler der erlösung],* but for intercession, many other mediators."[66]

Almost immediately after the *Confutatio* was read, Melanchthon began work on his *Apology of the Augsburg Confession,* a document considerably longer than the original *Confession.* When the diet recessed in September, he had not been afforded the opportunity to have this work read before the assembly. Revised and completed in the spring of 1531 and published together with the *Augsburg Confession,* the *Apology* was far more critical of the Catholic position than the original *Confession* had been. Melanchthon's initial point of attack in the article dealing with the saints centers on the issue of living versus dead: "They do not effect anything else than that the saints should be honored; likewise, that the saints who live pray for others; as though, indeed, the invocation of dead saints were on that account necessary. They cite Cyprian, because he asked Cornelius while yet alive to pray for his brothers when departing. By this example they prove the invocation of the dead." He goes on to note that "even supposing that the saints pray for the Church ever so much, yet it does not follow that they are to be invoked." Melanchthon further criticizes the distinction the Catholics had drawn between types of mediators: "Although they make a distinction between mediators of *intercession* and mediators ... of *redemption*, yet they plainly make the saints mediators of redemption."[67]

What is most interesting about the *Apology,* however, is that Melanchthon did not stop with a reiteration and amplification of the points made in the *Confession;*

---

[65] Article 21: "Of the Worship of the Saints," *Augsburg Confession,* in *Concordia,* 16; CT 57–59.

[66] "Vom Dienst der Heiligen" / "De Cultu Sanctorum," in *Die Confutatio der Confessio Augustana vom 3. August 1530,* ed. Herbert Immenkötter, Corpus Catholicorum, vol. 33 (Münster: Aschendorff, 1979), 124–26, 128.

[67] Article 21(9): "Of the Invocation of Saints," *Apology of the Augsburg Confession,* in *Concordia,* 104–5; CT 343, 345, 347.

nor was he content with a mere rebuttal of the arguments made in the *Confutatio*. Instead, Melanchthon proceeded with a full-scale condemnation, revisiting every major evangelical objection to the cult of the saints.[68]

Permeating the *Apology*, assertions of the fundamental tenet of *sola Scriptura* revolve around two loci: "No testimony concerning the praying of the dead is extant in the Scriptures ...," and "neither a command, nor a promise, nor an example can be produced from the Scriptures concerning the invocation of saints...." Melanchthon acknowledges that in the *Apology* he focuses almost exclusively upon abuses on the part of the educated elite: "Here we do not as yet recite the abuses of the common people [how manifest idolatry is practiced at pilgrimages]. We are still speaking of the opinions of the doctors." He, nonetheless, does attribute much of the disorder among the popular classes to the failures of the elite. Because of their false teachings, for example, "in public opinion the blessed Virgin has succeeded altogether to the place of Christ." The elite are also heavily responsible for the spread of superstition: "With the learned this error also prevails, namely, that to each saint a particular administration has been committed, that Anna bestows riches ..., Sebastian keeps off pestilence, Valentine heals epilepsy, George protects horsemen. These opinions have clearly sprung from heathen examples." Furthermore, these "fabulous stories concerning the saints" were the product of "certain triflers" who "have invented stories ... in which there are nothing but superstitious examples concerning certain prayers, certain fastings, and certain additions of service for bringing in gain." Indeed, "the bishops, theologians, and monks applaud these monstrous and wicked stories."[69]

In particular, Melanchthon faults the cloistered—"foolish monks"—for teaching people superstitions about the saints. He writes: "Some of us have seen a doctor of theology dying, for consoling whom a certain theologian, a monk, was employed. He pressed on the dying man nothing but this prayer: 'Mother of grace, protect us from the enemy; receive us in the hour of death.'" He continues with another example: "In a certain monastery we ... have seen a statue of the blessed Virgin, which moved automatically by a trick ... so as to seem either to turn away from [those who did not make a large offering] or nod to those making request." In this, as in additional instances, he attributes to monks—and to others in the church—motivations of economic greed: "Many learned and excellent men long before these times deplored the abuses of the Mass, confidence in monastic observances, services to the saints intended to yield a revenue...." Finally, he associates

---

[68] These objections are identified in chap. 1 above as revolving around *sola Scriptura*, saints' associations with the cloister, socioeconomic abuses, superstition, and disorder.

[69] "Article 21," *Apology*, 104–7; *CT* 345, 347, 351, 353–55.

such unsavory practices as indulgence peddling with abuses involving the cult of the saints, particularly those practices undertaken out of economic greed. Citing 1 Cor. 3:8, he writes: "'Every man shall receive his own reward according to his own labor,' i.e., they cannot mutually bestow their own merits, the one upon the other, as the monks sell the merits of their orders." Melanchthon ends this section on the saints by beseeching Emperor Charles "not to assent to the violent counsels of our adversaries, but to seek other honorable ways of so establishing harmony that godly consciences are not burdened, that no cruelty is exercised against innocent men, as we have hitherto seen, and that sound doctrine is not suppressed in the Church."[70]

In reviewing the problems addressed at the disputations, diets, and colloquies discussed above, one notes that the cult of the saints was rarely the primary subject of debate. Except among the Swiss, where the topic of images carried so much weight, the saints were almost always relegated to an ancillary position, overshadowed by the mass, authority, or other more ponderous issues. Nonetheless, the saints clearly did not fade away over the years in question. If anything, Melanchthon, in the *Apology*, allots them considerably more space than many earlier evangelical writers had done. In analyzing the activities of these meetings, one can hardly ignore the resilience of the cult of the saints as a minor, yet tenacious matter. Perhaps it is largely because the cult of the saints remained a convenient vehicle for the airing of a variety of confessional disagreements that it not only endured, but also maintained a vital presence in sixteenth-century German society, popular piety, and religious discourse.

THE ERFURT INCIDENT

As if to underscore the utility of the cult in religious disputes, the *Pfaffensturm* (parson storm or riot) that disturbed the peace of Erfurt between 1521 and 1525 coalesced in large part around the issue of the saints.[71] One of Thuringia's leading cities—center of trade, producer of woad, home to a prestigious university—Erfurt, by the end of the fifteenth century, enjoyed and endured a complex political status, one reflective of that of the empire itself. The city, located within Electoral Saxony after the division of the territory in 1485, continued from time to time to attract the interest of Albertine Saxony. To make matters even more complicated, Erfurt's nominal overlord

---

[70] "Article 21," *Apology*, 106–8; *CT* 349, 351, 353, 355, 357. Regarding economic greed, he writes that adversaries "invent these things, not in order to treat the saints with honor, but to defend lucrative services"; ibid., 105; *CT* 351.

[71] This reconstruction of the chronology of the Erfurt incident relies heavily upon Scribner, "Civic Unity and the Reformation in Erfurt," in *Popular Culture*, 185–216; Weiss, *Ein fruchtbar Bethlehem*, 68–81; Kleineidam, *Universitas*, 3:2–35.

was the archbishop of Mainz. By the beginning of the sixteenth century, however, the city had become nearly autonomous, an enviable—albeit precarious—status.[72]

During the years 1509 through 1516, for instance, Erfurt came close to losing its jealously guarded autonomy because of a series of political upheavals brought on primarily by social and economic strains. While these events had settled down in 1516, by 1520 tensions began mounting again. Initially, the issue was economic. Trade was declining steadily in the city, largely because of increased customs tariffs imposed by the archbishop of Mainz. While the resulting protests began by targeting the tariff issue, old concerns soon blended with new, and the clergy became a handy target. In difficult economic times, the clerics—with their immunity from taxation, not to mention their frequently cited greed—understandably came under harsh criticism. Such criticism was exacerbated by the fact that by 1520, Martin Luther had acquired a following among students and humanists in the university. Two of the more prominent Martinists were Luther's friend and fellow Augustinian Johannes Lang, and Justus Jonas, who began preaching the new theology in late 1520.[73] Clearly, the two interest groups fed on one another: those feeling the economic pinch whose resentment led to anticlericalism and those embracing evangelical tenets whose revised theology produced anti-Romanism. The common denominator was, of course, hostility to the Roman Catholic clergy and its supporters.

The discord neared a peak on 6–7 April 1521, when Luther stopped in Erfurt en route to the Diet of Worms. Welcomed by the council, the university, and many townspeople, Luther preached a rousing sermon to an overflowing crowd at the Augustinerkirche. The subject was justification by faith alone and the futility of seeking salvation through works. Among other points, he warned against relying on the efficacy of such things as pilgrimages "to St. James or St. Peter's." He furthermore lashed out once again at the Treasury of Merits: "I say that none of the saints, no matter how holy they were, attained salvation by their works. Even the holy mother of God did not become good, was not saved, by her virginity or her motherhood, but rather by the will of faith and the works of God, and not by her purity, or her own works."[74]

In addition to his warm reception at the church, Luther was honored with a feast by the university.[75] After he had proceeded to Weimar, however, he learned—

---

[72] Scribner, "Civic Unity," 186–87.

[73] Scribner, "Civic Unity," 194–95.

[74] *Sermon Preached at Erfurt on the Journey to Worms*, in *LW,* 51:60–66; WA 7:808–13.

[75] Weiss, *Ein fruchtbar Bethlehem*, 68. Weiss notes that the University's *Rechnungsbuch* records: "Thirty-one *Schneeberger Groschen* is what the reception for the honorable Doctor Martin Luther cost." Weiss adds, "That was about as much as a journeyman earned in twenty-one days" (68).

as did the people of Erfurt—that his works had been "damned and forbidden."[76] Luther's followers in Erfurt, particularly students, reacted by protesting this ban. When members of the orthodox clergy attempted to muzzle such support for Luther, the situation grew intense. During the evening of 10 June 1521 and throughout the following two days, the protest became an "organized riot" or *Pfaffensturm*.[77] As the riot escalated, once again economic, social, and religious concerns melded. Students were joined in their protests not only by some university professors (primarily humanists) but also by apprentices, journeymen, and peasants who had come to town for market day.[78]

In the midst of the *Pfaffensturm*, the council found itself in a difficult position. Not wanting an intervention from Mainz, members sought measures to avoid destruction of the archbishop's properties. On the other hand, the evangelical movement was a formidable force, one which the government could ill afford to further inflame. The council, therefore, attempted to quiet the situation by offering the orthodox clergymen protection in exchange for their renunciation of certain traditional privileges. Taxes were the key issue; indeed, the protesters called for a clergyman to bear the same burdens as any other burgher, a clear example of an area in which the evangelical message bolstered specific socioeconomic concerns. In addition to renouncing their privileged tax status, the clergy were also asked to compensate for never having paid property taxes by surrendering the amount of 10,000 gulden.[79]

Despite concessions, however, the discord persisted, with religious questions moving to the forefront. By early 1522, the *Pfaffensturm* swirled around the volatile issue of the cult of the saints, an issue which—unlike scholarly debates over fine points of theology—"touched the emotions of simple Christians the most powerfully."[80] This is not to imply that the role of the saints was unique in the religious traditions of Erfurt; rather, it helps explain the manner in which issues such as the cult of the saints led to the intimate involvement of "simple Christians" in public discourse during the remainder of Erfurt's *Pfaffensturm*.[81]

---

[76] Weiss, *Ein fruchtbar Bethlehem*, 68, citing WA-T, 3:3357 A.

[77] Scribner, "Civic Unity," 196.

[78] The parallels with the later Peasants' War are striking: the blending of socioeconomic and religious issues, the cross-class makeup of the protesters, and the involvement of both rural and urban participants.

[79] Weiss quotes the *Stadtarchiv* to this effect: "*Die priesterschaft soll thun als burger*," adding, "*und bürgerliche Lasten mittragen*"; *Ein fruchtbar Bethlehem*, 71.

[80] Kleineidam, *Universitas*, 3:12.

[81] While the saints certainly caused the most discord, other issues debated were fasts, the efficacy of good works, the role of priests, and private masses; Weiss, *Ein fruchtbar Bethlehem*, 74.

The cult of the saints serves as a central focus in perhaps the most interesting pamphlet published during the parson storm, *A Short Sermon concerning God's Saints*, by Johannes Femelius. Femelius, an Erasmian humanist who had supported Luther prior to his break with Rome, wrote the piece in the hope of setting the record straight on the issue of the saints. He defines his goal in this way: "It shall be clearly demonstrated in Scripture that the saints pray for us—passionately and lovingly cry out for our salvation...."[82] The bulk of this work consists of explications of various biblical passages that support his thesis.[83] The intriguing aspect of Femelius's pamphlet, therefore, comes not in his broader text but in his opening pages. Curiously, while attempting to convince the public of the truth of his viewpoint, Femelius starts off by blatantly insulting the ordinary people of Erfurt.[84] First, he derisively addresses his tract "to all the doctors of Erfurt, be they young or old, man or woman." He further goes on to advise people to buy his pamphlet—"spare a small amount of money"—before making up their minds on the subject of the saints, condescendingly referring to his desired readership as "Doctor Hans and Doctor Klaus."[85] He continues by designating the ongoing debate over the saints a "disputation,"[86] while expressing his concern that plain people—"they want even women to have a say"—are not learned enough in Scripture to judge such things.[87]

Femelius's pamphlet was published in 1522, an extremely significant year in the confessional history of Erfurt. By that year, evangelical preachers had been selected in at least four parishes.[88] Antonius Musa had begun preaching at St. Moritz in May 1521; Egidius Mechler, a former Franciscan, was preaching the new theology in Erfurt before July 1522;[89] while Peter Bamberger served St. Martin within the Walls

---

[82]Johannes Femelius, *Ein kurz Sermon, so die Heiligen Gottes belangen* ([Erfurt]: Hans Knappe, [1522]), esp. Ai, Köhler 733/1868.

[83]Among the passages Femelius cites are John 5:45: "Do not think that [Christ] will accuse you to the Father: there is one that accuseth you, even Moses, in whom ye trust" (Aiii^v); Luke 16:27: "Then [a certain rich man] said, I pray thee therefore, father [Abraham], that thou wouldest send him [Lazarus] to my father's house" (Bi^v); 2 Pet. 1:13–15: "Yea, I think it meet as long as I am in this tabernacle, to stir you up by putting you in remembrance; / Knowing that shortly I must put off this my tabernacle, even as our Lord Jesus Christ hath shewed me. / Moreover I will endeavour that ye may be able after my decease to have these things always in remembrance" (Bii^v); Rom. 8:26: "Likewise the Spirit also helpeth our infirmities: for we know not what we should pray for as we ought: but the Spirit itself maketh intercession for the saints according to the will of God" (Ci^v).

[84]Bagchi also makes this point in *Luther's Earliest Opponents*, 213.

[85]Femelius, *Ein kurz Sermon*, A.

[86]Bagchi uses this term as well, but I have found no other reference to an official disputation in Erfurt at this time; *Luther's Earliest Opponents*, 213.

[87]Femelius, *Ein kurz Sermon*, Ai. The contrast between Femelius's attitude toward "everyman" (*ydermann*) and the evangelical celebration of "everyman" (*Karsthans*) could not be more dramatic.

[88]Scribner, "Civic Unity," 196 n. 54.

[89]He became pastor of St. Bartholomew's in 1523. Martin Bauer claims his evangelical preaching

in the same year.[90] Pastor Georg Forchheim, who died 30 June 1522, was succeeded at St. Michael's by Johann Culsamer the next month. In addition, Johannes Lang preached frequently at St. Michael's between 1522 and 1525.[91] First Forchheim, and subsequently Culsamer and Lang, became thoroughly caught up in the *Pfaffensturm* as it evolved into a protracted theological debate between the evangelicals and the imposing pastor of St. Mary's, fearless representative of Old Believers, Bartholomaeus Arnoldi von Usingen.

Usingen had been chosen pastor of St. Mary's in early 1522. Johannes Lang informed Luther about Usingen's appointment, but initially Usingen, Luther's old teacher and fellow Augustinian, seemed a possible ally of the evangelicals. As Usingen made his views known, it became clear that his sympathies lay in more traditional directions. By spring of 1522, opposition to Usingen and his views had become pronounced. In April of that year, Lang renounced his office of prior and exhorted others to follow his example.[92] As Lang proceeded to gain a notable following, pamphlets and sermons abounded, debating such concerns as fasts, private masses, the role of the clergy, masses for the dead, the veneration of the saints, and the like. This was, indeed, a war of words at least for the moment; lurking under the surface was the potential that social and economic grievances might provoke "Doctor Hans and Doctor Klaus" to resort to more violent activities. Luther, fearing such a development, counseled Lang to avoid the mistakes of Wittenberg. In a letter dated 12 April 1522, he writes: "Above all, be careful that the people of Erfurt do not imitate our uproar by getting rid of images, the mass in one kind, and so forth."[93] The council likewise feared an escalation into turbulence, but once again felt itself hemmed in by conflicting political considerations. Erfurt's relationship with the archbishop of Mainz precluded its siding with the reformers, while fear of popular revolt prevented it from taking action against the evangelical movement. The council, therefore, resolved to remain neutral in matters of theology and to intervene only if disagreement appeared about to turn violent.[94]

In late April 1522 the council felt compelled to take action. The episode in question began on 20 April, with Usingen's delivery of "one of his greatest sermons" in

---

dated to the winter of 1520–21; *Evangelische Theologen in und um Erfurt im 16. bis 18. Jahrhundert: Beiträge zur Personen- und Familiengeschichte Thüringens* (Neustadt an der Aisch: Degener, 1992), 226.

[90] WA 10(2):168.

[91] In addition, the evangelical movement was also strong in St. Bartholomew's and Merchants' parishes *(Kaufmannskirche); Scribner, "Civic Unity," 196.

[92] MacKinnon, *Luther and the Reformation*, 3:105–6.

[93] WA Br. 2:494–95.

[94] Scribner, "Civic Unity," 197.

St. Mary's on the feast day of Erfurt's city patron, St. Adolar—a sermon which force-fully defended the veneration of the saints.[95] Usingen's sermon clearly touched a chord with the evangelical preachers, who decidedly outnumbered the orthodox clerics, thus setting off a series of highly contentious responses. One of the most bit-ing and direct answers to Usingen's sermon came from his primary opponent in this debate, Johannes Culsamer. Almost immediately, Culsamer's point-by-point *Refuta-tion of the Sermon Delivered at Erfurt by Doctor Bartholomaeus Usingen* appeared in print. Culsamer's major rebuttals in the pamphlet echo those of other similar exchanges: Usingen says the saints must be invoked; Scripture says Jesus should be invoked; Usingen defends an intercessor between man and Christ by using the anal-ogy that to address a prince, one must go through his servant; Scripture (1 Tim. 2:5) says Christ is the only intercessor.[96] Beginning with Usingen's sermon and Cul-samer's refutation, the *Pfaffensturm* became an increasingly boisterous pulpit war *(Kanzelkrieg)*, pitting Usingen, Femelius, and Conrad Cling[97] against Culsamer, Lang, Forchheim, Musa, Mechler, and Bamberger. As the war became more and more heated, the council reluctantly stepped in, demanding to interview the two main contenders, Usingen and Culsamer, and admonishing them to preach only what could be supported by Scripture. Because of the overwhelming numbers on the evangelical side, the council also promised Usingen safe conduct in the streets of Erfurt.[98]

Despite the council's interference, the *Pfaffensturm* continued, much to the growing distress of Martin Luther. In a letter dated 26 June 1522, Luther expressed to Lang his apprehensions about the deteriorating situation.[99] Lang responded by inviting Luther to visit the city, an invitation Luther declined primarily because he was under the ban. Instead, Luther responded to the crisis in Erfurt with a letter dated 10 July 1522, choosing the contentious debate over the cult of the saints as his vehicle for instruction. Luther begins his *Epistle or Instruction on the Saints to the Church at Erfurt* by noting: "It has come to my attention, dear brothers, that quarrels and discord have sprung up among you about unimportant matters, namely the veneration of the saints." Plainly, Luther's intention was to mediate, and his convic-tion revolved around alleviation of discord rather than elucidation of doctrine. He

---

[95] Kleineidam, *Universitas*, 16.

[96] Johannes Culsamer, *Ein Widerlegung etlicher Sermon geschechen zu Erfurt von Doktor Bartholomaeo Usingen* (Erfurt: [Mattes Maler], 1522), Bii[r-v], Köhler 1004/2552.

[97] Bauer, *Evangelische Theologen*, 142.

[98] Scribner, "Civic Unity," 197. While Scribner argues that the council pursued a policy of theolog-ical neutrality and "noncommitment" (197), its demand that the two preach only what could be sup-ported by Scripture seems to suggest a partiality for the evangelical position of *sola Scriptura*.

[99] WA Br. 2:565–66.

writes, for example: "I implore in Christ that your preachers stay away from questions about the saints in heaven and the dead and turn the people away from examining them, for there is no end to such things...."[100] This advice, however, failed to have the desired effect; therefore, in the fall of 1522 (20–22 October), Luther paid a visit to Erfurt, accompanied by Melanchthon, Johann Agricola, and Jakob Probst.[101] Once again he attempted to stem the turmoil in the city, this time by preaching two sermons: one at St. Michael's on 21 October and one at Kaufmannskirche on 22 October.[102]

Luther's best efforts notwithstanding, the *Pfaffensturm* raged on to such an extent that by June 1523 urban and rural violence had led to vandalism of several parsonages and to a number of deaths.[103] While other topics came to share the spotlight, the cult of the saints continued to occupy the most prominent role in the controversy.[104] One notable pamphlet produced during this period is Balthasar Stanberger's *Dialogue between Peter and a Peasant*, published in Erfurt in 1523.[105] This particular piece demonstrates the continuing controversy over the saints while it also exemplifies the tendency of evangelicals to make use of the saints—in this case biblical, but nonbiblical as well—as models of righteousness and good behavior, and at times, purveyors of sound doctrine. In this instance, St. Peter is the model who instructs the peasant about errors in belief concerning the saints—first, about the error of endowing them with intercessory powers.

At the beginning of Stanberger's pamphlet, for instance, the peasant recognizes St. Peter, kneels, and exclaims: "Oh, almighty Gatekeeper of Christ, you great

---

[100]See *Epistel oder Unterricht von den Heiligen*, 159–68. Ironically, *adiaphora*, which in some instances promoted consensus, in this case seem to have created discord. This is particularly interesting in light of views concerning the effects of theological uncertainty on the medieval church; see Joseph Lortz, *Wie kam es zur Reformation? Ein Vortrag* (Einsiedeln: Johannes, 1955).

[101]Concerning this visit, Scribner notes that the university and the council took little notice; "Civic Unity," 197; while MacKinnon writes that Luther "was enthusiastically acclaimed and feasted"; *Luther and the Reformation*, 3:106.

[102]WA 10(3):352–71.

[103]Scribner, "Civic Unity," 197.

[104]In 1523 Lang composed a new liturgy for the church in Erfurt; on 5 July 1523, Culsamer celebrated the first communion in two kinds at St. Michael's; on 13 July 1523, Mechler married, with Lang marrying in the same year; in January 1525, Culsamer married. In each of the works published in Erfurt during the *Pfaffensturm*, attacks upon the cult of the saints are featured: In 1522: Güttel, *Ein selig neu Jahr*. In 1523: *Ein Dialogus oder Gespräch zwischen einem Vater und Sohn; Ein Gespräch zwischen vier Personen*; Güttel, *Von apostolischem Amt und Eigenschaft*; Lange, *Ein Sermon von menschlicher Schwachheit*. In 1524: *Ein Gespräch auf das kürzest zwischen einem Christen und Juden*; Benedikt Gretzinger, *Ein unüberwindlich Beschirmbüchlin von Hauptartikeln der göttlichen Geschrift*, (Augsburg: Heinrich Steiner, 1525), Köhler 679/ 1773; Eberlin, *Ein Sermon zu den Christen in Erfurt*.

[105]Balthasar Stanberger, *Dialogus zwischen Petro und einem Bauern* (Erfurt: Michael Buchführer, 1523), in Bentzinger, *Die Wahrheit*, 296–315.

intercessor and helper who sits at Christ's side, help me with your intercession with Christ to attain eternal life...." St. Peter answers him: "Oh, dear brother, stand up and be quiet, for I am a man like you! I cannot be your helper and intercessor...I do not deserve veneration, for Christ alone is a helper and intercessor...."[106] Further in the pamphlet, St. Peter instructs the peasant on the false teachings of the pope:

Peasant: Oh, dear Apostle and Prince of Heaven, Peter, you are, indeed, one of God's high saints. The pope names you a pope in Rome, a Prince of Heaven, a helper of all wretched prisoners, Gatekeeper for Christ, in whom we all shall take refuge....

Peter: Oh, God in Heaven, how do I, a poor fisherman and mender of fishnets, merit this veneration and high title? I have never sought veneration; rather, I have ascribed everything to God, my salvation, as you see in my writings. And, concerning this, with godly inspiration and God's order appears Martin Luther, my brother and fellow Apostle of Jesus Christ, who tells the truth about the pope and his followers, that I was never a pope in Rome....[107]

Finally, Peter explains the motives behind the self-serving claims of the pope and his followers: "It is all a matter of greed, what one does with Our Lord's robe at Trier, without knowing to whom it belongs; one does likewise with the blessed Mother Anne and the baked saints of Erfurt. God says: 'Put your faith in me, not bones, or the robe, or the saints, or penny-cakes!'"[108] Ironically and significantly, Stanberger makes full use of the traditional respect his readers were likely to hold for St. Peter's authority in an effort to discredit the veneration of Peter and the other saints as well as to undermine papal claims of apostolic succession based on orthodox belief concerning Peter's role.

Ultimately, Erfurt's *Pfaffensturm* was settled by a coalition of religious and secular authorities who acted on the recognition that the discord was threatening the city's unity and autonomy. An Erfurt official, writing in 1533, explains the settlement in this way: "A disunity has arisen in the German lands and in the Holy Empire over Christian doctrine and preaching, a disunity that the superior authorities have not yet been able to settle; so Erfurt cannot settle it. Therefore the Word of God is free inside and outside the city in so far as each is answerable to God and does not

---

[106]Stanberger, *Dialogus zwischen Petro und einem Bauern*, 298.

[107]Stanberger, *Dialogus zwischen Petro und einem Bauern*, 298–99.

[108]Stanberger, *Dialogus zwischen Petro und einem Bauern*, 300.

preach disobedience, nor allow the preaching of it, or burden the conscience of others." Thus the authorities of Erfurt opted for order instead of religious uniformity. Scribner points out the uniqueness of the Erfurt case in that prior to 1555, no other city guaranteed "the coexistence of opposing religious views...by a treaty of state." In addition, however, he reminds his readers that those who chose this *politique*-like solution were elites.[109] Among the plain people of Erfurt—those who were the most incited by the dispute over the saints and who a few years later supported the Peasants' War in large numbers—the sense of settlement remained decidedly cloudy.

THE FIRST SAXON VISITATION

The disturbances of the 1520s[110]—the false brethren in Wittenberg, the prophets in Zwickau, the *Pfaffensturm* in Erfurt, the Peasants' War—led many evangelicals, and ultimately Luther, to propose that measures be taken to assess and adjust the condition of the clergy and the churches. By October 1525, Luther was urging Elector John Frederick of Saxony to lend his authority to such an assessment. By November of that year, Luther had requested the traditional method, a church visitation; by the following November, Luther had outlined a plan of procedure, in which the communities of Electoral Saxony would subsidize the work of four visitors—two to look into economic concerns and two to look into religious matters—all of whom were charged with appraising the state of the church. Luther's hope was that the Saxon model would "become a happy example which all other German princes may fruitfully imitate."[111]

The visitation itself began in February 1527.[112] Initially, the visitors followed no prescribed agenda in their inquiry; by September, however, using information gathered by the first visitors as well as from Luther, Melanchthon had composed a set of seventeen articles as guidelines for visitors to follow.[113] In January 1528, Luther

---

[109]Quoted in Scribner, "Civic Unity," 212, 213, 215–16.

[110]See, for example, Luther's *Eine treue Vermahnung zu allen Christen, sich zu hüten von Aufruhr und Empörung,* January 1522, in which he comments specifically upon the situation in Erfurt; in *Luthers Werke in Auswahl,* ed. Otto Clemen (Berlin: de Gruyter, 1950), 2:299–310; WA 8:670–87.

[111]Martin Luther, *Instructions for the Visitors of Parish Pastors,* in *LW* 40:272; WA 26:198–99.

[112]For an excellent discussion of the first Saxon visitation, see Brecht, *Martin Luther,* 2:259–73.

[113]The original seventeen included: the Doctrine, the Ten Commandments, True Christian Prayer, Tribulation, the Sacrament of Baptism, the Sacrament of the Body and Blood of the Lord, True Christian Penance, True Christian Confession, True Christian Satisfaction for Sin, the Human Order of the Church, Marriage, Free Will, Christian Freedom, the Turks, Daily Worship in the Church, the True Christian Ban, and the Office of Superintendents. In addition, in the second edition of 1538–39, Schools, the category of the first, second, and third divisions was added; Brecht, *Martin Luther,* 273–74. Editor Conrad Bergendoff

added a preface to the articles in which he carefully spelled out, among other things, the biblical sanction for the process of visitation; the papists' degradation of the procedure over time; and the evangelicals' worthy desire to reestablish "the true episcopal office and practice of visitation...because of the pressing need."[114]

While the "pressing need" included examination on fourteen subjects that clearly have little or nothing to do with the cult of the saints, in three of the original seventeen articles, problems with the saints are mentioned explicitly. First, in the article dealing with "True Christian Prayer," Melanchthon writes about the fallacy of "heedlessly" repeating prayers, with little expectation that God will hear such pleas. Quoting Ps. 115:6—"[Their idols] have ears, but they hear not"—he cautions against the traditional practice of appealing to mediators: "Many...seek help of St. Anthony, or St. Sebastian.... But whatever it may be, help should be sought from God."[115] In the article concerning "Daily Worship in the Church," he likewise targets the saints by enumerating sanctioned festival days and by admonishing that "a competent preacher ought to be able to show how to celebrate the festivals without superstition."[116] Finally, in his guidelines for examining the "Human Order of the Church," he warns against interpreting approval of the celebration of high festivals as endorsement of "prayers to the saints, for their intercession." He stresses instead the appropriate evangelical role for the saints: "We rightly honor the saints when we recognize that they are held up before us as a mirror of the grace and mercy of God.... Thus the people are to be aroused to faith and good works by the example of the saints...."[117]

In the closing paragraph of his preface to the visitors' instructions, Luther writes: "If some obstinately want to set themselves against us...we must separate these from ourselves as chaff on the threshing floor and refuse to accommodate ourselves to them."[118] Yet, as Luther became aware of the results of the first visitation, it is clear that he agonized over the "chaff" and over the "deplorable, miserable condition" in which he found his church.[119] Throughout the remainder of the sixteenth century, in

---

notes: "Melanchthon was the author of the *Instructions*, but Luther's ideas underlie the whole and some passages reflect his pen. Because of the endorsement of it by Luther, and the fact that he not only wrote the preface but made revisions in later editions, the work is generally included in the works of Luther"; *LW,* 40:266.

[114] *LW,* 2:271. See WA 26:175–240, for the text of the preface and instructions.

[115] *LW,* 2:279; "Von dem rechten Christlichen Gebet," WA 26:205.

[116] *LW,* 2:309; "Von teglichen Ubung ynn der Kirchen," WA 26:231–32.

[117] *LW,* 2:300; "Von menschlichen Kirchen Ordenung," WA 26:224–25.

[118] *LW,* 2:273; "Vorrhede," WA 26:200.

[119] *Small Catechism, Concordia,* 158. On the efficacy of visitation protocols in understanding the state of the church, see Strauss, *Luther's House of Learning,* 249–67; on the successes and failures of the Lutheran Reformation, see ibid., 300–7.

fact, evidence records that remnants of the Old Belief—including belief concerning the saints—continued to be embraced by ostensibly evangelical flocks. Indeed, while Luther does not explicitly mention abuse of the saints in the *Large Catechism*, he almost certainly has this in mind in passages such as the following, which deals with the First Commandment: "It is the intent of this commandment to require true faith and trust of the heart which settles upon the only true God, and clings to Him alone. That is as much as to say: 'See to it that you let Me alone be your God, and never seek another.'"[120]

Furthermore, anecdotal evidence suggests that at least some evangelical Christians continued to seek "others." During the second Nuremberg visitation (1560–61), for example, records disclose that in at least two locations—Altdorf and Hüll—the populace embraced images of the Virgin Mary, not as inspirational examples, but as efficacious mediators.[121] In the case of Hüll, in particular, a concerned neighboring pastor reported: "I have found there a distasteful and wicked idolatrous abuse. There are pilgrimages, processions around the altar with crosses, banners, lamps, and idolatrous pictures. The pictures are offered money, votive candles, and human hair. Children genuflect before the picture and offer petitions. The picture of the Madonna has two poles attached to it and is covered with rags and old and new church veils."[122] In 1565, one of the five Brandenburg-Ansbach-Kulmbach visitation instructions required determining "whether idols are being worshiped."[123] Moreover, considerable evidence exists to suggest the blatantly nonevangelical veneration of images in the period from 1553 to 1594.[124]

As one examines events occurring in the years between 1517 and 1531, it becomes evident that Huizinga's easy dismissal of the cult of the saints is by and large inaccurate. The cult of the saints obviously maintained a presence in the discourse of the period, as it did in the hearts and minds of many of the Christians—orthodox or evangelical—who lived through the early Reformation era. Exactly why the cult of the saints survived is a far more complex issue. Surely, questions of class enter into the formulation of an explanation. As Gerald Strauss writes, for instance: "The

---

[120]"Part First: The First Commandment," in the *Large Catechism, Concordia,* 169; *CT* 581.

[121]Gerhard Hirschmann, "The Second Nürnberg Church Visitation," in *Social History,* 365–66, 371.

[122]Quoted in Hirschmann, "The Second Nürnberg Church Visitation," 366.

[123]C. Scott Dixon, *The Reformation and Rural Society: The Parishes of Brandenburg-Ansbach-Kulmbach, 1528–1603,* Cambridge Studies in Early Modern History (Cambridge: Cambridge University Press, 1996), 64.

[124]Dixon notes episodes in Ansbach (1567), Ühlfeld (1582), Nuremberg, Weidenbach (1579), Wirsberg (1558), Seibelsdorf (1573), Wallmersbach, and Langenzenn (1553); Dixon, *The Reformation and Rural Society,* 172 and 172 n. 137. Gerald Strauss cites a 1594 report from Nassau-Wiesbaden in which the visitors describe the continuation of "unchristian" folkways, involving, among other things, the use of saints' names in amulets and spells; Strauss, *Luther's House of Learning,* 304.

strength of [popular] opposition has been consistently underestimated in traditional interpretations of the Protestant Reformation."[125] Class or gender analysis thus reveals much about sixteenth-century actions and beliefs that historians of earlier eras may have overlooked. In addition, moreover, some very pragmatic considerations—such as the usefulness of the saints, even to adherents of reformed faiths—also help to explain the tenacity with which the cult of the saints sustained its presence in early modern society.

[125]Strauss, *Luther's House of Learning*, 302. Strauss's claim, of course, is far less true now than it was in 1978. Nonetheless, his point remains useful.

Persistence OF THE SAINTS

CHAPTER 7

At the beginning, this study posed two central questions concerning the cult of the saints: Why did Reformation leaders so strongly and so universally denounce the cult? And did the cult readily disappear from Protestant areas? The response to the former question has emerged throughout the course of the study. Reformers, no matter what their stripe, objected to the cult primarily because they believed that those who venerated and invoked the saints did so in violation of Holy Scripture, in violation of social order, in violation of godly law, and in violation of reliance on faith alone. The written record of the early Reformation period resounds with these themes and condemnations. The response to the latter question, however, is considerably more complex.

Did the cult of the saints disappear? The easiest answer is quite simply, no. The number of times that the saints became an issue of dispute throughout the early Reformation era proves their persistence. In addition, as numerous historians, as well as contemporary observers and critics, point out, remnants of traditional piety persisted in Protestant areas possibly even for centuries. Robert Kolb sums this point up well: "When the pious peasant confronted a crisis and turned not only to his Savior and Lord, Jesus Christ, of whom his pastor spoke at every worship service, but also to the village patron saint or the appropriate auxiliary saint, of whom his grandmother had always spoken so fondly, the battle had to be fought again."[1]

Casual or clandestine invocation of the saints was at the same time accompanied by recognition of their continued significance in more official ways, such as in the retention of ecclesiastical calendars and of certain holidays.[2] Despite his harsh criticism of many traditional practices, Johann Eberlin advocated the observance of such saints' days as Annunciation, Ascension, Candlemas, Sts. Peter and Paul Day, St. John the Baptist Day, All Saints' Day, and the feast days of the patron of each

---

[1] Kolb, *For All the Saints*, 18.
[2] About calendars, see Kolb, *For All the Saints*, 140–44, and Kolb, "Festivals," 618–20. This particular theme promises to be of considerable interest in future research on the topic of the saints.

church.[3] In the case of Zurich, similarly, authorized festivals proclaimed in 1526 included: St. Stephen's Day, Annunciation, Assumption, Candlemas, All Saints' Day, Twelve Apostles' Day, St. John the Baptist Day, St. Mary Magdalene Day, and Sts. Felix and Regula Day. The proclamation was accompanied by the "reformed" caution that while no one was to work or force servants to work on such days, playing or dancing on the eves would not be tolerated.[4] By 1530, Zurich's ordinance concerning holidays was somewhat more vague; nonetheless, it continued to allow "until further notice" celebration of "Twelve Apostles' Day, and also other holidays which we have traditionally observed."[5] Similar provisions existed in many other Protestant communities.

Along with the enduring qualities described above, the saints also retained a role in Protestant areas because of their utility as exemplars or models. Works such as Porta's *Jungfrawenspiegel* demonstrate clearly the service that the saints performed in this regard. In addition, saints' prophecies—often critical of the church and society—sometimes proved useful to reformers seeking to reinforce their condemnation of traditional practices and behaviors.[6] A prime example is Andreas Osiander's appropriation of one of the apocalyptical prophecies of the twelfth-century St. Hildegard of Bingen. In this particular vision, "the most beautiful, loveliest image that had a female form" spoke to St. Hildegard, condemning many sacred and secular ills of the period, and saying, among other things, "The false priests are self-satisfied, for they have the honor of their priestly station without performing their duties; and that should not be."[7] In his foreword, Osiander points out that the papacy had not heeded this or, for that matter, the many other like prophecies that had "shown God's anger" through the ages.[8] For this reason, in Osiander's view, the papacy and the Roman church stood thoroughly discredited.

---

[3]Johann Eberlin, *Der Zehnte Bundesgenosse* (Basel: Pamphilus Gengenbach, 1521), in *Flugschriften*, ed. Laube, 1:75.

[4]Zurich, Bürgermeister, Rat und Grosser Rat, *Ordnung und Erkenntnis eines ehrsamen Rats der Stadt Zürich betreffend den Ehebruch, Kindertauf, Feiertage, Gemein Gebet* (n.p., n.d.), Aiii^v–Aiv, Köhler 886/2233. Saints Felix and Regula were possibly legendary martyred siblings who were Zurich's patrons. First accounts of them appear in the thirteenth century.

[5]Zurich, Bürgermeister, Rat und Grosser Rat, *Christenlich Ansehung*, Aiiii. See Kolb, *For All the Saints*, 139–44, on this point.

[6]Robert Scribner makes this point in *For the Sake of Simple Folk*, 184–85.

[7]*Sankt Hildegarden Weissagung über die Papisten und genannten Geistlichen*, with a foreword by Andreas Osiander (n.p., 1527), Aii^v, Aiii^v, Köhler 372/1036. A similar example puts forth the prophecies of St. Brigitta (1303–72): *Dies Büchlein zeigt an die Weissagung von zukünftiger Betrübnis und wird genannt die Bürde der Welt* (Augsburg: Schönsperger, 1522), Köhler 1031/2594. A Catholic example is *Dies seind etlich erschrockenliche Wunderzeichen, so Gott der Herr der lutherischen Materien uns zu warnen für Augen gestellt hat* (n.p., n.d.), Köhler 569/1458.

[8]*Sankt Hildegarden Weissagung*, Ai^v.

The saints could indeed be useful—so useful, in fact, that Osiander, who in 1525 had condemned the *Salve Regina* because it was "not more than four hundred years old,"[9] by 1527 seemed comfortable employing the vision of a twelfth-century saint to bolster his cause. While one interpretation of Osiander's seeming inconsistency might be sheer hypocrisy, the use of such prophecies was effective, as Robert Scribner notes, "largely because the propagandists also believed [them] to be true."[10] Clearly, this is one further instance which suggests that Protestant theologians often broke with the cult of the saints gradually and at times delivered inconsistent messages concerning the cult of the saints.

In his work on the Hessian Reformation, Johannes Schilling provides additional insight into the use of the saints as exemplars. One fascinating and revealing episode involves the installation of a monument on the grounds of a newly opened hospital, housed in the former Haina Cloister. The monument, commissioned by Landgrave Philip in 1542, depicts on the left, the landgrave with the Hessian coat of arms; to his right, a harpy; at far right, St. Elizabeth, "the Ancestress of the House of Hesse."[11] On the significance of this grouping, Schilling writes:

> With the founding of the hospital, so proclaimed the monument, the landgrave took his place alongside the noble saint who was so universally popular in her homeland. As Elizabeth had fed poor Lazarus, so other poor people of Haina would find a place of refuge. Surely, the idea also was to give Elizabeth a new function, a role to play: no longer would she be the cultish, venerated saint—the landgrave had had her relics removed forcibly from the shrine in St. Elizabeth's Church—but rather an example as servant and benefactress of the poor and the sick.[12]

In the instance of St. Elizabeth—and presumably numerous other saints of similar pedigree—usefulness extended far beyond emulation of her exemplary life. St. Elizabeth was, in addition, a symbol of continuity in authority and leadership; while her relics disappeared forever, Elizabeth herself persisted in her new incarnation.[13]

Elizabeth's evolution is indicative of the fact that perceptions of the saints and sainthood underwent translation throughout the course of the sixteenth century. Reformers frequently placed emphasis upon the saints as living members of the Christian community, resisting—but not wholly eradicating—the view of saints as

---

[9] Osiander, *Grund und Ursach*, Li.

[10] Scribner, *For the Sake of Simple Folk*, 184.

[11] Schilling, *Klöster und Mönche*, 223. The reference is to Elizabeth of Thuringia, 1207–31.

[12] Schilling, *Klöster und Mönche*, 224.

[13] This seems an especially valuable line of further research. Surely many other saints of similar status maintained a distinguished presence however altered by confessional restraints.

dead paragons. Ironically, after Luther's death in 1546, some of his followers began to ascribe to him many of the attributes and abilities of traditional dead saints. One finds numerous accounts of the incombustibility of items associated with Luther as well as images of the reformer—accounts dating from as early as 1521 (even prior to Luther's death) to as late as 1736.[14] Early Zwingli biographer Oswald Myconius likewise professed to have found the unburned heart of the Swiss reformer amidst the ashes of his body after Kappel.[15]

Concerning episodes of this nature, Scribner notes, "Such reports show unmistakable traces of the Catholic cult of the saints."[16] Papal legate Aleander made a similar comment in his account of Luther's progress to Worms in 1521: "Martin is pictured with a halo and a dove above his head. The people kiss these pictures. Such a quantity have been sold that I was not able to obtain one.... In the background is John Hus, whom Luther has recently proclaimed his saint."[17] While it is tempting to conclude that accounts of this nature were "ways of indicating Luther's sainthood," some historians object to this conclusion. Kurt Aland, for example, writes: "The Reformers are not 'substitute saints' for Protestants; they are men with all their weaknesses, just as theologians have always been."[18] It is interesting to point out here, however, that one of the major evangelical positions vis-à-vis dead saints is that, in fact, they are saints "not because they are without sin or have become saintly through works...but...through [the holiness] of the Lord Christ."[19] Indeed, Luther and Zwingli both celebrated the fact that saints had also been weak humans and thus sinners; this made them more realistic models for other fallible mortals.

Finally, it is crucial to address once again the key concept of intercessor. Traditional concerns, which had underscored the need for saints as mediators, held that "Christ is a harsh judge; I must have an intercessor."[20] One might certainly be tempted to conclude that such need for an intercessor likely diminished as reformers stressed direct contact with the deity. Perhaps surprisingly, the opposite seems to have been true. Among the reformers, belief in the need for an intercessor persisted although the identity of the mediator underwent a significant transition. Pamphleteer

---

[14] Robert Scribner, "Incombustible Luther: The Image of the Reformer in Early Modern Germany," in *Popular Culture and Popular Movements*, 323–53. Other historians who address this include: Soergel, *Wondrous in His Saints*, 147; Bainton, *Here I Stand*, 192.

[15] Scribner, "Incombustible Luther," 328.

[16] Scribner, "Incombustible Luther," 328.

[17] Quoted in Bainton, *Here I Stand*, 175.

[18] Aland, *Four Reformers*, 79.

[19] WA 28:177, Plass 3978/1247.

[20] Stanberger, *Ein Dialogus*, Fiᵛ. For Catholic statements to this effect, see, for example, Johannes Dietenberger, *Wie man die Heiligen ehren soll* (n.p., 1524), Giiiiᵛ, Köhler 1027/2588; Fabri, *Epistola…de invocatione et intercessione Mariae*, Gii.

Philipp Melhofer explains: "Our only helper, protector, and savior is God; therefore, only he should be invoked.... You will invoke me and live, the Old Testament attests. / Now, God is holy, and we are unholy—indeed, wretched sinners. Therefore, we do not want to approach God for ourselves; rather we must find a path to him. / The only path is Christ."[21] Thus, the traditional invocation of saints as mediators between sinners and Christ was *officially* overridden by the assertion that Christ himself— although in very recent memory deemed too "harsh" a "judge" to be approached directly—must now begin to serve as the only intercessor between human beings and an even more formidable God the Father. Clearly, despite the numerous attempts to discard the pantheon of intercessors, belief in the need for intercession endured.[22] Consequently—whether naively, clandestinely, or subversively—many fledgling Protestants at least occasionally found solace and a sense of divine imma- nence by invoking a more comforting, less threatening mediator. It seems equally clear that as long as this traditional mind-set persisted—and as long as Christians remained sinners—Robert Kolb's hypothetical peasant occasionally addressing his grandmother's saint remained a likely, albeit unsanctioned, scenario.

---

[21] Melhofer, *Offenbarung*, Bvii.

[22] Scribner goes so far as to suggest that in Lutheran iconography Luther himself came to be depicted "as mediator between Christ and ordinary Christians"; Scribner, "Incombustible Luther," 332.

DISPUTATIONS, DIETS, AND COLLOQUIES

DISPUTATION, DIET, OR COLLOQUY	DATES	RELATIONSHIP TO THE CULT OF THE SAINTS
Heidelberg Disputation	April–May 1518	Forty theses; thesis 6 deals with indulgences
Diet of Augsburg	1518	Cajetan declares Luther's view of penance and indulgences the two major issues of contention
Leipzig Disputation	June–July 1519	Two major issues: authority of pope and primacy of Rome; saints addressed through issues of good works and indulgences
Diet of Worms	April–May 1521	Edict of Worms addresses Luther's error concerning indulgences
Riga Disputation	June 1522	Twenty-four theses—Indulgences, pilgrimages, and veneration of saints addressed
First Diet of Nuremberg	November 1522– March 1523	Attempt to enforce Edict of Worms and silence heresy
First Zurich Disputation	January 1523	Sixty-seven *Schlußreden*—three deal with saints, including the longest (20)
Second Zurich Disputation	October 1523	Meets in the wake of iconoclasm: two days devoted to the mass; one to images—resolves to do away with mass and images
Second Diet of Nuremberg	January–April 1524	Attempt to enforce Edict of Worms
Third Zurich Disputation	1524	Reiterates decisions of Second Disputation

DISPUTATION, DIET, OR COLLOQUY	DATES	RELATIONSHIP TO THE CULT OF THE SAINTS
Fourth Zurich Disputation	1524	Reiterates decisions of Second Disputation
Appenzell Disputation	July 1524	Seven theses, including one dealing with indulgences and one dealing with the veneration of saints
Waldshut Colloquy	April 1526	Eighteen theses, including one dealing with images and one dealing with intercessors and pilgrimages
Baden-Aargau Disputation	May–June 1526	Seven theses, including one dealing with the saints and the Virgin Mary as mediators and one dealing with images
First Diet of Speyer	June–August 1526	Attempts to deal with abuses fail
Synod of Homberg	October 1526	158 theses, including those dealing with ceremonies, invocation of saints, *Ave Maria*
Düsseldorf Disputation	1527	Ten theses, including those dealing with issue of mediators, veneration of images
Bern Disputation	January 1528	Ten theses, including one dealing with Christ as the only mediator and one dealing with the veneration of images
Second Diet of Speyer	March 1529	Attempts enforcement of Edict of Worms
Diet of Augsburg	June–September 1530	*Augsburg Confession, Confutatio,* and *Apology of the Augsburg Confession* (1531)

APPENDIX 2

This appendix lists publications that identify Jesus as the only legitimate intercessor between God and man, see chap. 2, n. 91. These works are also listed in the bibliography.

A. S. *Ein Epistel, meinen lieben Brüdern in Christo Jesu zugeschrieben.* N.p., 1523, Aii.

Amsdorf, Nikolaus von. *Wider die Lügenprediger des hohen Doms zu Magdeburg.* Wittenberg: [Nickel Schirlentz], 1525, Aiii.

Artikel, darinne etlike Misbruke by den Parren des Förstensdoms Lüneborg entdecket werden. [Magdeburg: Hans Barth], 1528. Giii (Köhler [q.v.] 1077/2725).

[Berckenmeyer, Jörg.] *Ein Register der heiligen göttlichen Geschrift.* Halle, 1525, Aii.

Bucer, Martin. *An ein christlichen Rat und Gemein der Stadt Weißenberg: Summari seiner Predigt daselbst getan.* [Strassburg: Johann Schott, 1523], Diii^v.

————. *Verantwortung M. Bucers auf das ihm seine Widerwärtigen zum ärgsten zumessen.* [Strassburg: Johann Schott], 1523. Div^v (Köhler [q.v.] 1114/2845).

Bugenhagen, Johannes. *Von dem christlichen Glauben und rechten guten Werken.* Wittenberg: Georg Rhau, 1526. Aiiii (Köhler [q.v.] 1153–56/2928).

Capito, Wolfgang Fabricius. *Von drei Straßburger Pfaffen und den geäußerten Kirchengütern.* [Strassburg: Wolfgang Köpfel], 1525. Ei^v (Köhler [q.v.] 1132/2900).

Christliche Unterrichtung eins Pfarrherrn an seinen Herrn, ein Fürsten des heiligen Reichs, auf vierzig Artikel und Punkten gestellt. [N.p.], 1526. Bi (Köhler [q.v.] 1062/2679).

[Comander, Johannes.] *Überdiese nachkommenden Schlußreden wollen wir, der Pfarrer zu Sankt Martin zu Chur samt anderen, einem jeden Antwort und Bericht geben.* [Augsburg: Melchior Ramminger, 1526.] Art. 12, n.p. (Köhler [q.v.] 360/1006).

Culsamer, Johannes. *Ein Widerlegung etlicher Sermon geschechen zu Erfurt von Doktor Bartholomaeo Usingen.* Erfurt: [Mattes Maler], 1522. Bii^v (Köhler [q.v.] 1004/2552).

Eberlin, Johann. *Ein schöner Spiegel eins christlichen Lebens.* Strassburg: Johannes Schwan, 1524. B–B^v (Köhler [q.v.] 52/148).

————. *Ein Sermon zu den Christen in Erfurt.* [Erfurt: Johannes Loersfeld], 1524, Bi^v–Bii^v.

[Gengenbach, Pamphilus.] *Der evangelisch Bürger.* Zwickau: Jörg Gastel, 1524, Aiiii^v (Köhler [q.v.] 463/1251).

Georg von Polenz, Bf. von Samland. *Ein Sermon am Christtag in der Domkirch zu Königsberg gepredigt.* [Augsburg: Melchior Ramminger, 1524.]

Goldschmidt, Sebastian. *Ein Unterweisung etlicher Artikel, so Bruder Mattheiß öffentlich gepredigt hat.* [Worms: Peter Schöffer, 1525], Biiii.

[Greifenberger, Hans]. *Dies Büchel zeigt an, wie wir also weit geführt sind von der Lehre unsers Meisters Christo.* [Munich: Hans Schobser], 1523.

———. *Dies Büchlin zeigt an die falschen Propheten.* [Augsburg: Philipp Ulhart, 1523?], Bi.

Gretzinger, Benedikt. *Hauptartikel und fürnehmlich Punkten der göttlichen Geschrift.* [Wittenberg: Johann Rhau-Grunenberg], 1524, Eiiii^v.

———. *Hauptartikel und fürnehmste Stück unsers Christentums.* [Wittenberg: Johann Rhau-Grunenberg, 1525], Gii^v.

———. *Ein unüberwindlich Beschirmbüchlin von Hauptartikeln der göttlichen Geschrift.* Augsburg: Heinrich Steiner, 1525. Fii^v (Köhler [q.v.] 679/1773).

Groner, Johannes. *Zu Trost allen armen Gewissen: Ein klein Büchlin.* Wittenberg: Hans Lufft, 1524. Hi^v (Köhler [q.v.] 1068/2701).

Güttel, Kaspar. *Schutzrede wider etliche ungezähmte freche Clamanten.* Wittenberg: [Johann Rhau-Grunenberg, 1522], Cii (Köhler [q.v.] 17/72).

———. *Von apostolischem Amt und Eigenschaft der Bischof, Pfarrer und Prädikanten.* [Erfurt: Wolfgang Stürmer], 1523, Bi^v.

———. *Von merklichen Mißbräuchen wider das klare göttliche Wort.* [Zwickau]: Gabriel Kantz, 1528. Av (Köhler [q.v.] 1235/3116).

Handlung und Disputation, so zwischen Friedrich Mecum und Johann Korbach geschehen. N.p., 1527. Biii (Köhler [q.v.] 138/378).

Herman, Nikolaus. *Ein Mandat Jesu Christi an alle seine getreuen Christen.* Wittenberg: Nickel Schirlentz, 1524. In *Flugschriften*, ed. Clemen, 2:261 [q.v.].

Heyden, Sebald. *Daß der einig Christus unser Mittler und Fürsprech sei bei dem Vater, nicht sein Mutter noch die Heiligen.* [Leipzig: Michael Blum, 1526.]

Hug, Michael. *Ein kurzer, aber christlicher und fast nützlicher Sermon von dem rechten, wahren und lebendigen Glauben.* [Augsburg: Heinrich Steiner], 1524. Aiii^{r-v} (Köhler [q.v.] 372/1040).

Ich kann nit viel Neues, erdenken, ich will der Katzen die Schellen anhenken. [Strasburg: Matthias Schürer Erben, 1525.] n.p. (Köhler [q.v.] 1315/3418).

Karlstadt, Andreas. *Ein Frage, ob auch jemand möge selig werden ohn die Fürbit Mariä.* [Nuremberg: Hieronymus Höltzel], 1524. Aii^v (Köhler [q.v.] 87/238).

[Krautwald, Valentin.] *Von Gnaden Gottes, ihrem ordentlichen Gang und schnellen Lauf.* [Strasburg: Balthasar Beck, 1528.] Av (Köhler [q.v.] 1864/4766).

Lonicer, Johannes. *Berichtbüchlin.* N.p., n.d., Aiiii.

Lotzer, Sebastian. *Eine heilsame Ermahnung an die Einwohner von Horb.* [Augsburg: Jörg Nadler], 1523. In *Flugschriften,* ed. Laube, 1:255 [q.v.].

Luther, Martin. *Predigt zu Zwickau am Mittwoch nach Quasimodogeniti vormittags,* 30 April 1522, WA 10(3):106.

————. *Predigt am Johannistage,* 24 June 1522, WA 10(3):203.

————. *Sermon von dem unrechten Mammon,* 17 August 1522, WA 10(3):280.

Mayer, Sebastian. *Widerrufung an ein löbliche Freistadt Straßburg.* [Augsburg: Philipp Ulhart], 1524, Cii.

Melhofer, Philipp. *Offenbarung der allerheimlischsten Heimlichkeit der jetzigen Baalspriester.* [Augsburg: Philipp Ulhart, ca. 1529], Bvii–Bviii.

Mirisch, Melchior, Eberhard Weidensee, Johannes Fritzhans [and others]. *Doctor Melchior Mirisch, Doctor Eberhardus Weidensee, Johannes Fritzhans samt andern Predigern des Evangelii der Stadt Magdeburg erbieten sich, dies nachgedruckten Artikel zu erhalten.* [Magdeburg: Hans Knappe], 1524, Aii^v (Köhler [q.v.] 982/2484.)

Oekolampad, Johannes. *Von Anrufung der Heiligen.* Basel: Adam Petri, 1526, Avi^v–Avii, Bv^v (Köhler [q.v.] 814/2038).

[Osiander, Andreas.] *Grund und Ursach aus der heiligen Schrift, wie und warum die Pröpst zu Nürnberg die Mißbrauch bei der heiligen Meß geändert haben.* [Zwickau: Jörg Gastel, 1525], Li (Köhler [q.v.] 18–19/74).

Rhegius, Urbanus. *Die neu Lehr samt ihrer Verlegung.* [Strassburg: Johann Knobloch], 1527, Ciii (Köhler [q.v.] 770–71/1946).

Sachs, Hans. *Disputation zwischen einem Chorherren und Schuhmacher.* [Bamberg: Georg Erlinger], 1524. In *Die Wahrheit,* ed. Bentzinger, 362.

Sattler, Michael. *Brüderlich Vereinigung etzlichen Kinder Gottes sieben Artikel betreffend. Item ein Sendbrief Michael Sattlers an eine Gemeine Gottes samt seinem Martyrium.* N.p., 1527. In *Flugschriften,* ed. Clemen, 2:328 [q.v.].

[Schwarzenberg, Johann von.] *Beschwörung der alten teufelischen Schlangen mit dem göttlichen Wort.* Nuremberg: Hans Hergot, 1525, Gi^v (Köhler [q.v.] 274–77/785).

Ein Sendbrief von einem jungen Studenten zu Wittenberg an seine Eltern in Schwabenland von wegen der Lutherischen Lehre zugeschrieben. Augsburg: Melchior Ramminger, 1523. In *Flugschriften,* ed. Clemen, 1:15 [q.v.].

Ein Sermon von der Anbetung, gepredigt von einem Karmelit. [Augsburg: Melchior Ramminger], 1522, Aiii.

Stanberger, Balthasar. *Dialogus zwischen Petro und einem Bauern.* Erfurt: Michael Buchführer, 1523. In *Flugschriften,* ed. Clemen, 3:201 [q.v.].

Stör, Thomas. *Von dem christlichen Weingarten.* [Bamberg: Georg Erlinger, 1524.] In *Flugschriften,* ed. Laube, 1:372 [q.v.].

Ein tröstliche Disputation auf Frag und Antwort gestellet, von zweien Handwerksmännern. N.p., n.d., Gii^v–Giii (Köhler [q.v.] 680–81/1774).

Vögeli, Jörg. *Schirmred eines laiischen Bürgers zu Konstanz wider den Pfarrer von Überlingen.* N.p., n.d., Hi^v.

Wilhelm, Graf von Isenburg. *In diesem Büchlein unterrichtet der wohlgeborn mein G. H. von Isenburg den ehrsame Rat von Köln.* N.p., n.d., Aiiii^v (Köhler [q.v.] 1557/ 4039).

———. *Kurze Erklärung der prinzipal Artikel meins G. H. von Isenburg, der halben sein Gnad als ein Ketzer wider die Billigkeit wird angegen.* N.p., n.d., Aiiii^v (Köhler [q.v.] 1558/4041).

———. *Kurzer Bericht und Anzeige aus heiliger, göttlicher Geschrift, wie Gott in seinen Heiligen zu loben ist.* N.p.: Jakob Schmidt, 1526, Aiiii^{r-v}.

Wurm, Matthias. *Trost Klostergefanger.* N.p., n.d., Ai^v.

Zwingli, Huldrich (Ulrich). *Ein christenliche, fast nützliche und tröstliche Epistel an die Gläubigen zu Eslingen.* N.p., 1526, Aii^v.

———. *Die erst kurze Antwort über Ecken sieben Schlusreden.* N.p., [1526], Aii^v.

———. *Ein Gegenwurf und Widerwehr wider Hieronymum Emser.* Zurich: C. Froschauer, 1525, Fiii.

———. *Eine Predigt über die ewigreine Jungfrau Maria, die Mutter Jesus Christi, unseres Erlösers.* Zurich, 1522. In Emidio Campi, *Zwingli und Maria: Eine reformationsgeschichtliche Studie.* Zurich: Theologischer, 1997, 144.

———. *Huldreich Zwinglis sämtliche Werke.* Vol. 1, *Werke 1510–Januar 1523,* 385–428.

———. *Huldreich Zwinglis sämtliche Werke.* Vol. 3, *Werke 1524–März 1525,* 272.

———. *Huldreich Zwinglis sämtliche Werke.* Vol. 5, *Werke April 1526–Juni 1527.* Corpus Reformatorum. Zurich: Theologischer, 1982, 190, 278.

Appendix 3

This key provides abbreviations to indicate reformers' works in which the scriptural references that follow are used to condemn the invocation of saints and/or the veneration of images. Scriptural citations included in the second part of Appendix 3 are from the Authorized (King James) Version of the Bible.

Key to Works Cited in this Appendix

A. S.
: A. S. *Ein Epistel, meinen lieben Brüdern in Christo Jesu zugeschrieben*. N.p., 1523.

Amsdorf
: Amsdorf, Nikolaus von. *Wider die Lügenprediger des hohen Doms zu Magdeburg.* Wittenberg: [Nickel Schirlentz], 1525.

Artikel
: *Artikel, darinne etlike Misbruke by den Parren des Förstensdoms Lüneborg entdecket werden*. [Magdeburg: Hans Barth], 1528.

[Berckenmeyer]
: [Berckenmeyer, Jörg.] *Ein Register der heiligen göttlichen Geschrift*. Halle, 1525.

Billicanus
: Billicanus, Theobald. *An die christelich Kirch-Versammlung einem ehrsamen Rat und Gemein der Stadt Weil Sendbrief*. [Augsburg: Melchior Ramminger], 1522.

Bucer *(Rat)*
: Bucer, Martin. *An ein christlichen Rat und Gemein der Stadt Weißenberg: Summari seiner Predigt daselbst getan.* [Strassburg: Johann Schott, 1523.]

Bucer *(Bild)*
: ———. *Daß einigerlei Bild beiden Gottgläubigen an Orten, da sie verehrt, nit mögen geduldet werden.* [Strassburg: Johann Knobloch, 1530.]

Bucer *(Grund)*
: ———. *Grund und Ursach aus göttlicher Schrift der Neuerungen zu Straßburg vorgenommen.* [Strassburg: Wolfgang Köpfel], 1525.

Eberlin
: Eberlin, Johann. *Ein schöner Spiegel eins christlichen Lebens*. Strassburg: Johannes Schwan, 1524.

Eckstein	Eckstein, Utz. *Dialogus. Ein hübsche Disputation, die Christus hat mit Adam ton.* [Zurich: C. Froschauer, 1526.]
[Gengenbach]	[Gengenbach, Pamphilus.] *Der evangelisch Bürger.* Zwickau: Jörg Gastel, 1524.
Goldschmidt	Goldschmidt, Sebastian. *Ein Unterweisung etlicher Artikel, so Bruder Mattheiß öffentlich gepredigt hat.* [Worms: Peter Schöffer, 1525.]
[Greifenberger] *(Büchel)*	[Greifenberger, Hans.] *Dies Büchel zeigt an, wie wir also weit geführt sind von der Lehre unsers Meisters Christo.* [Munich: Hans Schobser], 1523.
Greifenberger *(Büchlin)*	Greifenberger, Hans. *Dies Büchlin zeigt an die falschen Propheten.* [Augsburg: Philipp Ulhart, 1523?]
Gretzinger *(Punkten)*	Gretzinger, Benedikt. *Hauptartikel und fürnehmlich Punkten der göttlichen Geschrift.* [Wittenberg: Johann Rhau-Grunenberg], 1524.
Gretzinger *(Stück)*	———. *Hauptartikel und fürnehmste Stück unsers Christentums.* [Wittenberg: Johann Rhau–Grunenberg, 1525.]
Güttel *(Dialogus)*	Güttel, Kaspar. *Dialogus oder Gesprächbüchlein, wie christlich und evangelisch zu leben.* N.p., 1523.
Güttel *(Amt)*	———. *Von apostolischem Amt und Eigenschaft der Bischof, Pfarrer und Prädikanten.* [Erfurt: Wolfgang Stürmer], 1523.
Hätzer	Hätzer, Ludwig. *Ein Urteil Gottes unsers Ehegemahl, wie man sich mit allen Götzen und Bildnissen halten soll.* Zurich: C. Froschauer, 1523.
Heyden	Heyden, Sebald. *Daß der einig Christus unser Mittler und Fürsprech sei bei dem Vater, nicht sein Mutter noch die Heiligen.* [Leipzig: Michael Blum, 1526.]
Hug	Hug, Michael. *Ein kurzer, aber christlicher und fast nützlicher Sermon von dem rechten, wahren und lebendigen Glauben.* [Augsburg: Heinrich Steiner], 1524.
Ich kann	*Ich kann nit viel Neues, erdenken, ich will der Katzen die Schellen anhenken.* [Strassburg: Matthias Schürer Erben, 1525.]
Karlstadt	Karlstadt, Andreas. *Von Abtuhung der Bilder.* Wittenberg: Nickell Schyrlentz, 1522.
Lonicer	Lonicer, Johannes. *Berichtbüchlin.* N.p., n.d.

Luther *(Adel)*	Luther, Martin. *An den christlichen Adel deutscher Nation von des christlichen Standes Besserung.* WA 6:381–469.
Luther *(Epistel)*	———. *Epistel oder Unterricht von den Heiligen an die Kirche zu Erfurt.* WA 10(2):159–68.
Luther *(Predigt)*	———. *Predigt am Johannistage.* WA 10(3):201–8.
Luther *(Erfurt)*	———. *Sermon D. Martini Luthers geschehen zu Erfurdt am Sontag Quasimodogeniti.* WA 7: 808–13.
Luther *(Mammon)*	———. *Ein Sermon von dem unrechten Mammon.* WA 10(3):283–92.
Luther *(Visitatoren)*	———. *Unterricht der Visitatoren an die Pfarrherrn im Kurfürstentum zu Sachsen (1528).* WA 26:175–240; *LW* 40:269–320.
Luther ("Bilder")	———. "Von dem Bildersturmen," in *Wider die himmlischen Propheten, von den Bildern und Sakrament.* WA 18:67–84.
Luther *(Abgott)*	———. *Wider den neuen Abgott und alten Teufel der zu Meißen sol erhoben werden.* WA 15(1):170–98.
Melhofer	Melhofer, Philipp. *Offenbarung der allerheimlischsten Heimlichkeit der jetzigen Baalspriester.* [Augsburg: Philipp Ulhart, ca. 1529.]
Mirisch	Mirisch, Melchior, Eberhard Weidensee, Johannes Fritzhans and others. *Doctor Melchior Mirisch, Doctor Eberhardus Weidensee, Johannes Fritzhans samt andern Predigern des Evangelii der Stadt Magdeburg erbieten sich, dies nachgedruckten artikel zu erhalten.* [Magdeburg: Hans Knappe], 1524.
[Peringer]	[Peringer, Diepold.] *Ein Sermon, geprediget vom Bauern zu Wörd bei Nürnberg, von dem freien willen des Menschen, auch von Anrufung der Heiligen.* [Augsburg: Silvan Otmar, 1524.]
Pollio	Pollio, Symphorianus. *Göttlicher und päpstlicher Recht Vergleichung.* N.p., 1530.
Rhegius	Rhegius, Urbanus. *Die neu Lehr samt ihrer Verlegung.* [Strassburg: Johann Knobloch], 1527.
Sachs	Sachs, Hans. *Disputation zwischen einem Chorherren und Schuhmacher.* [Bamberg: Georg Erlinger], 1524.

Sattler	Sattler, Michael. *Brüderlich Vereinigung etzlichen Kinder Gottes sieben Artikel betreffend. Item ein Sendbrief Michael Sattlers an eine Gemeine Gottes samt seinem Martyrium.* N.p., 1527.
Schenck	Schenck von Stauffenberg, Jakob. *Sendbrief an seine Geschweihen.* [Speyer: Jakob Schmidt], 1524.
Schmid	Schmid, Konrad. *Antwort auf etlich Widerred derer, so die Predigt, durch ihn getan, geschmät.* [Zurich: C. Froschauer], 1522.
Sermon	*Ein Sermon von der Anbetung, gepredigt von einem Karmelit.* [Augsburg: Melchior Ramminger], 1522.
Sickingen	Sickingen, Franz von. *Ein Sendbrief zu Unterrichtung etlicher Artikel christlichen Glaubens.* Wittenberg: [Johann Rhau–Grunenberg], 1522.
Spelt	Spelt, Heinrich. *Ein wahre Deklaration oder Erklärung der Profession, Gelübden und Leben, so die falschen Geistlichen tun.* [Augsburg: Heinrich Steiner], 1523.
Tröstliche	*Ein tröstliche Disputation auf Frag und Antwort gestellet, von zweien Handwerksmännern.* N.p., n.d.
Vögeli	Vögeli, Jörg. *Schirmred eines laiischen Bürgers zu Konstanz wider den Pfarrer von Überlingen.* N.p, n.d.
Wilhelm	Wilhelm, Graf Von Isenburg. *Kurzer Bericht und Anzeige aus heiliger, göttlicher Geschrift, wie Gott in seinen Heiligen zu loben ist.* N.p.: Jakob Schmidt, 1526.
Wurm	Wurm, Matthias. *Christenlich kurz Vermahnung zum andern Mal an Jakob Kornkauf, von Fasten, Feiertagen, Beichten.* Strassburg: Johannes Schwan, 1524.
Zeuleys	Zeuleys, Ulrich. *Daß die heiligen für Gott nicht anzurufen, ein kurzer Unterricht.* N.p., 1524.
Ziegler	Ziegler, Clemens. *Ein kurz Register und Auszug der Bibel, in welchem man findet, was Abgötterei sei.* N.p., 1524.
Zurich	Zurich, Bürgermeister, Rat und Grosser Rat. *Christliche Antwort dem hochwürdigen Herren Hugo, Bischof zu Konstanz, über die Unterricht beider Artikel der Bilder und der Mess.* Zurich: Hans Hager, 1524.
Zwingli *(Compar)*	Zwingli, Huldrich. *Ein Antwort, Valentino Compar gegeben.* Zurich: Hans Hager, [1525].

Zwingli *(Epistel)*   ————. *Ein christenliche, fast nützliche und tröstliche Epistel an die Gläubigen zu Eslingen.* N.p., 1526.

Zwingli *(Antwort)*   ————. *Die erst kurze Antwort über Ecken sieben Schlusreden.* N.p., [1526].

Zwingli *(Gegenwurf)*   ————. *Ein Gegenwurf und Widerwehr wider Hieronymum Emser.* Zurich: C. Froschauer, 1525.

Zwingli *(Glauben)*   ————. *Von wahrem und falschem Glauben.* Zurich: C. Froschauer, 1526.

♦

Scriptural References Used against the Saints and Images

Old Testament

Genesis

31:33—35. And Laban went into Jacob's tent, and into Leah's tent, and into the two maidservants' tents; but he found them not. Then went he out of Leah's tent, and entered into Rachel's tent. / Now Rachel had taken the images, and put them in the camel's furniture, and sat upon them. And Laban searched all the tent, but found them not. / And she said to her father, "Let it not displease my lord that I cannot rise up before thee; for the custom of women is upon me." And he searched, but found not the images.

Zwingli *(Compar)*

Exodus

20:3—5. Thou shalt have no other gods before me. / Thou shalt not make unto thee any graven images, or any likeness of any thing that is in heaven above, or that is in the earth beneath, or that is in the water under the earth: / Thou shalt not bow down thyself to them, nor serve them: for I the Lord thy God am a jealous God, visiting the iniquity of the fathers upon the children unto the third and fourth generation of them that hate me....

Bucer *(Bild);* Eckstein; Hätzer; Karlstadt; Luther ("Bilder"); [Peringer]; Sickingen; Wilhelm; Wurm; Zeuleys; Zurich; Zwingli *(Compar)*

20:22—23. And the Lord said unto Moses, "Thus thou shalt say unto the children of Israel, 'Ye have seen that I have talked with you from heaven. / Ye shall not make with me gods of silver, neither shall ye make unto you gods of gold.'"

Hätzer

32:4—6. And he received them at their hand, and fashioned it with a graving tool, after he had made it a molten calf: and they said, "These be thy gods, O Israel, which brought thee up out of the land of Egypt." / And when Aaron saw it, he built an altar before it; and Aaron made proclamation, and said, "To morrow is a feast to the Lord." / And they rose up early on the morrow, and offered burnt offerings, and brought peace offerings; and the people sat down to eat and to drink, and rose up to play.

Ziegler; Zwingli *(Compar)*

34:13—17. But ye shall destroy their altars, break their images, and cut down their groves: / For thou shalt worship no other god: for the Lord, whose name is Jealous, is a jealous God: / Lest thou make a covenant with the inhabitants of the land, and they go a whoring after their gods, and do sacrifice unto their gods, and one call thee, and thou eat of his sacrifice; / And thou take of their daughters unto thy sons, and their daughters go a whoring after their gods, and make thy sons go a whoring after their gods. / Thou shalt make thee no molten gods.

Billicanus; Hätzer; Wilhelm

Leviticus

6:12—13. And the fire upon the altar shall be burning in it; it shall not be put out: and the priest shall burn wood on it every morning, and lay the burnt offering in order upon it; and he shall burn thereon the fat of the peace offerings. / The fire shall ever be burning upon the altar; it shall never go out.

Ziegler

20:8. And ye shall keep my statutes, and do them: I am the lord which sanctify you.

Melhofer; Wilhelm; Zwingli *(Gegenwurf)*

26:1. Ye shall make you no idols nor graven image, neither rear you up a standing image, neither shall ye set up any image of stone in your land, to bow down unto it: for I am the Lord your God.

Hätzer; Pollio; Wilhelm; Ziegler, cited as Leviticus 25; Zwingli *(Gegenwurf)*

NUMBERS

23:5−7. And the Lord put a word in Balaam's mouth, and said, "Return unto Balak, and thus thou shalt speak." / And he returned unto him, and, lo, he stood by his burnt sacrifice, he, and all the princes of Moab. / And he took up his parable, and said, "Balak the king of Moab hath brought me from Aram, out of the mountains of the east, saying, 'Come, curse me Jacob, and come, defy Israel.'"

Luther *(Abgott)*

24:1−5. And when Balaam saw that it pleased the Lord to bless Israel, he went not, as at other times, to seek for enchantments, but he set his face toward the wilderness. / And Balaam lifted up his eyes, and he saw Israel abiding in his tents according to their tribes; and the spirit of God came upon him. / And he took up his parable, and said, "Balaam the son of Beor hath said, and the man whose eyes are open hath said: / He hath said, which heard the words of God, which saw the vision of the Almighty, falling into a trance, but having his eyes open: / 'How goodly are thy tents, O Jacob, and thy tabernacles, O Israel!'"

Karlstadt; Luther *(Abgott)*

25:1−4. And Israel abode in Shittim, and the people began to commit whoredom with the daughters of Moab. / And they called the people unto the sacrifices of their gods: and the people did eat, and bowed down to their gods. / And Israel joined himself unto Baalpeor: and the anger of the Lord was kindled against Israel. / And the Lord said unto Moses, "Take all the heads of the people, and hang them up before the Lord against the sun, that the fierce anger of the Lord may be turned away from Israel."

Hätzer; Zwingli *(Glauben)*

DEUTERONOMY

4:23−28. Take heed unto yourselves, lest ye forget the covenant of the Lord your God, which he made with you, and make you a graven image, or the likeness of any thing, which the Lord thy God hath forbidden thee. / For the Lord thy God is a consuming fire, even a jealous God. / When thou shalt beget children, and children's children, and ye shall have remained long in the land, and shall corrupt yourselves, and make a graven image, or the likeness of any thing, and shall do evil in the sight of the Lord thy God, to provoke him to anger: / I call heaven and earth to witness against you this day, that ye shall soon utterly perish from off the land whereunto ye go over Jordan to possess it; ye shall not prolong your days upon it, but shall utterly be destroyed. / And the Lord shall scatter you among the nations, and ye shall be left few in number among the heathen, whither the Lord shall lead you. / And there ye shall serve gods, the work of men's hands, wood and stone, which neither see, nor hear, nor eat, nor smell.

Hätzer; Wurm; Ziegler; Zwingli *(Compar);* Zwingli *(Glauben)*

5:6−9. I am the Lord thy God, which brought thee out of the land of Egypt, from the house of bondage. / Thou shalt have none other gods before me. / Thou shalt not make thee any graven image, or any likeness of any thing that is in heaven above, or that is in the earth beneath, or that is in the waters beneath the earth: / Thou shalt not bow down thyself unto them, nor serve them: for I the Lord thy God am a jealous God, visiting the iniquity of the fathers upon the children unto the third and fourth generation of them that hate me. . . .

Amsdorf; Bucer *(Grund);* Hätzer; *Ich kann;* Lonicer; Pollio; Spelt; Wilhelm; Wurm; Zwingli *(Compar);* Zwingli *(Glauben)*

6:5. And thou shalt love the Lord thy God with all thine heart, and with all thy soul, and with all thy might.

Sickingen; Spelt; Zwingli *(Compar)*

7:5−6. But thus shall ye deal with them; ye shall destroy their altars, and break down their images, and cut down their groves, and burn their graven images with fire. / For thou art an holy people unto the Lord thy God: the Lord thy God hath chosen thee to be a special people unto himself, above all people that are upon the face of the earth.

Hätzer; Karlstadt; Pollio; Wilhelm; Wurm; Zwingli *(Compar);* Zwingli *(Glauben)*

DEUTERONOMY, *continued*

11:16–17. Take heed to yourselves, that your heart be not deceived, and ye turn aside, and serve other gods, and worship them; / And then the Lord's wrath be kindled against you, and he shut up the heaven, that there be no rain, and that the land yield not her fruit; and lest ye perish quickly from off the good land which the Lord giveth you.

Wurm; Zwingli *(Glauben)*

12:1–13. These are the statutes and judgments, which ye shall observe to do in the land, which the Lord God of thy fathers giveth thee to possess it, all the days that ye live upon the earth. / Ye shall utterly destroy all the places, wherein the nations which ye shall possess served their gods, upon the high mountains, and upon the hills, and under every green tree: / And ye shall overthrow their altars, and break their pillars, and burn their groves with fire; and ye shall hew down the graven images of their gods, and destroy the names of them out of that place. / Ye shall not do so unto the Lord your God. / But unto the place which the Lord your God shall choose out of all your tribes to put his name there, even unto his habitation shall ye seek, and thither thou shalt come: / And thither ye shall bring your burnt offerings, and your sacrifices, and your tithes, and heave offerings of your hand, and your vows, and your freewill offerings, and the firstlings of your herds and of your flocks: / And there ye shall eat before the Lord your God, and ye shall rejoice in all that ye put your hand unto, ye and your households, wherein the Lord thy God hath blessed thee. / Ye shall not do after all the things that we do here this day, every man whatsoever is right in his own eyes. / For ye are not as yet come to the rest and to the inheritance, which the Lord your God giveth you. / But when ye go over Jordan, and dwell in the land which the Lord your God giveth you to inherit, and when he giveth you rest from all your enemies round about, so that ye dwell in safety; / Then there shall be a place which the Lord your God shall choose to cause his name to dwell there; thither shall ye bring all that I command you; your burnt offerings, and your sacrifices,

your tithes, and the heave offering of your hand, and all your choice vows which ye vow unto the Lord: / And ye shall rejoice before the Lord your God, ye, and your sons, and your daughters, and your menservants, and your maidservants, and the Levite that is within your gates; forasmuch as he hath no part nor inheritance with you. / Take heed to thyself that thou offer not thy burnt offerings in every place that thou seest....

Hätzer, cited as Deuteronomy 11; Heyden; Lonicer; Wurm; Ziegler

13:1–5. If there arise among you a prophet, or a dreamer of dreams, and giveth thee a sign or a wonder, / And the sign or the wonder come to pass, whereof he spake unto thee, saying, "Let us go after other gods, which thou hast not known, and let us serve them"; / Thou shalt not hearken unto the words of that prophet, or that dreamer of dreams: for the Lord your God proveth you, to know whether ye love the Lord your God with all your heart and with all your soul. / Ye shall walk after the Lord your God, and fear him, and keep his commandments, and obey his voice, and ye shall serve him, and cleave unto him. / And that prophet, or that dreamer of dreams, shall be put to death; because he hath spoken to turn you away from the Lord your God, which brought you out of the land of Egypt, and redeemed you out of the house of bondage, to thrust thee out of the way which the Lord thy God commanded thee to walk in. So shalt thou put the evil away from the midst of thee.

Hätzer; Luther *(Abgott)*; Zwingli *(Glauben)*

27:15. Cursed be the man that maketh any graven or molten image, an abomination unto the Lord, the work of the hands of the craftsman, and putteth it in a secret place. And all the people shall answer and say, "Amen."

Hätzer; Pollio; Wurm; Zwingli *(Glauben)*

29:17–20. And ye have seen their abominations, and their idols, wood and stone, silver and gold, which were among them: / Lest there should be among you man, or woman, or family, or tribe, whose heart turneth away this day from the Lord our God, to go and serve the gods of these nations; lest there should be among you a

DEUTERONOMY, *continued*

root that beareth gall and wormwood; / And it come to pass, when he heareth the words of this curse, that he bless himself in his heart, saying, "I shall have peace, though I walk in the imagination of mine heart, to add drunkenness to thirst": / The Lord will not spare him, but then the anger of the Lord and his jealousy shall smoke against that man, and all the curses that are written in this book shall lie upon him, and the Lord shall blot out his name from under heaven.

Wurm

32:16–19. They provoked him to jealousy with strange gods, with abominations provoked they him to anger. / They sacrificed unto devils, not to God; to gods whom they knew not, to new gods that came newly up, whom your fathers feared not. / Of the Rock that begat thee thou art unmindful, and hast forgotten God that formed thee. / And when the Lord saw it, he abhorred them, because of the provoking of his sons, and of his daughters.

Melhofer; Wilhelm; Zwingli *(Compar);* Zwingli *(Gegenwurf);* Zwingli *(Glauben)*

JOSHUA

24:19–20. And Joshua said unto the people, "Ye cannot serve the Lord: for he is an holy God; he is a jealous God; he will not forgive your transgressions nor your sins. / If ye forsake the Lord, and serve strange gods, then he will turn and do you hurt, and consume you, after that he hath done you good."

Hätzer, cited as Joshua 27; Zwingli *(Glauben)*

JUDGES

10:15–16. And the children of Israel said unto the Lord, "We have sinned: do thou unto us whatsoever seemeth good unto thee; deliver us only, we pray thee, this day." / And they put away the strange gods from among them, and served the Lord and his soul was grieved for the misery of Israel.

Hätzer; Zwingli *(Glauben)*

1 SAMUEL

7:3. And Samuel spake unto all the house of Israel, saying, "If ye do return unto the Lord with all your hearts, then put away the strange gods and Ashtaroth from among you, and prepare your hearts unto the Lord, and serve him only: and he will deliver you out of the hand of the Philistines."

Hätzer, cited as 1 Kings 7; Zwingli *(Glauben),* cited as 1 Kings 7

2 SAMUEL

22:1–3. And David spake unto the Lord the words of this song in the day that the Lord had delivered him out of the hand of all his enemies and out of the hand of Saul: / And he said, "The Lord is my rock, and my fortress, and my deliverer; / The God of my rock; in him will I trust: he is my shield, and the horn of my salvation, my high tower, and my refuge, my saviour; thou savest me from violence."

Gretzinger *(Stück),* cited as 2 Kings 22; [Peringer], cited as 2 Kings 22; Wilhelm, cited as 2 Kings 22

1 KINGS

12:28. Whereupon the king took counsel, and made two calves of gold, and said unto them, "It is too much for you to go up to Jerusalem: behold thy gods, O Israel, which brought thee up out of the land of Egypt."

Zwingli *(Compar)*

18:21–22. And Elijah came unto all the people, and said, "How long halt ye between two opinions? If the Lord be God, follow him: but if Baal, then follow him." And the people answered him not a word. / Then said Elijah unto the people, "I, even I only remain a prophet of the Lord; but Baal's prophets are four hundred and fifty men."

Güttel *(Dialogus)*

2 KINGS

11:17–18. And Jehoiada made a covenant between the Lord and the king and the people, that they should be the Lord's people; between

2 KINGS, *continued*

the king also and the people. / And all the people of the land went into the house of Baal, and brake it down; his altars and his images brake they in pieces thoroughly, and slew Mattan the priest of Baal before the altars. And the priest appointed officers over the house of the Lord.

Gretzinger *(Stück),* cited as 4 Kings 11

17:37—39. And the statutes, and the ordinances, and the law, and the commandment, which he wrote for you, ye shall observe to do for evermore; and ye shall not fear other gods. / And the covenant that I have made with you ye shall not forget; neither shall ye fear other gods. / But the Lord your God ye shall fear; and he shall deliver you out of the hand of all your enemies.

Wilhelm, cited as 4 Kings 17; Zwingli *(Compar),* cited as 4 Kings 17

18:4. He removed the high places, and brake the images, and cut down the groves, and brake in pieces the brasen serpent that Moses had made: for unto those days the children of Israel did burn incense to it: and he called it Nehushtan.

Hätzer, cited as 4 Kings 18; Karlstadt, cited as 4 Kings 18; Pollio, cited as 4 Kings 18; Wurm, cited as 4 Kings 18

23:4. And the king commanded Hilkiah the high priest, and the priests of the second order, and the keepers of the door, to bring forth out of the temple of the Lord all the vessels that were made for Baal, and for the grove, and for all the host of heaven: and he burned them without Jerusalem in the fields of Kidron, and carried the ashes of them unto Beth-el.

Hätzer, cited as 4 Kings 23

23:14—15. And he brake in pieces the images, and cut down the groves, and filled their places with the bones of men. / Moreover the altar that was at Beth-el, and the high place which Jeroboam the son of Nebat, who made Israel to sin, had made, both that altar and the high place he

brake down, and burned the high place, and stamped it small to powder, and burned the grove.

Hätzer, cited as 4 Kings 23

2 CHRONICLES

16:7—9. And at that time Hanani the seer came to Asa king of Judah, and said unto him, "Because thou hast relied on the king of Syria, and not relied on the Lord thy God, therefore is the host of the king of Syria escaped out of thine hand. / Were not the Ethiopians and the Lubims a huge host, with very many chariots and horsemen? yet, because thou didst rely on the Lord, he delivered them into thine hand. / For the eyes of the Lord run to and fro throughout the whole earth, to shew himself strong in the behalf of them whose heart is perfect toward him. Herein thou hast done foolishly: therefore from henceforth thou shalt have wars."

Gretzinger *(Stück)*

33:15. And he took away the strange gods, and the idol out of the house of the Lord, and all the altars that he had built in the mount of the house of the Lord, and in Jerusalem, and cast them out of the city.

Hätzer

PSALMS

7:1—2. O Lord my God, in thee do I put my trust: save me from all them that persecute me, and deliver me: / Lest he tear my soul like a lion, rending it in pieces, while there is none to deliver.

Zwingli *(Compar)*

9:13—14. Have mercy upon me, O Lord; consider my trouble which I suffer of them that hate me, thou that liftest me up from the gates of death: / That I may shew forth all thy praise in the gates of the daughter of Zion: I will rejoice in thy salvation.

Heyden

18:1—7. I will love thee, O Lord, my strength. / The Lord is my rock, and my fortress, and my deliverer; my God, my strength, in whom I will trust; my buckler, and the horn of my salvation,

PSALMS, *continued*

and my high tower. / I will call upon the Lord, who is worthy to be praised: so shall I be saved from mine enemies. / The sorrows of death compassed me, and the floods of ungodly men made me afraid. / The sorrows of hell compassed me about: the snares of death prevented me. / In my distress I called upon the Lord, and cried unto my God: he heard my voice out of his temple, and my cry came before him, even into his ears. / Then the earth shook and trembled; the foundations also of the hills moved and were shaken, because he was wroth.

[Berckenmeyer], cited as Psalm 17; Gretzinger *(Stück)*, cited as Psalm 17; [Peringer], cited as Psalm 17; Wilhelm, cited as Psalm 17; Zwingli *(Compar)*, cited as Psalm 17

30:4. Sing unto the Lord, O ye saints of his, and give thanks at the remembrance of his holiness.

[Berckenmeyer], cited as Psalm 29

31:23. O love the Lord, all ye his saints: for the Lord preserveth the faithful, and plentifully rewardeth the proud doer.

[Berckenmeyer], cited as Psalm 30

60:10–12. Wilt thou not, O God, which hadst cast us off? And thou, O God, which didst not go out with our armies? / Give us help from trouble: for vain is the help of man. / Through God we shall do valiantly: for he it is that shall tread down our enemies.

Zwingli *(Compar)*

62:7–8. In God is my salvation and my glory: the rock of my strength, and my refuge, is in God. / Trust in him at all times; ye people, pour out your heart before him: God is a refuge for us. Selah.

Schmid, cited as Psalm 61

63:1–4. O God, thou art my God; early will I seek thee: my soul thirsteth for thee, my flesh longeth for thee in a dry and thirsty land, where no water is; / To see thy power and thy glory, so

as I have seen thee in the sanctuary. / Because thy lovingkindness is better than life, my lips shall praise thee. / Thus will I bless thee while I live: I will lift up my hands in thy name.

Gretzinger *(Punkten)*; Gretzinger *(Stück)*, cited as Psalm 62; Heyden

72:18. Blessed be the Lord God, the God of Israel, who only doeth wondrous things.

Luther *(Abgott)*, cited as Psalm 71

73:28. But it is good for me to draw near to God; I have put my trust in the Lord God, that I may declare all thy works.

Gretzinger *(Stück)*

86:1–5. Bow down thine ear, O Lord, hear me: for I am poor and needy. / Preserve my soul; for I am holy: O thou my God, save thy servant that trusteth in thee. / Be merciful unto me, O Lord: for I cry unto thee daily. / Rejoice the soul of thy servant: for unto thee, O Lord, do I lift up my soul. / For thou, Lord, art good, and ready to forgive; and plenteous in mercy unto all them that call upon thee.

Heyden, cited as Psalm 85; [Peringer], cited as Psalm 85

86:9–12. All nations whom thou hast made shall come and worship before thee, O Lord; and shall glorify thy name. / For thou art great, and doest wondrous things: thou art God alone. / Teach me thy way, O Lord; I will walk in thy truth: unite my heart to fear thy name. / I will praise thee, O Lord my God, with all my heart: and I will glorify thy name for evermore.

Gretzinger *(Stück)*; [Peringer]; Wilhelm, cited as Psalm 85

96:5. For all the gods of the nations are idols: but the Lord made the heavens.

Zwingli *(Compar)*, cited as Psalm 95

97:7. Confounded be all they that serve graven images, that boast themselves of idols: worship him, all ye gods.

Zwingli *(Compar)*, cited as Psalm 96

PSALMS, *continued*

106:36. And they served their idols: which were a snare unto them.

Hätzer, cited as Psalm 105

115:1—11. Not unto us, O Lord, not unto us, but unto thy name give glory, for thy mercy, and for thy truth's sake. / Wherefore should the heathen say, "Where is now their God?" / But our God is in the heavens: he hath done whatsoever he hath pleased. / Their idols are silver and gold, the work of men's hands. / They have mouths, but they speak not: eyes have they, but they see not: / They have ears, but they hear not: noses have they, but they smell not: / They have hands, but they handle not: feet have they, but they walk not: neither speak they through their throat. / They that make them are like unto them; so is every one that trusteth in them. / O Israel, trust thou in the Lord: he is their help and their shield. / Ye that fear the Lord, trust in the Lord: he is their help and their shield.

A.S., cited as Psalm 113; Heyden, cited as Psalm 113; Luther *(Visitatoren),* cited as Psalm 114; Zwingli *(Compar),* cited as Psalm 113; Zwingli *(Glauben),* cited as Psalm 114

118:5—9. I called upon the Lord in distress: the Lord answered me, and set me in a large place. / The Lord is on my side; I will not fear: what can man do unto me? / The Lord taketh my part with them that help me: therefore shall I see my desire upon them that hate me. / It is better to trust in the Lord than to put confidence in man. / It is better to trust in the Lord than to put confidence in princes.

Gretzinger *(Stück);* [Peringer], cited as Psalm 117

118:22. The stone which the builders refused is become the head stone of the corner.

Gretzinger *(Stück),* cited as Psalm 117

149:1. Praise ye the Lord. Sing unto the Lord a new song, and his praise in the congregation of saints.

[Berckenmeyer]

150:1. Praise ye the Lord. Praise God in his sanctuary: praise him in the firmament of his power.

Gretzinger *(Stück);* Lonicer; Luther *(Abgott); Sermon;* Sickingen; Wilhelm

ISAIAH

1:13—14. Bring no more vain oblations; incense is an abomination unto me; the new moons and sabbaths, the calling of assemblies, I cannot away with; it is iniquity, even the solemn meeting. / You new moons and your appointed feasts my soul hateth: they are a trouble unto me; I am weary to bear them.

Zwingli *(Compar)*

3:11. Woe unto the wicked! It shall be ill with him: for the reward of his hands shall be given him.

Ziegler

5:20. Woe unto them that call evil good, and good evil; that put darkness for light, and light for darkness; that put bitter for sweet, and sweet for bitter!

Zwingli *(Compar)*

6:3. And one cried unto another, and said, "Holy, holy, holy, is the Lord of hosts: the whole earth is full of glory."

[Berckenmeyer]

12:2. Behold, God is my salvation; I will trust, and not be afraid: for the Lord JEHOVAH is my strength and my song; he also is become my salvation.

Gretzinger *(Stück);* [Peringer]; Wilhelm

16:5. And in mercy shall the throne be established: and he shall sit upon it in truth in the tabernacle of David, judging, and seeking judgment, and hasting righteousness.

Heyden

19:1—2. The burden of Egypt. Behold, the Lord rideth upon a swift cloud, and shall come

ISAIAH, *continued*

into Egypt: and the idols of Egypt shall be moved at his presence, and the heart of Egypt shall melt in the midst of it. / And I will set the Egyptians against the Egyptians: and they shall fight every one against his brother, and every one against his neighbour; city against city, and kingdom against kingdom.

Ziegler

37:38. And it came to pass, as he was worshipping in the house of Nisroch his god, that Adrammelech and Sharezer his sons smote him with the sword; and they escaped into the land of Armenia: and Esar-haddon his son reigned in his stead.

Ziegler, cited as Isaiah 36

40:18–19. To whom then will ye liken God? Or what likeness will ye compare unto him? / The workman melteth a graven image, and the goldsmith spreadeth it over with gold, and casteth silver chains.

Zwingli *(Compar)*

41:10. Fear thou not; for I am with thee: be not dismayed; for I am thy God: I will strengthen thee; yea, I will help thee; yea, I will uphold thee with the right hand of my righteousness.

Wilhelm

42:8. I am the Lord: that is my name: and my glory will I not give to another, neither my praise to graven images.

Hätzer; Zeuleys; Ziegler; Zwingli *(Glauben)*

42:17. They shall be turned back, they shall be greatly ashamed, that trust in graven images, that say to the molten images, "Ye are our gods."

Hätzer

43:7. Even every one that is called by my name: for I have created him for my glory, I have formed him; yea, I have made him.

Heyden

43:11–12. "I, even I, am the Lord; and beside me there is no saviour. / I have declared, and have saved, and I have shewed, when there was no strange god among you: therefore ye are my witnesses," saith the Lord, "that I am God."

Gretzinger *(Stück);* Güttel *(Dialogus);* Heyden; Melhofer; [Peringer]; Wilhelm; Ziegler; Zwingli *(Gegenwurf);* Zwingli *(Glauben)*

44:6–20. Thus saith the Lord the King of Israel, and his redeemer the Lord of hosts; "I am the first, and I am the last; and beside me there is no God. / And who, as I, shall call, and shall declare it, and set it in order for me since I appointed the ancient people? and the things that are coming, and shall come, let them shew unto them. / Fear ye not, neither be afraid: have not I told thee from that time and have declared it? ye are even my witnesses. Is there a God beside me? yea, there is no God; I know not any. / They that make a graven image are all of them vanity; and their delectable things shall not profit; and they are their own witnesses; they see not, nor know; that they may be ashamed. / Who hath formed a god, or molten a graven image that is profitable for nothing? / Behold, all his fellows shall be ashamed: and the workmen, they are of men: let them stand up; yet they shall fear, and they shall be ashamed together. / The smith with the tongs both worketh in the coals, and fashioneth it with hammers, and worketh it with the strength of his arms: yea, he is hungry, and his strength faileth: he drinketh no water, and is faint. / The carpenter stretcheth out his rule; he marketh it out with a line; he fitteth it with planes, and he marketh it out with the compass, and maketh it after the figure of a man, according to the beauty of a man; that it may remain in the house. / He heweth him down cedars and taketh the cypress and the oak, which he strengtheneth for himself among the trees of the forest: he planteth an ash, and the rain doth nourish it. / Then shall it be for a man to burn: for he will take thereof, and warm himself; yea, he kindleth it, and baketh bread; yea, he maketh a god, and worshippeth it; he maketh it a graven image, and falleth down thereto. / He burneth part thereof in the fire; with part thereof he eateth flesh; he roasteth roast, and is satisfied: yea, he warmeth himself, and saith, 'Aha, I am

ISAIAH, *continued*

warm, I have seen the fire': / And the residue thereof he maketh a god, even his graven image: he falleth down unto it, and worshippeth it, and prayeth unto it, and saith, 'Deliver me; for thou art my god.' / They have not known nor understood: for he hath shut their eyes, that they cannot see; and their hearts, that they cannot understand. / And none considereth in his heart, neither is there knowledge nor understanding to say, 'I have burned part of it in the fire; yea, also I have baked bread upon the coals thereof; I have roasted flesh, and eaten it: and shall I make the residue thereof an abomination? shall I fall down to the stock of a tree?' / He feedeth on ashes: a deceived heart hath turned him aside, that he cannot deliver his soul, nor say, 'Is there not a lie in my right hand?'"

> Hätzer; Karlstadt; Zwingli *(Compar)*, uses only vv. 9–20; Zwingli *(Glauben)*, uses only vv. 9–20

45:16. They shall be ashamed, and also confounded, all of them: they shall go to confusion together that are makers of idols.

> Zwingli *(Compar)*

46:9. Remember the former things of old: for I am God, and there is none else; I am God, and there is none like me.

> Ziegler

48:12. Hearken unto me, O Jacob and Israel, my called; I am he; I am the first, I also am the last.

> Heyden

49:15. Can a woman forget her sucking child, that she should not have compassion on the son of her womb? Yea, they may forget, yet will I not forget thee.

> Heyden

49:26. And I will feed them that oppress thee with their own flesh; and they shall be drunken with their own blood, as with sweet wine: and all flesh shall know that I the Lord am thy Saviour and thy Redeemer, the mighty One of Jacob.

> Melhofer

51:1. Hearken to me, ye that follow after righteousness, ye that seek the Lord: look unto the rock whence ye are hewn, and to the hole of the pit whence ye are digged.

> Heyden

52:6. Therefore my people shall know my name: therefore they shall know in that day that I am he that doth speak: "behold, it is I."

> Zwingli *(Gegenwurf)*

65:3–4. A people that provoketh me to anger continually to my face; that sacrificeth in gardens, and burneth incense upon altars of brick; / Which remain among the graves, and lodge in the monuments, which eat swine's flesh, and broth of abominable things is in their vessels....

> Ziegler

66:1. Thus saith the Lord, "The heaven is my throne, and the earth is my footstool: where is the house that ye build unto me? And where is the place of my rest?"

> Wilhelm

66:3. He that killeth an ox is as if he slew a man; he that sacrificeth a lamb, as if he cut off a dog's neck; he that offereth an oblation, as if he offered swine's blood; he that burneth incense, as if he blessed an idol. Yea, they have chosen their own ways, and their soul delighteth in their abominations.

> Gretzinger *(Stück)*; Ziegler

JEREMIAH

2:11–13. Hath a nation changed their gods, which are yet no gods? But my people have changed their glory for that which doth not profit. / Be astonished, O ye heavens, at this, and be horribly afraid, be ye very desolate, saith the Lord. / For my people have committed two evils; they have forsaken me the fountain of living

JEREMIAH, *continued*

waters, and hewed them out cisterns, broken cisterns, that can hold no water.

Pollio; Zwingli *(Compar)*; Zwingli
(Gegenwurf)

2:28. But where are thy gods that thou hast
made thee? Let them arise, if they can save thee
in the time of thy trouble: for according to the
number of thy cities are thy gods, O Judah.

Zwingli *(Compar)*; Zwingli *(Gegenwurf)*

8:19. Behold the voice of the cry of the
daughter of my people because of them that
dwell in a far country: Is not the Lord in Zion? Is
not her king in her? Why have they provoked me
to anger with their graven images, and with
strange vanities?

Ziegler

9:13–15. And the Lord saith, "Because they
have forsaken my law which I set before them,
and have not obeyed my voice, neither walked
therein; / But have walked after the imagination
of their own heart, and after Baalim, which their
fathers taught them": Therefore thus saith the
Lord of hosts, the God of Israel; "Behold I will
feed them, even this people, with wormwood,
and give them water of gall to drink."

Ziegler

10:3–5. For the customs of the people are
vain: for one cutteth a tree out of the forest, the
work of the hands of the workman, with the ax. /
They deck it with silver and with gold; they fasten it with nails and with hammers, that it move
not. / They are upright as the palm tree, but speak
not: they must needs be borne, because they cannot go. Be not afraid of them; for they cannot do
evil, neither also is it in them to do good.

Karlstadt

10:14–15. Every man is brutish in his knowledge: every founder is confounded by the graven
image: for his molten image is falsehood, and
there is no breath in them. / They are vanity, and

the work of errors: in the time of their visitation
they shall perish.

Hätzer; Zwingli *(Glauben)*

13:9–10. Thus saith the Lord, "After this
manner will I mar the pride of Judah, and the
great pride of Jerusalem. / This evil people,
which refuse to hear my words, which walk in
the imagination of their heart, and walk after
other gods, to serve them, and to worship them,
shall even be as this girdle, which is good for
nothing."

Hätzer; Zwingli *(Glauben)*

17:5. Thus saith the Lord; "Cursed be the man
that trusteth in man, and maketh flesh his arm,
and whose heart departeth from the Lord."

Gretzinger *(Stück)*; Heyden; Wilhelm;
Zeuleys; Zwingli *(Gegenwurf)*; Zwingli
(Glauben)

17:7. Blessed is the man that trusteth in the
Lord, and whose hope the Lord is.

Wilhelm

23:1–2. "Woe be unto the pastors that destroy
and scatter the sheep of my pasture!" saith the
Lord. / Therefore thus saith the Lord God of
Israel against the pastors that feed my people; "Ye
have scattered my flock, and driven them away,
and have not visited them: behold, I will visit
upon you the evil of your doings," saith the Lord.

Ziegler

23:13. And I have seen folly in the prophets of
Samaria; they prophesied in Baal, and caused my
people Israel to err.

Zwingli *(Compar)*

23:27. Which think to cause my people to
forget my name by their dreams which they tell
every man to his neighbour, as their fathers have
forgotten my name for Baal.

Zwingli *(Compar)*

23:28. "The prophet that hath a dream, let
him tell a dream; and he that hath my word, let

JEREMIAH, *continued*

him speak my word faithfully. What is the chaff to the wheat?" saith the Lord.

Heyden

24:7. And I will give them an heart to know me, that I am the Lord: and they shall be my people, and I will be their God: for they shall return unto me with their whole heart.

Heyden

29:12. Then shall ye call upon me, and ye shall go and pray unto me, and I will hearken unto you.

Melhofer; Wilhelm

33:8. And I will cleanse them from all their iniquity, whereby they have sinned against me; and I will pardon all their iniquities, whereby they have sinned, and whereby they have transgressed against me.

Wilhelm

51:47. Therefore, behold, the days come, that I will do judgment upon the graven images of Babylon: and her whole land shall be confounded, and all her slain shall fall in the midst of her.

Ziegler

EZEKIEL

6:3–7. And say, "Ye mountains of Israel, hear the word of the Lord God"; Thus saith the Lord God to the mountains, and to the hills, to the rivers, and to the valleys; "Behold, I even I, will bring a sword upon you, and I will destroy your high places. / And your altars shall be desolate, and your images shall be broken: and I will cast down your slain men before your idols. / And I will lay the dead carcases of the children of Israel before their idols; and I will scatter your bones round about your altars. / In all your dwelling places the cities shall be laid waste, and the high places shall be desolate; that your altars may be laid waste and made desolate, and your idols may be broken and cease, and your images may be cut

down, and your works may be abolished. / And the slain shall fall in the midst of you, and ye shall know that I am the Lord."

Hätzer; Zwingli *(Glauben)*

14:2–8. And the word of the Lord came unto me, saying, / "Son of man, these men have set up their idols in their heart, and put the stumblingblock of their iniquity before their face: should I be enquired of at all by them? / Therefore speak unto them, and say unto them, 'Thus saith the Lord God; Every man of the house of Israel that setteth up his idols in his heart, and putteth the stumblingblock of his iniquity before his face, and cometh to the prophet; I the Lord will answer him that cometh according to the multitude of his idols; / That I may take the house of Israel in their own heart, because they are all estranged from me through their idols.' / Therefore say unto the house of Israel, 'Thus saith the Lord God; Repent, and turn yourselves from your idols; and turn away your faces from all your abominations.' / For every one of the house of Israel, or of the stranger that sojourneth in Israel, which separateth himself from me, and setteth up his idols in his heart, and putteth the stumblingblock of his iniquity before his face, and cometh to a prophet to enquire of him concerning me; I the Lord will answer him by myself: / And I will set my face against that man, and will make him a sign and a proverb, and I will cut him off from the midst of my people; and ye shall know that I am the Lord."

Zwingli *(Gegenwurf)*; Zwingli *(Glauben)*

18:5–9. "But if a man be just, and do that which is lawful and right, / And hath not eaten upon the mountains, neither hath lifted up his eyes to the idols of the house of Israel, neither hath defiled his neighbour's wife, neither hath he come near to a menstruous woman, / And hath not oppressed any, but hath restored to the debtor his pledge, hath spoiled none by violence, hath given his bread to the hungry, and hath covered the naked with a garment; / He that hath not given forth upon usury, neither hath taken any increase, that hath withdrawn his hand from iniquity, hath executed true judgment between man and man, / Hath walked in my statutes, and hath

EZEKIEL, *continued*

kept my judgments, to deal truly; he is just, he shall surely live," saith the Lord God.

Zwingli *(Gegenwurf)*

22:4. Thou art become guilty in thy blood that thou hast shed; and hast defiled thyself in thine idols which thou hast made; and thou hast caused thy days to draw near, and art come even unto thy years: therefore have I made thee a reproach unto the heathen, and a mocking to all countries.

Ziegler

36:22–23. Therefore say unto the house of Israel, "Thus saith the Lord God; 'I do not this for your sakes, O house of Israel, but for mine holy name's sake, which ye have profaned among the heathen, whither ye went. / And I will sanctify my great name, which was profaned among the heathen, which ye have profaned in the midst of them; and the heathen shall know that I am the Lord," saith the Lord God, "when I shall be sanctified in you before their eyes."

[Berckenmeyer]

39:7. So will I make my holy name known in the midst of my people Israel; and I will not let them pollute my holy name any more: and the heathen shall know that I am the Lord, the Holy One in Israel.

Ziegler

44:12–13. "Because they ministered unto them before their idols, and caused the house of Israel to fall into iniquity; therefore have I lifted up mine hand against them," saith the Lord God, "and they shall bear their iniquity. / And they shall not come near unto me, to do the office of a priest unto me, nor to come near to any of my holy things, in the most holy place: but they shall bear their shame, and their abominations which they have committed."

Ziegler

DANIEL

3:1. Nebuchadnezzar the king made an image of gold, whose height was threescore cubits, and the breadth thereof six cubits: he set it up in the plain of Dura, in the province of Babylon.

Ziegler

5:22–23. And thou his son, O Belshazzar, hast not humbled thine heart, though thou knewest all this; / But hast lifted up thyself against the Lord of heaven; and they have brought the vessels of his house before thee, and thou, and thy lords, thy wives, and thy concubines, have drunk wine in them; and thou hast praised the gods of silver, and gold, of brass, iron, wood, and stone, which see not, nor hear, nor know: and the God in whose hand thy breath is and whose are all thy ways, hast thou not glorified....

Ziegler

HOSEA

9:10. I found Israel like grapes in the wilderness; I saw your fathers as the firststripe in the fig tree at her first time: but they went to Baalpeor, and separated themselves unto that shame; and their abominations were according as they loved.

Karlstadt

13:4. Yet I am the Lord thy God from the land of Egypt, and thou shalt know no god but me: for there is no saviour beside me.

Heyden; Wilhelm

MICAH

1:7. And all the graven images thereof shall be beaten to pieces, and all the hires thereof shall be burned with the fire, and all the idols thereof will I lay desolate: for she gathered it of the hire of an harlot, and they shall return to the hire of an harlot.

Hätzer; Zwingli *(Glauben)*

HABAKKUK

2:18–19. What profiteth the graven image that the maker thereof hath graven it; the molten image, and a teacher of lies, that the maker of his

HABAKKUK, *continued*

work trusteth therein, to make dumb idols? / Woe unto him that saith to the wood, "Awake"; to the dumb stone, "Arise, it shall teach!" Behold, it is laid over with gold and silver, and there is no breath at all in the midst of it.

Hätzer; Karlstadt; Zwingli *(Glauben)*

MALACHI

2:11. Judah hath dealt treacherously, and an abomination is committed in Israel and in Jerusalem; for Judah hath profaned the holiness of the Lord which he loved, and hath married the daughter of a strange god.

Ziegler

New Testament

MATTHEW

4:10. Then saith Jesus unto him, "Get thee hence, Satan: for it is written, 'Thou shalt worship the Lord thy God, and him only shalt thou serve.'"

A.S.; Gretzinger *(Stück)*; [Peringer]; Sachs; Sickingen; Zeuleys; Ziegler

6:6–7. But thou, when thou prayest, enter into thy closet, and when thou hast shut thy door, pray to thy Father which is in secret; and thy Father which seeth in secret shall reward thee openly. / But when ye pray, use not vain repetitions, as the heathen do: for they think that they shall be heard for their much speaking.

Zwingli *(Compar)*

6:9. After this manner therefore pray we: "Our Father which art in heaven, Hallowed be thy name."

A.S.; Lonicer; Sickingen

6:24. No man can serve two masters: for either he will hate the one, and love the other; or else he will hold to the one, and despise the other. Ye cannot serve God and mammon.

Heyden

10:8–9. Heal the sick, cleanse the lepers, raise the dead, cast out devils: freely ye have received, freely give. / Provide neither gold, nor silver, nor brass in your purses. . . .

Zwingli *(Compar)*

11:28. Come unto me, all ye that labour and are heavy laden, and I will give you rest.

Gretzinger *(Punkten)*; Gretzinger *(Stück)*; Heyden; [Peringer]; Sachs; Zeuleys; Zwingli *(Antwort)*; Zwingli *(Gegenwurf)*

12:46–50. While he yet talked to the people, behold, his mother and his brethren stood without, desiring to speak with him. / Then one said unto him, "Behold, thy mother and thy brethren stand without, desiring to speak with thee." / But he answered and said unto him that told him, "Who is my mother? and who are my brethren?" / And he stretched forth his hand toward his disciples, and said, "Behold my mother and my brethren! / For whosoever shall do the will of my Father which is in heaven, the same is my brother, and sister, and mother."

Heyden; Zeuleys

16:18–19. And I say also unto thee, "That thou art Peter, and upon this rock I will build my church; and the gates of hell shall not prevail against it. / And I will give unto thee the keys of the kingdom of heaven: and whatsoever thou shalt bind on earth shall be bound in heaven: and whatsoever thou shalt loose on earth shall be loosed in heaven."

Heyden; Luther *(Adel)*

18:19–20. Again I say unto you, "That if two of you shall agree on earth as touching any thing that they shall ask, it shall be done for them of my Father which is in heaven. / For where two or three are gathered together in my name, there am I in the midst of them."

Zwingli *(Gegenwurf)*; Zwingli *(Glauben)*

19:17. And he said unto him, "Why callest thou me good? there is none good but one, that

MATTHEW, *continued*

is, God: but if thou wilt enter into life, keep the commandments."

Heyden

21:42. Jesus saith unto them, "Did ye never read in the scriptures, 'The stone which the builders rejected, the same is become the head of the corner: this is the Lord's doing, and it is marvellous in our eyes'?"

Gretzinger *(Stück)*

22:32. I am the God of Abraham, and the God of Isaac, and the God of Jacob? God is not the God of the dead, but of the living.

Vögeli

22:37. Jesus said unto him, "Thou shalt love the Lord thy God with all thy heart, and with all thy soul, and with all thy mind."

Sickingen; Spelt

23:4. For they bind heavy burdens and grievous to be borne, and lay them on men's shoulders; but they themselves will not move them with one of their fingers.

Zwingli *(Glauben)*

23:9. And call no man your father upon the earth: for one is your Father, which is in heaven.

Zwingli *(Gegenwurf)*

24:1–2. And Jesus went out, and departed from the temple: and his disciples came to him for to shew him the buildings of the temple. / And Jesus said unto them, "See ye not all these things? verily I say unto you, 'There shall not be left here one stone upon another, that shall not be thrown down.'"

Ziegler

24:14. And this gospel of the kingdom shall be preached in all the world for a witness unto all nations; and then shall the end come.

Zwingli *(Compar)*

24:24. For there shall arise false Christs, and false prophets, and shall shew great signs and wonders; insomuch that, if it were possible, they shall deceive the very elect.

Luther *(Abgott);* Rhegius

25:40. And the King shall answer and say unto them, "Verily I say unto you, 'Inasmuch as ye have done it unto one of the least of these my brethren, ye have done it unto me.'"

Luther *(Predigt);* Pollio; Wurm; Zwingli *(Compar)*

28:19–20. Go ye therefore, and teach all nations, baptizing them in the name of the Father, and of the Son, and of the Holy Ghost: / Teaching them to observe whatsoever I have commanded you: and, lo, I am with you always, even unto the end of the world. Amen.

Heyden

MARK

5:8–9. For he said unto them, "Come out of the man, thou unclean spirit." / And he asked him, "What is thy name?" And he answered, saying, "My name is Legion: for we are many."

Zwingli *(Glauben)*

6:7–8. And he called unto him the twelve, and began to send them forth by two and two; and gave them power over unclean spirits; / And commanded them that they should take nothing for their journey, save a staff only; no scrip, no bread, no money in their purse. . . .

Zwingli *(Compar)*

10:18. And Jesus said unto him, "Why callest thou me good? there is none good but one, that is, God."

Heyden

12:32–33. And the scribe said unto him, "Well, Master, thou hast said the truth: for there is one God; and there is none other but he: / And to love him with all the heart, and with all the understanding, and with all the soul, and with all the strength, and to love his neighbour as

MARK, *continued*

himself, is more than all whole burnt offerings and sacrifices."

Gretzinger *(Stück)*

LUKE

1:38. And Mary said, "Behold the handmaid of the Lord; be it unto me according to thy word." And the angel departed from her.

Heyden; Schenck

6:43–45. For a good tree bringeth not forth corrupt fruit: neither doth a corrupt tree bring forth good fruit. / For every tree is known by his own fruit. For of thorns men do not gather figs, nor of a bramble bush father they grapes. / A good man out of the good treasure of his heart bringeth forth that which is good; and an evil man out of the evil treasure of his heart bringeth forth that which is evil: for of the abundance of the heart his mouth speaketh.

Wilhelm

8:15. But that on the good ground are they, which in an honest and good heart, having heard the word, keep it, and bring forth fruit with patience.

Zwingli *(Compar)*

9:23–24. And he said to them all, "If any more will come after me, let him deny himself, and take up his cross daily, and follow me. / For whosoever will save his life shall lose it: but whosoever will lose his life for my sake, the same shall save it."

Heyden

10:4. Carry neither purse, nor scrip, nor shoes: and salute no man by the way.

Zwingli *(Compar)*

10:22. All things are delivered to me of my Father: and no man knoweth who the Son is, but

the Father; and who the Father is, but the Son, and he to whom the Son will reveal him.

Heyden

11:9. And I say unto you, "Ask, and it shall be given you; seek, and ye shall find; knock, and it shall be opened unto you."

Hug

11:27–28. And it came to pass, as he spake these things, a certain woman of the company lifted up her voice, and said unto him, "Blessed is the womb that bare thee, and the paps which thou hast sucked." / But he said, "Yea, rather, blessed are they that hear the word of God, and keep it."

Heyden

18:19. And Jesus said unto him, "Why callest thou me good? none is good, save one, that is, God."

Zwingli *(Gegenwurf)*; Zwingli *(Glauben)*

20:17–18. And he beheld them, and said, "What is this then that is written, 'The stone which the builders rejected, the same is become the head of the corner?' / Whosoever shall fall upon that stone shall be broken; but on whomsoever it shall fall, it will grind him to powder."

Gretzinger *(Stück)*

20:38. For he is not a God of the dead, but of the living: for all live unto him.

Vögeli

JOHN

1:6–8. There was a man sent from God, whose name was John. / The same came for a witness, to bear witness of the Light, that all men through him might believe. / He was not that Light, but was sent to bear witness of that Light.

A.S.

1:18. No man hath seen God at any time; the only begotten Son, which is in the bosom of the Father, he hath declared him.

Zwingli *(Compar)*

JOHN, *continued*

2:3—4. And when they wanted wine, the mother of Jesus saith unto him, "They have no wine." / Jesus saith unto her, "Woman, what have I to do with thee? mine hour is not yet come."

A. S.; Heyden

4:21—24. Jesus saith unto her, "Woman, believe me, the hour cometh, when ye shall neither in this mountain, nor yet at Jerusalem, worship the Father. / Ye worship ye know not what: we know what we worship: for salvation is of the Jews. / But the hour cometh, and now is, when the true worshippers shall worship the Father in spirit and in truth: for the Father seeketh such to worship him. / God is a Spirit: and they that worship him must worship him in spirit and in truth."

A. S.; Heyden; Luther *(Abgott)*

5:19. Then answered Jesus and said unto them, "Verily, verily, I say unto you, 'The Son can do nothing of himself, but what he seeth the Father do: for what things soever he doeth, these also doeth the Son likewise.'"

Heyden; Zwingli *(Compar)*

6:51. I am the living bread which came down from heaven: if any man eat of this bread, he shall live for ever: and the bread that I will give is my flesh, which I will give for the life of the world.

Heyden; Zwingli *(Compar)*

7:16. Jesus answered them, and said, "My doctrine is not mine, but his that sent me."

Zwingli *(Compar)*

8:28. Then said Jesus unto them, "When ye have lifted up the Son of man, then shall ye know that I am he, and that I do nothing of myself; but as my Father hath taught me, I speak these things."

Schenck

10:25—27. Jesus answered them, "I told you, and ye believed not: the works that I do in my Father's name, they bear witness of me. / But ye believe not, because ye are not of my sheep, as I said unto you. / My sheep hear my voice, and I know them, and they follow me."

Zwingli *(Compar)*

12:49. For I have not spoken of myself; but the Father which sent me, he gave me a commandment what I should say, and what I should speak.

Heyden

14:6. Jesus saith unto him, "I am the way, the truth, and the life: no man cometh unto the Father, but by me."

Artikel; Eberlin; Gretzinger *(Punkten);* Greifenberger *(Büchlin);* [Greifenberger] *(Büchel);* Gretzinger *(Stück),* cited as John 13; Heyden; Hug; Melhofer; Mirsch; Sickingen; Wilhelm; Zwingli *(Gegenwurf);* Zwingli *(Glauben)*

14:13. And whatsoever ye shall ask in my name, that will I do, that the Father may be glorified in the Son.

Zeuleys

14:26. But the Comforter, which is the Holy Ghost, whom the Father will send in my name, he shall teach you all things, and bring all things to your remembrance, whatsoever I have said unto you.

Luther *(Abgott)*

15:1. I am the true vine, and my Father is the husbandman.

Heyden

15:4. Abide in me, and I in you. As the branch cannot bear fruit of itself, except it abide in the vine; no more can ye, except ye abide in me.

Heyden

15:5. I am the vine, ye are the branches: He that abideth in me, and I in him, the same bringeth forth much fruit: for without me ye can do nothing.

Wilhelm

JOHN, *continued*

16:13—14. Howbeit when he, the Spirit of truth, is come, he will guide you into all truth: for he shall not speak of himself; but whatsoever he shall hear, that shall he speak: and he will shew you things to come. / He shall glorify me: for he shall receive of mine, and shall shew it unto you.

Heyden

16:23. And in that day ye shall ask me nothing. Verily, verily, I say unto you, "Whatsoever ye shall ask the Father in my name, he will give it you."

Heyden; Pollio; Wilhelm

16:24. Hitherto have ye asked nothing in my name: ask, and ye shall receive, that your joy may be full.

A. S.

ACTS

4:7—12. And when they had set them in the midst, they asked, "By what power, or by what name, have ye done this?" / Then Peter, filled with the Holy Ghost, said unto them, "Ye rulers of the people, and elders of Israel, / If we this day be examined of the good deed done to the impotent man, by what means he is made whole; / Be it known unto all, and to all the people of Israel, that by the name of Jesus Christ of Nazareth, whom ye crucified, whom God raised from the dead, even by him doth this man stand here before you whole. / This is the stone which was set at nought of you builders, which is become the head of the corner. / Neither is there salvation in any other: for there is none other name under heaven given among men, whereby we must be saved."

A. S.; Gretzinger *(Stück);* Güttel *(Amt);*
Karlstadt; [Peringer]; *Tröstliche;* Wilhelm;
Zeuleys

10:26. But Peter took him up, saying, "Stand up; I myself also am a man."

Gretzinger *(Stück);* [Peringer]; Vögeli;
Wilhelm

12:21—23. And upon a set day Herod, arrayed in royal apparel, sat upon his throne, and made an oration unto them. / And the people gave a shout, saying, "It is the voice of a god, and not of a man." / And immediately the angel of the Lord smote him, because he gave not God the glory: and he was eaten of worms, and gave up the ghost.

Gretzinger *(Stück);* [Peringer]; Wilhelm

14:11—15. And when the people saw what Paul had done, they lifted up their voices, saying in the speech of Lycaonia, "The gods are come down to us in the likeness of men." / And they called Barnabas, Jupiter; and Paul, Mercurius, because he was the chief speaker. / Then the priest of Jupiter, which was before their city, brought oxen and garlands unto the gates, and would have done sacrifice with the people. / Which when the apostles, Barnabas and Paul, heard of, they rent their clothes, and ran in among the people, crying out, / And saying, "Sirs, why do ye these things? We also are men of like passions with you, and preach unto you that ye should turn from these vanities unto the living God, which made heaven, and earth, and the sea, and all things that are therein...."

Gretzinger *(Stück);* [Peringer]; Wilhelm

15:20. But that we write unto them, that they abstain from pollutions of idols, and from fornication, and from things strangled, and from blood.

Zwingli *(Glauben)*

17:21—23. (For all the Athenians and strangers which were there spent their time in nothing else, but either to tell, or to hear some new thing.) / Then Paul stood in the midst of Mars' hill, and said, "Ye men of Athens, I perceive that in all things ye are too superstitious. / For as I passed by, and beheld your devotions, I found an altar with this inscription, 'TO THE UNKNOWN GOD.' Whom therefore ye ignorantly worship, him declare I unto you."

Luther *(Epistel);* Ziegler, Zwingli *(Antwort)*

ACTS, *continued*

21:25. As touching the Gentiles which believe, we have written and concluded that they observe no such thing, save only that they keep themselves from things offered to idols, and from blood, and from strangled, and from fornication.

Zwingli *(Antwort)*

26:18. To open their eyes, and to turn them from darkness to light, and from the power of Satan unto God, that they may receive forgiveness of sins, and inheritance among them which are sanctified by faith that is in me.

[Berckenmeyer]

ROMANS

1:7. To all that be in Rome, beloved of God, called to be saints: Grace to you and peace from God our Father, and the Lord Jesus Christ.

[Berckenmeyer]; Goldschmidt; Vögeli

1:21–25. Because that, when they knew God, they glorified him not as God, neither were thankful; but became vain in their imaginations, and their foolish heart was darkened. / Professing themselves to be wise, they became fools, / And changed the glory of the uncorruptible God into an image made like to corruptible man, and to birds, and fourfooted beasts, and creeping things. / Wherefore God also gave them up to uncleanness through the lusts of their own hearts, to dishonour their own bodies between themselves: / Who changed the truth of God into a lie, and worshipped and served the creature more than the Creator, who is blessed for ever. Amen.

Zwingli *(Compar)*

2:10–11. But glory, honour, and peace, to every man that worketh good, to the Jew first, and also to the Gentile: / For there is no respect of persons with God.

Vögeli

3:23–26. For all have sinned, and come short of the glory of God; / Being justified freely by his grace through the redemption that is in Christ Jesus: / Whom God hath set forth to be a propitiation through faith in his blood, to declare his righteousness for the remission of sins that are past, through the forbearance of God. / To declare, I say, at this time his righteousness: that he might be just, and the justifier of him which believeth in Jesus.

Gretzinger *(Stück)*; Luther *(Abgott)*; Vögeli; Wilhelm; Zwingli *(Gegenwurf)*

5:1–2. Therefore being justified by faith, we have peace with God through our Lord Jesus Christ: / By whom also we have access by faith into this grace wherein we stand, and rejoice in hope of the glory of God.

Gretzinger *(Stück)*; Luther *(Abgott)*; Luther *(Predigt)*; Zeuleys

5:15. But not as the offence, so also is the free gift. For if through the offence of one many be dead, much more the grace of God, and the gift by grace, which is by one man, Jesus Christ, hath abounded unto many.

Luther *(Abgott)*

5:17. For if by one man's offence death reigned by one; much more they which receive abundance of grace and of the gift of righteousness shall reign in life by one, Jesus Christ.

Eberlin; Luther *(Abgott)*

5:19–21. For as by one man's disobedience many were made sinners, so by the obedience of one shall many be made righteous. / Moreover the law entered, that the offence might abound. But where sin abounded, grace did much more abound: / That as sin hath reigned unto death, even so might grace reign through righteousness unto eternal life by Jesus Christ our Lord.

Vögeli

7:14–15. For we know that the law is spiritual: but I am carnal, sold under sin. / For that which I do I allow not: for what I would, that do I not; but what I hate, that do I.

Wilhelm

ROMANS, *continued*

8:3—4. For what the law could not do, in that it was weak through the flesh, God sending his own Son in the likeness of sinful flesh, and for sin, condemned sin in the flesh: / That the righteousness of the law might be fulfilled in us, who walk not after the flesh, but after the Spirit.

> Zwingli *(Gegenwurf)*; Zwingli *(Glauben)*

8:32—34. He that spared not his own Son, but delivered him up for us all, how shall he not with him also freely give us all things? / Who shall lay any thing to the charge of God's elect? It is God that justifieth. / Who is he that condemneth? It is Christ that died, yea rather, that is risen again, who is even at the right hand of God, who also maketh intercession for us.

> Eberlin; Goldschmidt; Gretzinger *(Stück)*; Luther *(Predigt)*; Luther *(Visitatoren)*; Rhegius; Vögeli

10:11—15. For the scripture saith, "Whosoever believeth on him shall not be ashamed." / For there is no difference between the Jew and the Greek: for the same Lord over all is rich unto all that call upon him. / For whosoever shall call upon the name of the Lord shall be saved. / How then shall they call on him in whom they have not believed? and how shall they believe in him of whom they have not heard? and how shall they hear without a preacher? / And how shall they preach, except they be sent? as it is written, "How beautiful are the feet of them that preach the gospel of peace, and bring glad tidings of good things!"

> A. S.; Gretzinger *(Stück)*; Goldschmidt; Güttel *(Amt)*; Heyden; Melhofer; Wilhelm; Zeuleys; Zwingli *(Compar)*

12:4—5. For as we have many members in one body, and all members have not the same office: / So we, being many, are one body in Christ, and every one members one of another.

> [Berckenmeyer]; Vögeli

12:13. Distributing to the necessity of saints; given to hospitality.

> Luther *(Abgott)*

14:23. And he that doubteth is damned if he eat, because he eateth not of faith: for whatsoever is not of faith is sin.

> Wurm

15:1—3. We then that are strong ought to bear the infirmities of the weak, and not to please ourselves. / Let every one of us please his neighbour for his good to edification. / For even Christ pleased not himself; but, as it is written, "The reproaches of them that reproached thee fell on me."

> Wurm

15:16. That I should be the minister of Jesus Christ to the Gentiles, ministering the gospel of God, that the offering up of the Gentiles might be acceptable, being sanctified by the Holy Ghost.

> [Berckenmeyer]

15:18—21. For I will not dare to speak of any of those things which Christ hath not wrought by me, to make the Gentiles obedient, by word and deed, / Through mighty signs and wonders, by the power of the Spirit of God; so that from Jerusalem, and round about unto Illyricum, I have fully preached the gospel of Christ. / Yea, so have I strived to preach the gospel, not where Christ was named, lest I should build upon another man's foundation: / But as it is written, "To whom he was not spoken of, they shall see: and they that have not heard shall understand."

> Zwingli *(Compar)*

15:24—25. Whensoever I take my journey into Spain, I will come to you: for I trust to see you in my journey, and to be brought on my way thitherward by you, if first I be somewhat filled with your company. / But now I go unto Jerusalem to minister unto saints.

> Ziegler

ROMANS, *continued*

16:1–2. I commend unto you Phebe our sister, which is a servant of the church which is at Cenchrea: / That ye receive her in the Lord, as becometh saints, and that ye assist her in whatsoever business she hath need of you: for she hath been a succourer of many, and of myself also.

[Berckenmeyer]; Sattler

16:17–18. Now I beseech you, brethren, mark them which cause divisions and offences contrary to the doctrine which ye have learned; and avoid them. / For they that are such serve not our Lord Jesus Christ, but their own belly; and by good words, and fair speeches deceive the hearts of the simple.

Zwingli *(Compar)*

1 CORINTHIANS

1:1–2. Paul, called to be an apostle of Jesus Christ through the will of God, and Sosthenes our brother, / Unto the church of God which is at Corinth, to them that are sanctified in Christ Jesus, called to be saints, with all that in every place call upon the name of Jesus Christ our Lord, both theirs and ours....

[Berckenmeyer]; Sattler; Vögeli

1:13. Is Christ divided? was Paul crucified for you? or were ye baptized in the name of Paul?

Tröstliche, cited as 1 Corinthians 3; Wilhelm; Zeuleys, cited as 1 Corinthians 4

1:30–31. But of him are ye in Christ Jesus, who of God is made unto us wisdom, and righteousness, and sanctification, and redemption: / That, according as it is written, "He that glorieth, let him glory in the Lord."

Heyden; Luther *(Erfurt)*; Pollio; Rhegius; Wilhelm

3:16–17. Know ye not that ye are the temple of God, and that the Spirit of God dwelleth in you? / If any man defile the temple of God, him

shall God destroy; for the temple of God is holy, which temple ye are.

Luther *(Abgott)*; Vögeli

4:7. For who maketh thee to differ from another? and what hast thou that thou didst not receive? now if thou didst receive it, why dost thou glory, as if thou hadst not received it?

Heyden

5:11. But now I have written unto you not to keep company, if any man that is called a brother be a fornicator, or covetous, or an idolater, or a railer, or a drunkard, or an extortioner; with such an one no not to eat.

Ziegler; Zwingli *(Antwort)*; Zwingli *(Compar)*; Zwingli *(Glauben)*

6:2. Do ye not know that the saints shall judge the world? and if the world shall be judged by you, are ye unworthy to judge the smallest matters?

[Berckenmeyer]; Vögeli

6:9. Know ye not that the unrighteous shall not inherit the kingdom of God? Be not deceived: neither fornicators, nor idolaters, nor adulterers, nor effeminate, nor abusers of themselves with mankind.

Zwingli *(Compar)*

7:14. For the unbelieving husband is sanctified by the wife, and the unbelieving wife is sanctified by the husband: else were your children unclean; but now are they holy.

[Berckenmeyer]

8:4. As concerning therefore the eating of those things that are offered in sacrifice unto idols, we know that an idol is nothing in the world, and that there is none other God but one.

Heyden; Karlstadt; Zwingli *(Compar)*; Zwingli *(Glauben)*

I CORINTHIANS, *continued*

10:4. And did all drink the same spiritual drink: for they drank of that spiritual Rock that followed them: and that Rock was Christ.

Heyden

10:6–7. Now these things were our examples, to the intent we should not lust after evil things, as they also lusted. / Neither be ye idolaters, as were some of them; as it is written, "The people sat down to eat and drink, and rose up to play."

Ziegler; Zwingli *(Antwort);* Zwingli *(Compar);* Zwingli *(Glauben)*

12:2. Ye know that ye were Gentiles, carried away unto these dumb idols, even as ye were led.

Zwingli *(Antwort);* Zwingli *(Compar);* Zwingli *(Glauben)*

12:13. For by one Spirit are we all baptized into one body, whether we be Jews or Gentiles, whether we be bond or free; and have been all made to drink into one Spirit.

Vögeli

16:1. Now concerning the collection for the saints, as I have given order to the churches of Galatia, even so do ye.

[Berckenmeyer]

2 CORINTHIANS

1:1–2. Paul, an apostle of Jesus Christ by the will of God, and Timothy our brother, unto the church of God which is at Corinth, with all the saints which are in all Achaia: / Grace be to you and peace from God, our Father, and from the Lord Jesus Christ.

Vögeli

6:16. And what agreement hath the temple of God with idols? for ye are the temple of the living God; as God hath said, "I will dwell in them, and walk in them; and I will be their God, and they shall be my people."

Eckstein; Zwingli *(Antwort)*

9:12–13. For the administration of this service not only supplieth the want of the saints, but is abundant also by many thanksgivings unto God; / Whiles by the experiment of this ministration they glorify God for your professed subjection unto the gospel of Christ, and for your liberal distribution unto them, and unto all men....

[Berckenmeyer]

GALATIANS

3:28. There is neither Jew nor Greek, there is neither bond nor free, there is neither male nor female: for ye are all one in Christ Jesus.

Heyden

5:6. For in Jesus Christ neither circumcision availeth any thing, nor uncircumcision; but faith which worketh by love.

Wurm

5:19–21. Now the works of the flesh are manifest, which are these; Adultery, fornication, uncleanness, lasciviousness, / Idolatry, witchcraft, hatred, variance, emulations, wrath, strife, seditions, heresies, / Envyings, murders, drunkenness, revellings, and such like: of which I tell you before, as I have also told you in time past, that they which do such things shall not inherit the kingdom of God.

Zwingli *(Antwort);* Zwingli *(Glauben)*

EPHESIANS

2:19–22. Now therefore ye are no more strangers and foreigners, but fellow-citizens with the saints, and of the household of God; / And are built upon the foundation of the apostles and prophets, Jesus Christ himself being the chief corner stone; / In whom all the building fitly framed together groweth unto an holy temple in the Lord; / In whom ye also are builded together for an habitation of God through the Spirit.

Gretzinger *(Stück);* Heyden; Wilhelm

3:16–19. That he would grant you, according to the riches of his glory, to be strengthened with might by his Spirit in the inner man; / That Christ may dwell in your hearts by faith; that ye,

EPHESIANS, *continued*

being rooted and grounded in love, / May be able to comprehend with all saints what is the breadth, and length, and depth, and height; / And to know the love of Christ, which passeth knowledge, that ye might be filled with all fulness of God.

Gretzinger *(Stück);* Wilhelm

4:4–6. There is one body, and one Spirit, even as ye are called in one hope of your calling; / One Lord, one faith, one baptism, / One God and Father of all, who is above all, and through all, and in you all.

Heyden; Vögeli

6:12. For we wrestle not against flesh and blood, but against principalities, against powers, against the rulers of the darkness of this world, against spiritual wickedness in high places.

Luther *(Epistel)*

PHILIPPIANS

2:11. And that every tongue should confess that Jesus Christ is Lord, to the glory of God the Father.

A.S.

COLOSSIANS

1:12–14. Giving thanks unto the Father, which hath made us meet to be partakers of the inheritance of the saints in light: / Who hath delivered us from the power of darkness, and hath translated us into the kingdom of his dear Son: / In whom we have redemption through his blood, even the forgiveness of sins....

[Berckenmeyer]; Vögeli

3:11–13. Where there is neither Greek nor Jew, circumcision nor uncircumcision, Barbarian, Scythian, bond nor free: but Christ is all, and in all. / Put on therefore, as the elect of God, holy and beloved, bowels of mercies, kindness, humbleness of mind, meekness, longsuffering; / forbearing one another, and forgiving one another,

if any man have a quarrel against any: even as Christ forgave you, so also do ye.

[Berckenmeyer]; Vögeli

I THESSALONIANS

1:9. For they themselves shew of us what manner of entering in we had unto you, and how ye turned to God from idols to serve the living and true God....

Zwingli *(Antwort);* Zwingli *(Compar);* Zwingli *(Glauben)*

I TIMOTHY

1:12–13. And I thank Christ Jesus our Lord, who hath enabled me, for that he counted me faithful, putting me into the ministry; / Who was before a blasphemer, and a persecutor, and injurious: but I obtained mercy, because I did it ignorantly in unbelief.

Pollio

1:15–17. This is a faithful saying, and worthy of all acceptation, that Christ Jesus came into the world to save sinners; of whom I am chief. / Howbeit for this cause I obtained mercy, that in me first Jesus Christ might shew forth all long-suffering, for a pattern to them which should hereafter believe on him to life everlasting. / Now unto the King eternal, immortal, invisible, the only wise God, be honour and glory for ever and ever. Amen.

[Berckenmeyer]; Gretzinger *(Stück)*

2:5–6. For there is one God, and one mediator between God and men, the man Christ Jesus; / Who gave himself a ransom for all, to be testified in due time.

Bucer *(Rat);* [Gengenbach]; Gretzinger *(Punkten),* cited as 1 Timothy 6; Gretzinger *(Stück);* Heyden; Hug; Lonicer; Luther *(Abgott);* Pollio; Rhegius; Sattler; Wilhelm; Zeuleys; Zwingli *(Antwort);* Zwingli *(Epistel);* Zwingli *(Gegenwurf);* Zwingli *(Glauben)*

5:9–10. Let not a widow be taken into the number under threescore years old, having been the wife of one man, / Well reported of for good

1 TIMOTHY, *continued*

works; if she have brought up children, if she have lodged strangers, if she have washed the saints' feet, if she have relieved the afflicted, if she have diligently followed every good work.

Luther *(Abgott)*

TITUS

3:10. A man that is a heretick after the first and second admonition reject....

Luther *(Epistel)*

HEBREWS

2:9–11. But we see Jesus, who was made a little lower than the angels for the suffering of death, crowned with glory and honour; that he by the grace of God should taste death for every man. / For it became him, for whom are all things, and by whom are all things, in bringing many sons unto glory, to make the captain of their salvation perfect through sufferings. / For both he that sanctifieth and they who are sanctified are all of one: for which cause he is not ashamed to call them brethren.

[Berckenmeyer]; Heyden

6:9–10. But, beloved, we are persuaded better things of you, and things that accompany salvation, though we thus speak. / For God is not unrighteous to forget your work and labour of love, which ye have shewed toward his name, in that ye have ministered to the saints, and do minister.

[Berckenmeyer]

7:25–27. Wherefore he is able also to save them to the uttermost that come unto God by him, seeing he ever liveth to make intercession for them. / For such an high priest became us, who is holy, harmless, undefiled, separate from sinners, and made higher than the heavens; / Who needeth not daily, as those high priests, to offer up sacrifice, first for his own sins, and then for the people's: for this he did once, when he offered up himself.

Gretzinger *(Stück);* Heyden; Hug

8:6. But now hath he obtained a more excellent ministry, by how much also he is the mediator of a better covenant, which was established upon better promises.

Hug; Pollio

9:15. And for this cause he is the mediator of the new testament, that by means of death, for the redemption of the transgressions that were under the first testament, they which are called might receive the promise of eternal inheritance.

[Berckenmeyer]; Hug; Pollio; Rhegius

12:22–24. But ye are come unto mount Sion, and unto the city of the living God, the heavenly Jerusalem, and to an innumerable company of angels, / To the general assembly and church of the firstborn, which are written in heaven, and to God the Judge of all, and to the spirits of just men made perfect, / And to Jesus the mediator of the new covenant, and to the blood of sprinkling, that speaketh better things than that of Abel.

[Berckenmeyer]; Pollio

13:24. Salute all them that have the rule over you, and all the saints. They of Italy salute you.

Gretzinger *(Stück);* Wilhelm

1 PETER

1:18–21. Forasmuch as ye know that ye were not redeemed with corruptible things, as silver and gold, from your vain conversation received by tradition from your father; / But with the precious blood of Christ, as of a lamb without blemish and without spot: / Who verily was foreordained before the foundation of the world, but was manifest in these last times for you, / Who by him do believe in God, that raised him up from the dead, and gave him glory; that your faith and hope might be in God.

Vögeli

2:9. But ye are a chosen generation, a royal priesthood, an holy nation, a peculiar people; that ye should shew forth the praises of him who

1 PETER, *continued*

hath called you out of darkness into his marvellous light....

[Berckenmeyer]

4:3. For the time past of our life may suffice us to have wrought the will of the Gentiles, when we walked in lasciviousness, lusts, excess of wine, revellings, banquetings, and abominable idolatries....

Zwingli *(Antwort);* Zwingli *(Compar);* Zwingli *(Glauben)*

4:18. And if the righteous scarcely be saved, where shall the ungodly and the sinner appear?

Luther *(Mammon)*

1 JOHN

2:1–2. My little children, these things write I unto you, that ye sin not. And if any man sin, we have an advocate with the Father, Jesus Christ the righteous: / And he is the propitiation for our sins: and not for ours only, but also for the sins of the whole world.

Eberlin; Gretzinger *(Stück);* Heyden; Hug; Luther *(Visitatoren);* Pollio; Rhegius; Sachs; Wilhelm; Zeuleys; Zwingli *(Antwort);* Zwingli *(Epistel)*

4:9–10. In this was manifested the love of God toward us, because that God sent his only begotten Son into the world, that we might live through him. / Herein is love, not that we loved God, but that he loved us, and sent his Son to be the propitiation for our sins.

Gretzinger *(Stück);* Heyden

5:21. Little children, keep yourselves from idols. Amen.

Zwingli *(Antwort);* Zwingli *(Compar);* Zwingli *(Glauben)*

JUDE

1:3. Beloved, when I gave all diligence to write unto you of the common salvation, it was needful

for me to write unto you, and exhort you that ye should earnestly contend for the faith which was once delivered unto the saints.

[Berckenmeyer]

REVELATION

5:8–9. And when he had taken the book, the four beasts and four and twenty elders fell down before the Lamb, having every one of them harps, and golden vials full of odours, which are the prayers of the saints. / And they sung a new song, saying, "Thou art worthy to take the book, and to open the seals thereof: for thou wast slain, and hast redeemed us to God by thy blood out of every kindred, and tongue, and people, and nation...."

Heyden

13:7. And it was given unto him to make war with the saints, and to overcome them: and power was given him over all kindreds, and tongues, and nations.

[Berckenmeyer]; Luther *(Epistel)*

14:12–13. Here is the patience of the saints: here are they that keep the commandments of God, and the faith of Jesus. / And I heard a voice from heaven saying unto me, "Write, 'Blessed are the dead, which die in the Lord from henceforth': Yea," saith the Spirit, "that they may rest from their labours; and their works do follow them."

[Berckenmeyer]

16:5–6. And I heard the angel of the waters say, "Thou art righteous, O Lord, which art, and wast, and shalt be, because thou hast judged thus. / For they have shed the blood of saints and prophets, and thou hast given them blood to drink; for they are worthy."

[Berckenmeyer]

19:10. And I fell at his feet to worship him. And he said unto me, "See thou do it not: I am thy fellowservant, and of thy brethren that have the testimony of Jesus: worship God: for the testimony of Jesus is the spirit of prophecy."

[Peringer]

REVELATION, *continued*

22:8–9. And I John saw these things, and heard them. And when I had heard and seen, I fell down to worship before the feet of the angel which shewed me these things. / Then saith he unto me, "See thou do it not: for I am thy fellowservant, and of thy brethren the prophets, and of them which keep the sayings of this book: worship God."

> A. S.; Gretzinger *(Stück);* [Peringer], cited as Revelation 42[?]; Wilhelm

BIBLIOGRAPHY

SELECTED SIXTEENTH-CENTURY WORKS

Listed here are pamphlets and printed sources from the sixteenth century, including modern editions. Most of the pamphlets are found in *Flugschriften des frühen 16. Jahrhunderts,* edited by Hans-Joachim Köhler, Hildegard Hebenstreit-Wilfert, and Christoph Weismann, produced in microfiche by the Inter Documentation Co., 1978–87. The Köhler microform number is listed in the entries below for each such pamphlet.

Contemporary works are cited in full in the footnotes upon their first mention, with short-title references throughout the book.

A. S. *Ein Epistel, meinen lieben Brüdern in Christo Jesu zugeschrieben.* N.p., 1523. (Köhler [q.v.] 222/622.)

Adler, Caspar. *Ein Sermon von der Schul Christi.* [Augsburg: Sigmund Grimm], 1523. (Köhler [q.v.] 45/125.)

Alveldt, Augustin von. *Ein Vorklärung aus heller Warheit, ob das "Salve regina misericordiae" ein christlicher Lobesang sei oder nicht.* [Leipzig: Nickel Schmidt], 1527. (Köhler [q.v.] 780/1961.)

Amsdorf, Nikolaus von. *Wider die Lügenprediger des hohen Doms zu Magdeburg.* Wittenberg: [Nickel Schirlentz], 1525. (Köhler [q.v.] 14/61.)

Die Appellation und Protestation der evangelischen Stände auf dem Reichstage zu Speier 1529. Ed. Julius Ney. Quellenschriften zur Geschichte des Protestantismus. Darmstadt: Wissenschaftliche Buchgesellschaft, 1967.

Artikel, darinne etlike Misbruke by den Parren des Förstensdoms Lüneborg entdecket werden. [Magdeburg: Hans Barth], 1528. (Köhler [q.v.] 1077/2725.)

Bachman, Paul. *Ein Sermon des Abts zu Cellen in Aufnehmung der Reliquien Sancti Bennois.* Dresden: Wolfgang Stöckel, 1527. (Köhler [q.v.] 183/2966.)

Der Barfüßer zu Magdeburg Grund ihres Ordens. Magdeburg: [Heinrich Öttinger], 1526. (Köhler [q.v.] 433–34/1174.)

Beklagung eines Laien genannt Hans Schwalb, über viel Missbräuche christlichen Lebens. Augsburg: Melchior Ramminger, 1521. In *Flugschriften,* ed. Clemen, 1:347–57 [q.v.]. Leipzig: Rudolph Haupt, 1907.

Bentzinger, Rudolf, ed. *Die Warhheit muss ans Licht! Dialoge aus der Zeit der Reformation.* Frankfurt a/M: Röderberg, 1983.

[Berckenmeyer, Jörg.] *Ein Register der heiligen göttlichen Geschrift.* Halle, 1525. (Köhler [q.v.] 1655/4269.)

Bern, Disputation (1528). *Die Predigten so von den fremden Prädikanten, die zu Bern auf dem Gespräch gewesen, beschehen sind.* Zurich: C. Froschauer, 1528. (Köhler [q.v.] 772–74/1948.)

————. *Ratschlag haltender Disputation zu Bern.* [Zurich: C. Froschauer, 1528.] (Köhler [q.v.] 1805/4620.)

Berner Synodus mit den Schlussreden der Berner Disputation und dem Reformationsamt. Dokumente der Berner Reformation. Bern: Paul Haupt, 1978.

Die Beschwerung damit päpstliche Heiligkeit das Heilige Römische Reich und gemeine teutsche Nation beschweren. N.p., n.d. (Köhler [q.v.] 1776/4574.)

Billicanus, Theobald. *An die christelich Kirch-Versammlung einem ehrsamen Rat und Gemein der Stadt Weil Sendbrief.* [Augsburg: Melchior Ramminger], 1522. (Köhler [q.v.] 723/1839.)

Blarer, Ambrosius. *Wahrhaft Verantwortung an einen ehrsame weisen Rat zu Konstanz anzeigend, warum er aus dem Kloster gewichen.* [Augsburg: Simprecht Ruff], 1523. (Köhler [q.v.] 83/224.)

Brenz, Johannes. *Ein Sermon von den Heiligen.* [Ulm: Matthias Hoffischer, 1523.] (Köhler [q.v.] 87/233.)

Bucer, Martin. *An ein christlichen Rat und Gemein der Stadt Weißenberg: Summari seiner Predigt daselbst getan.* [Strassburg: Johann Schott, 1523.] (Köhler [q.v.] 1114–15/2846.)

————. *Daß einigerlei Bild bei den Gottgläubigen an Orten, da sie verehrt, nit mögen geduldet werden.* [Strassburg: Johann Knobloch, 1530.] (Köhler [q.v.] 1439/3824.)

————. *Grund und Ursach aus göttlicher Schrift der Neuerungen zu Straßburg vorgenommen.* [Strassburg: Wolfgang Köpfel], 1525. (Köhler [q.v.] 676–77/1770.)

————. *Verantwortung M. Bucers auf das ihm seine Widerwärtigen zum ärgsten zumessen.* [Strassburg: Johann Schott], 1523. (Köhler [q.v.] 1114/2845.)

Dies Büchlein zeigt an die Weissagung von zukünftiger Betrübnis und wird genannt die Bürde der Welt. Augsburg: Johann Schönsperger, 1522. (Köhler [q.v.] 1031/2594.)

Bugenhagen, Johannes. *Von dem christlichen Glauben und rechten guten Werken.* Wittenberg: Georg Rhau, 1526. (Köhler [q.v.] 1153–56/2928.)

Canons and Decrees of the Council of Trent. Translated by H. J. Schroeder. St. Louis: Herder, 1941.

Capito, Wolfgang Fabricius. *Von drei Straßburger Pfaffen und den geäußerten Kirchengütern.* [Strassburg: Wolfgang Köpfel], 1525. (Köhler [q.v.] 1132/2900.)

Christliche Unterrichtung eins Pfarrherrn an seinen Herrn, ein Fürsten des heiligen Reichs, auf vierzig Artikel und Punkten gestellt. N.p., 1526. (Köhler [q.v.] 1062/2679.)

Clemen, Otto, ed. *Flugschriften aus den ersten Jahren der Reformation.* 4 vols. Leipzig: von Rudolf Haupt, 1907–11.

Clichtoveus, Jodocus. *De veneratione sanctorum libri duo.* Cologne: Peter Quentel, 1525. (Köhler [q.v.] 209–10/594.)

[Comander, Johannes.] *Überdiese nachkommenden Schlußreden wollen wir, der Pfarrer zu Sankt Martin zu Chur samt anderen, einem jeden Antwort und Bericht geben.* [Augsburg: Melchior Ramminger, 1526.] (Köhler [q.v.] 360/1006.)

Concordia or Book of Concord: The Symbols of the Evangelical Lutheran Church. St. Louis: Concordia, 1950.

Die Confutatio der Confessio Augustana vom 3. August 1530. Edited by Herbert Immenkötter. Corpus Catholicorum, vol. 33. Münster: Aschendorff, 1979.

Cronberg, Hartmuth von. *Ein christliche Schrift und Vermahnung an alle Ständ des Römischen Reichs.* [Zwickau: Jörg Gastel, 1523.] (Köhler [q.v.] 231/643.)

Culsamer, Johannes. *Ein Widerlegung etlicher Sermon geschechen zu Erfurt von Doktor Bartholo-maeo Usingen.* Erfurt: [Mattes Maler], 1522. (Köhler [q.v.] 1004/2552.)

Die deutsche Vigile der gottlosen Papisten, Münch und Pfaffen. [Lübeck: Johan Balhorn, 1526 or 1527?] In *Flugschriften,* ed. Clemen, 3:121–45 [q.v.].

Deutscher Nation beschwerd von den Geistlichen. [Strassburg: Johann Schott, 1523.] (Köhler [q.v.] 983/2488.)

Ein Dialogus, das ist ein Gespräch zweier Personen, Christus und Christianus. [Nuremberg: Hieronymus Höltzel, 1524.] (Köhler [q.v.] 268/754.)

Ein Dialogus oder Gespräch zwischen einem Vater und Sohn die Lehre Martini Luthers und sonst andere Sachen des christlichen Glaubens belangend. Erfurt: Michael Buchführer, 1523. In *Flugschriften,* ed. Clemen, 1:25–47 [q.v.].

Diepolt, Johann. *Ein Sermon, an Sankt Mariae Magdalenae Tag geprediget zu Ulm.* [Augsburg: Philipp Ulhart, 1523.] (Köhler [q.v.] 456/1233.)

———. *Zwo nützlich Sermon, geprediget zu Ulm.* [Nuremberg: Johann Stuchs], 1523. (Köhler [q.v.] 394/1072.)

Dietenberger, Johannes. *Fragstück[e] an alle Christgläubigen.* Cologne: [Peter Quentel], 1530. (Köhler [q.v.] 604–6/1563.)

———. *Grund und Ursach aus der heiligen Schrift wie unbillig und unredlich das "Salve regina" wird unterlassen.* [Cologne: Peter Quentel], 1526. (Köhler [q.v.] 802/2016.)

———. *Wie man die Heiligen ehren soll.* N.p., 1524. (Köhler [q.v.] 1027/2588.)

Eberlin, Johann. *Ein freundlich[e] tröstliche Vermahnung an alle frommen Christen zu Augsburg.* [Augsburg: Philipp Ulhart, 1522.] (Köhler [q.v.] 233/652.)

[———]. *Ein klägliche Klag an den christlichen römischen Kaiser Carolum von wegen Doktor Luthers und Ulrich von Hutten. Der erst [bis XV.] Bundgenoß.* [Augsburg: Jörg Nadler, 1521.] (Köhler [q.v.] 232–33/648.)

[———]. *Das Lob der Pfarrer von dem unnützen Kosten.* [Augsburg: Sigmund Grimm & Marx Wirsung, 1522.] (Köhler [q.v.] 7/32.)

———. *Ein schöner Spiegel eins christlichen Lebens.* Strassburg: Johannes Schwan, 1524. (Köhler [q.v.] 52/148.)

———. *Ein Sermon zu den Christen in Erfurt.* [Erfurt: Johannes Loersfeld], 1524. (Köhler [q.v.] 53/149.)

[———]. *Wider die falsch scheinende[n] Geistlichen unter dem christlichen Haufen.* [Augsburg: Melchior Ramminger], 1524. (Köhler [q.v.] 49/136.)

———. *Der Zehnte Bundesgenosse.* Basel: Pamphilus Gengenbach, 1521. In *Flugschriften,* ed. Laube, 1:75–89 [q.v.].

Eckstein, Utz. *Dialogus. Ein hübsche Disputation, die Christus hat mit Adam ton.* [Zurich: C. Froschauer, 1526.] (Köhler [q.v.] 942/2348.)

Erasmus, Desiderius. *Colloquies.* Translated by Craig R. Thompson. Collected Works of Erasmus. Toronto: University of Toronto Press, 1997.

———. *The Essential Erasmus.* Edited by John P. Dolan. New York: New American Library, 1983.

Fabri, Johannes (von Leutkirch). *Christenliche Beweisung über sechs Artikel des unchristenlichen Ulrich Zwinglins.* Tübingen: Ulrich Morhart, 1526. (Köhler [q.v.] 668–72/1766.)

———. *Epistola… de invocatione et intercessione Mariae.* Vienna: Johann Singriener, 1529. (Köhler [q.v.] 607/1565.)

Ein fast schöne Unterweisung, aus der Heiligen Geschrift gegründet. [Augsburg: Heinrich Steiner], 1526. (Köhler [q.v.] 1579/4086.)

Femelius, Johannes. *Ein kurz Sermon, so die Heiligen Gottes belangen.* [Erfurt]: Hans Knappe, [1522]. (Köhler [q.v.] 733/1868.)

[Ferrarius (Montanus), Johannes.] *Was der durchleüchtige Fürst Philipp, Landgraf zu Hessen, mit den Klosterpersonen, Praffherren und Bildnissen in seinem Fürstentume fürgenommen hat.* N.p., 1528. (Köhler [q.v.] 1496/3937.)

Freisleben, Johannes. *Das "Salve regina" nach dem Richtscheid, das da heißt Graphitheopneustos, ermessen und abgericht.* [Regensburg: Paul Kohl, 1523.] (Köhler [q.v.] 1282/3300.)

Gebwiler, Hieronymus. *Beschirmung des Lobs und Ehren der hochgelobten himmlischen Königin Mariä.* [Strassburg: Johann Grüninger, 1523.] (Köhler [q.v.] 1475/3876.)

[Gengenbach, Pamphilus.] *Der evangelisch Bürger.* Zwickau: Jörg Gastel, 1524. (Köhler [q.v.] 463/1251.)

[———.] *Dies ist ein jämmerliche Klag über die Totenfresser.* [Strassburg: Johann Prüss, 1522.] (Köhler [q.v.] 244/674.)

Georg von Polenz, Bf. von Samland. *Ein Sermon am Christtag in der Domkirch zu Königsberg gepredigt.* [Augsburg: Melchior Ramminger, 1524.] (Köhler [q.v.] 461/1244.)

Ein Gespräch auf das kürzest zwischen einem Christen und Juden, auch einem Wirte samt seinem Hausknecht, den Eckstein Christum betreffend. [Erfurt: Michel Buchfürer], 1524. (Köhler [q.v.] 621/1608.)

Ein Gespräch zwischen vier Personen, wie sie ein Gezänk haben von der Wallfahrt im Grimmental, was für Unrat oder Büberei daraus entstanden sei. Erfurt: Wolfgang Stürmers, [1523 or 1524]. In *Die Wahrheit,* ed. Bentzinger, 270–95 [q.v.].

Gesprächbüchlin neu Karsthans. N.p., n.d. (Köhler [q.v.] 172/475.)

Goldschmidt, Sebastian. *Ein Unterweisung etlicher Artikel, so Bruder Mattheiß öffentlich gepredigt hat.* [Worms: Peter Schöffer, 1525.] (Köhler [q.v.] 1476/3879.)

Grebel, Nikolaus, and Johann Schweblin. *Ein Sermon auf Misercordia Domini zu(o) Pfortzhaim im Spital.* [Augsburg: Melchior Ramminger], 1524. In *Städtische Predigt in der Frühzeit der Reformation: Eine Untersuchung deutschen Flugschriften der Jahre 1522 bis 1529,* ed. Bernd Moeller and Karl Stackmann [q.v.]. Göttingen: Vandenhoeck & Ruprecht, 1996.

[Greifenberger, Hans.] *Dies Büchel zeigt an, wie wir also weit geführt sind von der Lehre unsers Meisters Christo.* [Munich: Hans Schobser], 1523. (Köhler [q.v.] 1079–2736.)

———. *Dies Büchlin zeigt an die falschen Propheten.* [Augsburg: Philipp Ulhart, 1523?] (Köhler [q.v.] 255/715.)

Gretzinger, Benedikt. *Hauptartikel und fürnehmlich Punkten der göttlichen Geschrift.* [Wittenberg: Johann Rhau-Grunenberg], 1524. (Köhler [q.v.] 1137/2910.)

———. *Hauptartikel und fürnehmste Stück unsers Christentums.* [Wittenberg: Johann Rhau-Grunenberg, 1525.] (Köhler [q.v.] 1055–56/2665.)

———. *Ein unüberwindlich Beschirmbüchlin von Hauptartikeln der göttlichen Geschrift.* Augsburg: Heinrich Steiner, 1525. (Köhler [q.v.] 679/1773.)

Groner, Johannes. *Zu Trost allen armen Gewissen: Ein klein Büchlin.* Wittenberg: Hans Lufft, 1524. (Köhler [q.v.] 1068/2701.)

Die gründlichen und rechten Hauptartikel aller Bauerschaft und Hintersassen der geistlichen und weltlichen Oberkeiten. Regensburg: Paul Kohl, n.d. (Köhler [q.v.] 1363/3599.)

Ein guter grober Dialogus deutsch, zwischen zweien guten Gesellen. [Augsburg: Melchior Ramminger, ca. 1521.] (Köhler [q.v.] 264/743.)

Güttel, Kaspar. *Dialogus oder Gesprächbüchlein von einem rechtgeschaffen Christenmenschen.* N.p., 1522. (Köhler [q.v.] 71–72/189.)

———. *Dialogus oder Gesprächbüchlein, wie christlich und evangelisch zu leben.* N.p., 1523. (Köhler [q.v.] 265/747.)

———. *Ein selig neu Jahr von neuen und alten Gezeiten.* Erfurt: [Matthew Maler], 1522. (Köhler [q.v.] 1189–90/2985.)

———. *Schutzrede wider etliche ungezähmte freche Clamanten.* Wittenberg: [Johann Rhau-Grunenberg, 1522.] (Köhler [q.v.] 17/72.)

———. *Von apostolischem Amt und Eigenschaft der Bischof, Pfarrer und Prädikanten.* [Erfurt: Wolfgang Stürmer], 1523. (Köhler [q.v.] 270/769.)

———. *Von merklichen Mißbräuchen wider das klare göttliche Wort.* [Zwickau]: Gabriel Kantz, 1528. (Köhler [q.v.] 1235/3116.)

Handlung und Disputation, so zwischen Friedrich Mecum und Johann Korbach geschehen. N.p., 1527. (Köhler [q.v.] 138/378.)

Hätzer, Ludwig. *Ein Urteil Gottes unsers Ehegemahl, wie man sich mit allen Götzen und Bildnissen halten soll.* Zurich: C. Froschauer, 1523. (Köhler [q.v.] 244/675.)

Hauer, Georg. *Ander zwo Predigt vom "Salve Regina."* Landshut: Johann Weißenburger, 1526. (Köhler [q.v.] 69/182.)

———. *Drei christlich Predigt vom "Salve Regina."* [Ingolstadt: Andreas Lutz, 1523.] (Köhler [q.v.] 1026/2586.)

Hausmann, Nikolaus, Wolfgang Zeuner, and Paul Lindenau. *Unterricht und Warnung an die Kirch zu Zwickau.* Zwickau: [Jörg Gastel, 1525]. (Köhler [q.v.] 290/841.)

Hedio, Caspar. *In die erst Epistel S. Joannis des Evangelisten ettliche Christlich Predigt.* [Strassburg: Johann Knobloch], 1524. In *Städtische Predigt,* ed. Moeller and Stackmann [q.v.].

Herman, Nikolaus. *Ein Mandat Jesu Christi an alle seine getreuen Christen.* Wittenberg: Nickel Schirlentz, 1524. In *Flugschriften,* ed. Clemen, 2:261–73 [q.v.].

Heyden, Sebald. *Daß der einig Christus unser Mittler und Fürsprech sei bei dem Vater, nicht sein Mutter noch die Heiligen.* [Leipzig: Michael Blum, 1526.] (Köhler [q.v.] 903/2261.)

Hug, Michael. *Ein kurzer, aber christlicher und fast nützlicher Sermon von dem rechten, wahren und lebendigen Glauben.* [Augsburg: Heinrich Steiner], 1524. (Köhler [q.v.] 372/1040.)

Ich kann nit viel Neues, erdenken, ich will der Katzen die Schellen anhenken. [Strassburg: Matthias Schürer Erben, 1525.] (Köhler [q.v.] 1315/3418.)

Im Land zu Meißen bei Freiburg im Jahr 1522 ist ein solch Wundergeburt von einer Kuh kommen. [Augsburg: Melchior Ramminger, 1523.] (Köhler [q.v.] 7/30.)

In rechter gründlicher, brüderlicher und christenlicher Liebe Gott recht zu erkennen. [Augsburg: Melchior Ramminger, 1520?] (Köhler [q.v.] 215/609.)

J. N. *Von der rechten Erhebung Bennos.* [Wittenberg: Hans Lufft], 1524. In *Flugschriften,* ed. Laube, 2:1343–47 [q.v.].

Karlstadt, Andreas. *Ein Frage, ob auch jemand möge selig werden ohn die Fürbit Mariä.* [Nuremberg: Hieronymus Höltzel], 1524. (Köhler [q.v.] 87/238.)

———. *Von Abtuhung der Bilder.* Wittenberg: Nickell Schyrlentz, 1522. In *Flugschriften,* ed. Laube, 1:105–27 [q.v.].

———. *Von dem Sabbat und geboten Feiertagen.* [Konstanz: Johann Schäffler, 1524.] (Köhler [q.v.] 70/186.)

————. *Von Gelübden Unterrichtung*. Wittenberg: [Nickel Schirlentz], 1521. (Köhler [q.v.] 134/362.)

Kattelsburger, Nikolaus. *Ein Missive oder Sendbrief von den falschen Lehren*. [Augsburg: Philipp Ulhart], 1524. (Köhler [q.v.] 725/1845.)

Keller, Andreas. *Ein Sermon auf den Tag der Verkündung Mariae, gepredigt zu Rottenburg*. [Augsburg: Heinrich Steiner], 1524. (Köhler [q.v.] 393/1069.)

Kettenbach, Heinrich von. *Ein Gespräch mit einem frommen Altmütterlein von Ulm*. Augsburg: Melchior Ramminger, 1523. In *Flugschriften*, ed. Clemen, 2:52–75 [q.v.].

————. *Ein Practica practiciert aus der heiligen Bibel auf viel zukünftig Jahr*. Bamberg: Georg Erlinger, 1523. In *Flugschriften*, ed. Clemen, 2:183–200 [q.v.].

————. *Ein Sermon zu der löblichen Stadt Ulm zu einem Valete*. Bamberg: Georg Erlinger, [1523]. In *Flugschriften*, ed. Clemen, 2:107–23 [q.v.].

Klag und Antwort von luthersichen und päpstischen Pfaffen über die Reformation, zu Regensburg ausgangen. "Lumbitsch auff dem Federmarck" [Nuremberg: Hieronymus Höltzel], n.d. (Köhler [q.v.] 342/964.)

Ein klärlich Anzeigung und Ausweisung eins christlichen und unchristlichen Lebens. [Speyer: Jakob Schmidt, 1523.] (Köhler [q.v.] 223/624.)

Köhler, Hans-Joachim, Hildegard Hebenstreit-Wilfert, and Christoph Weismann, eds. *Flugschriften des frühen 16. Jahrhunderts*. Microfiche Serie 1978. Zug: Inter Documentation Company, 1978–87.

[Krautwald, Valentin.] *Von Gnaden Gottes, ihrem ordentlichen Gang und schnellen Lauf*. [Strassburg: Balthasar Beck, 1528.] (Köhler [q.v.] 1864/4766.)

Lange, Johannes. *Ein Sermon von menschlicher Schwachheit*. Erfurt: [Wolfgang Stürmer, 1523]. (Köhler [q.v.] 1849/4727.)

Laube, Adolf, ed. *Flugschriften der frühen Reformationsbewegung (1518–1524)*. 2 vols. Vaduz, Liechtenstein: Topos, 1983.

Liliencron, Rochus, Freiherr von, ed. *Die Historischen Volkslieder der Deutschen vom 13. bis 16. Jahrhundert*. 5 vols. Leipzig: F. C.W. Vogel, 1867.

Linck, Wenzeslaus. *Artikel und Positiones, so durch Wenzeslaum Linck zu Altenburg gepredigt*. Grimma: [Wolfgang Stöckel], 1523. (Köhler [q.v.] 980/2470.)

————. *Ein schöne christliche Sermon von dem Ausgang der Kinder Gottes aus des Antichrists Gefängnis*. [Nuremberg: Hans Hergot], 1524. (Köhler [q.v.] 273/781.)

————. *Ein Sermon von Anrufung der Heiligen*. [Augsburg: Heinrich Steiner, 1523.] (Köhler [q.v.] 107/280.)

Locher, Johann [Johann Rott]. *Vom Ave-Maria-Läuten den Gläubigen fast fürderlich*. [Zwickau: Jörg Gastel], 1524. (Köhler [q.v.] 248/689.)

Lonicer, Johannes. *Berichtbüchlin*. N.p., n.d. (Köhler [q.v.] 225/631.)

Lotzer, Sebastian. *Eine heilsame Ermahnung an die Einwohner von Horb*. [Augsburg: Jörg Nadler], 1523. In *Flugschriften*, ed. Laube, 1:252–64 [q.v.].

Luther, Martin. *Ausgewählte Schriften*. 7 vols. Edited by Karin Bornkamm and Gerhard Ebeling. Frankfurt a/M: Insel, 1982.

————. *D. Martin Luthers Briefwechsel, D. Martin Luthers Werke: Kritische Gesamtausgabe*. 11 vols. Weimar: H. Böhlau, 1930.

————. *D. Martin Luthers Werke: Kritische Gesamtausgabe*. 57 vols. Weimar: H. Böhlau, 1883.

————. *Die Deutsche Bibel, D. Martin Luthers Werke: Kritische Gesamtausgabe*. 9 vols. Weimar: H. Böhlau, 1906.

————. *Luthers Werke in Auswahl.* 8 vols. Edited by Otto Clemen. Berlin: de Gruyter, 1950.

————. *Luther's Works.* 55 vols. Edited by Helmut T. Lehmann. Philadelphia: Muhlenberg, 1955.

————. *Tischreden, D. Martin Luthers Werke: Kritische Gesamtausgabe.* 6 vols. Weimar: H. Böhlau, 1912.

————. *What Luther Says: An Anthology.* Compiled by Ewald M. Plass. 3 vols. St. Louis: Concordia, 1959.

Marschalck, Haug. *Wer gern wöllt wissen, wie ich hieß, zu lesen mich hätt nit verdrieß.* N.p., n.d. (Köhler [q.v.] 42/110.)

Mayer, Sebastian. *Widerrufung an ein löbliche Freistadt Straßburg.* [Augsburg: Philipp Ulhart], 1524. (Köhler [q.v.] 147/405.)

Melhofer, Philipp. *Offenbarung der allerheimlichsten Heimlichkeit der jetzigen Baalspriester.* [Augsburg: Philipp Ulhart, ca. 1529.] (Köhler [q.v.] 1530–31/3982.)

Mirisch, Melchior, Eberhard Weidensee, Johannes Fritzhans [and others]. *Doctor Melchior Mirisch, Doctor Eberhardus Weidensee, Johannes Fritzhans samt andern Predigern des Evangelii der Stadt Magdeburg erbieten sich, dies nachgedruckten Artikel zu erhalten.* [Magdeburg: Hans Knappe], 1524. (Köhler [q.v.] 982/2484.)

Moeller, Bernd, and Karl Stackman. *Städtische Predigt in der Frühzeit der Reformation: Eine untersuchung deutschen Flugschriften der Jahre 1522 bis 1529.* Göttingen: Vandenhoeck & Ruprecht, 1996.

Ein neues Gespräch von zweien Gesellen, wie sie vom heiligen Wort Gottes geredt haben. [Augsburg: Heinrich Steiner], 1524. (Köhler [q.v.] 627/1628.)

[Oekolampad, Johannes.] *Canonici indocti Lutherani.* [Augsburg, 1519.] (Köhler [q.v.] 145/401.)

————. *De laudando in Maria Deo Sermo.* Basel: Andreas Cratander, 1521. (Köhler [q.v.] 627/1628.)

————. *Iudicium de doctore Martino Luthero.* [Basel], 1521. (Köhler [q.v.] 692/1521.)

————. *Ein Sermon von dem Vers im Magnificat* "Exultavit spiritus meus." [Augsburg: Sigmund Grimm & Marx Wirsung, 1520?] (Köhler [q.v.] 1100/2800.)

————. *Ein Sermon, wie wir Gott in Maria loben sollen.* [Augsburg: Sigmund Grimm & Marx Wirsung, 1521.] (Köhler [q.v.] 530/1351.)

————. *Von Anrufung der Heiligen.* Basel: Adam Petri, 1526. (Köhler [q.v.] 814/2038.)

[Osiander, Andreas.] *Grund und Ursach aus der heiligen Schrift, wie und warum die Pröpst zu Nürnberg die Mißbrauch bei der heiligen Meß geändert haben.* [Zwickau: Jörg Gastel, 1525.] (Köhler [q.v.] 18–19/74.)

Das Papstum mit seinen Gliedern gemalet und beschrieben. N.p., 1526. (Köhler [q.v.] 1294/3333.)

[Peringer, Diepold.] *Ein Sermon, gepredigt vom Bauern zu Wöhrd bei Nürnberg, von dem freien willen des Menschen, auch von Anrufung der Heiligen.* [Augsburg: Silvan Otmar, 1524.] (Köhler [q.v.] 375/1045.)

————. *Ein Sermon von der Abgötterei durch den Bauern, der weder schreiben noch lesen kann, gepredigt.* [Nuremberg: Hans Hergot, 1524.] (Köhler [q.v.] 1493/3922.)

Pollio, Symphorianus. *Göttlicher und päpstlicher Recht Vergleichung.* N.p., 1530. (Köhler [q.v.] 88/241.)

Porta, Conrad. *Jungfrawenspiegel. Faksimiledruck der Ausgabe von 1580.* Edited by Cornelia Niekus Moore. Bern: Peter Lang, 1990.

Prugner, Nikolaus, and Balthasar Hubmaier. *Achtunddreißig Schlußreden, so betreffende ein ganz christlich Leben.* [Strassburg: Johannes Schwan], 1524. (Köhler [q.v.] 144/396.)

Reuter, Simon. *Anntwort wider die Baalspfaffen.* [Bamberg: Georg Erlinger, 1523.] (Köhler [q.v.] 225/633.)

Rhegius, Urbanus. *Die neu Lehr samt ihrer Verlegung.* [Strassburg: Johann Knobloch], 1527. (Köhler [q.v.] 770–71/1946.)

Römer, Johannes. *Ein schöner Dialogus von den vier größten Beschwernissen eines jeglichen Pfarrers.* [Schlettstadt: Lazarus Schürer?], 1521. In *Flugschriften*, ed. Clemen, 3:49–91 [q.v.].

Rubius, Johannes. *Ein neues Büchlein on der löblichen Disputation in Leipzig.* [Leipzig: Valentin Schumann], 1519. In *Flugschriften*, ed. Laube, 2:1257–84 [q.v.].

Russ, Wolfgang. *Ein Sermon, in welcher der Mensch gereizt und ermahnt wird zu Lieb der evangelischen Lehre.* [Nuremberg: Hieronymus Höltzel, 1523.] (Köhler [q.v.] 1084/2745.)

Ryschner, Utz. *Eine schöne Unterweisung, daß wir in Christo alle Brüder und Schwestern sind.* [Augsburg: Heinrich Steiner], 1524. In *Flugschriften*, ed. Laube, 1:427 [q.v.].

Sachs, Hans. *Disputation zwischen einem Chorherren und Schuhmacher.* [Bamberg: Georg Erlinger], 1524. In Bentzinger, *Die Wahrheit*, 353–80.

———. *Etliche geistliche, in der Schrift gegründte Lieder, für die Laien zu singen.* [Augsburg: Philipp Ulhart], 1526. (Köhler [q.v.] 1587/4096.)

———. *Von einem Schuhmacher und Chorherren eine Disputation.* [Strassburg: Wolfgang Köpfel], 1524. (Köhler [q.v.] 1820/4666.)

———. *Die Wittenbergische Nachtigall.* [Bamberg: Georg Erlinger, 1523.] In *Flugschriften*, ed. Laube, 1:590–616 [q.v.].

Sankt Hildegarden Weissagung über die Papisten und genannten Geistlichen. With a foreword by Andreas Osiander. N.p., 1527. (Köhler [q.v.] 372/1036.)

Sattler, Michael. *Brüderlich Vereinigung etzlichen Kinder Gottes sieben Artikel betreffend. Item ein Sendbrief Michael Sattlers an eine Gemeine Gottes samt seinem Martyrium.* N.p., 1527. In *Flugschriften*, ed. Clemen, 2:325–37 [q.v.].

[Schappeler, Christoph.] *Verantwortung und Auflösung etlicher vermeinter Argument.* Augsburg: Melchior Ramminger, 1523. In *Flugschriften*, ed. Clemen, 2:339–413 [q.v.].

Schatzger [Schatzgeyer], Kaspar. *Von der lieben Heiligen Ehrung und Anrufung das erst deutsch Büchlin.* Munich: Hans Schobser, 1523. (Köhler [q.v.] 706–7/1811.)

Schenck von Stauffenberg, Jakob. *Sendbrief an seine Geschweihen.* [Speyer: Jakob Schmidt], 1524. (Köhler [q.v.] 139/385.)

Schmid, Konrad. *Antwort auf etlich Widerred derer, so die Predigt, durch ihn getan, geschmät.* [Zurich: C. Froschauer], 1522. (Köhler [q.v.] 1955/4988.)

Ein schöner Dialogus und Strafred von dem Schultheiß von Geißdorf mit seinem Schüler wider den Pfarrer daselbst. N.p., n.d. (Köhler [q.v.] 264/744.)

Schwanhauser, Johannes. *Ein Sermon, geprediget anno 1523 an dem 22. Sonntag nach Trinitatis, an aller Heiligen Tag.* [Bamberg: Georg Erlinger, 1523.] (Köhler [q.v.] 1042/2622.)

[Schwarzenberg, Johann von.] *Beschwörung der alten teufelischen Schlangen mit dem göttlichen Wort.* Nuremberg: Hans Hergot, 1525. (Köhler [q.v.] 274–77/785.)

Dies seind etlich erschrockenliche Wunderzeichen, so Gott der Herr der lutheranischen Materien uns zu warnen für Augen gestellt hat. N.p., n.d. (Köhler [q.v.] 569/1458.)

Seitz, Otto, ed. *Der authentische Text der Leipziger Disputation (1519).* Berlin: C. A. Schwetschke & Sohn, 1903.

Ein Sendbrief von einem jungen Studenten zu Wittenberg an seine Eltern in Schwabenland von wegen der Lutherischen Lehre zugeschrieben. Augsburg: Melchior Ramminger, 1523. In *Flugschriften*, ed. Clemen, 1:9–18 [q.v.].

Ein Sendbrief von einer ehrbaren Frau im ehelichen Stand an ein Klosterfrauen. [Augsburg: Heinrich Steiner, 1524.] (Köhler [q.v.] 170/466.)

Ein Sermon von der Anbetung, gepredigt von einem Karmelit. [Augsburg: Melchior Ramminger], 1522. (Köhler [q.v.] 270/763.)

Sickingen, Franz von. *Ein Sendbrief zu Unterrichtung etlicher Artikel christlichen Glaubens.* Wittenberg: [Johann Rhau-Grunenberg], 1522. (Köhler [q.v.] 215/606.)

Spelt, Heinrich. *Ein wahre Deklaration oder Erklärung der Profession, Gelübden und Leben, so die falschen Geistlichen tun.* [Augsburg: Heinrich Steiner], 1523. (Köhler [q.v.] 47/131.)

Stanberger, Balthasar. *Ein Dialogus oder Gespräch zwischen einem Prior, Laienbruder und Bettler, das Wort Gottes belangend.* N.p., n.d. (Köhler [q.v.] 1003/2546.)

———. *Dialogus zwischen Petro und einem Bauern.* Erfurt: Michael Buchführer, 1523. In *Flugschriften*, ed. Clemen, 3:200–14 [q.v.].

Staygmayer, Hans. *Ein kurze Unterrichtung von der wahren christlichen Bruderschaft.* [Augsburg: Philipp Ulhart], 1524. (Köhler [q.v.] 142/391.)

———. *Ein schöner Dialogus oder Gespräch von einem Mönch und Becken.* [Augsburg: Philipp Ulhart, 1524.] (Köhler [q.v.] 4/17.)

Stifel, Michael. *Wider Doktor Murnars falsch erdicht Lied von dem Untergang christlichs Glaubens.* [Strassburg: Reinhard Beck Erben, 1522?] (Köhler [q.v.] 249/695.)

Stör, Thomas. *Von dem christlichen Weingarten.* [Bamberg: Georg Erlinger, 1524.] In *Flugschriften*, ed. Laube, 1:357–96 [q.v.].

Ein tröstliche Disputation auf Frag und Antwort gestellet, von zweien Handwerksmännern. N.p., n.d. (Köhler [q.v.] 680–81/1774.)

Ulem, Hans. *Merkt ihr Laien, habt euch in Hut, secht der Geistlichen Übermut.* N.p., n.d. (Köhler [q.v.] 843/2117.)

Vögeli, Jörg. *Schirmred eines laiischen Bürgers zu Konstanz wider den Pfarrer von Überlingen.* N.p., n.d. (Köhler [q.v.] 1556/4035.)

Von etlichen Klagen, die der allmächtig Gott tut durch seine Knecht. N.p., 1525. (Köhler [q.v.] 411/1122.)

Von St. Johanns Trunk ein hübscher neuer Spruch. N.p., n.d. (Köhler [q.v.] 624/1616.)

Warnung und Ermahnung der christlichen Kirchen zu Germanien ihrer Tochter, daß sie ihre Verführer mit Feuer und Eisen ausrotten wolle. N.p., n.d. (Köhler [q.v.] 1884/4814.)

Weidensee, Eberhard, and Johannes Fritzhans. *Wie Doctor Cubito, Bonifacius und der Sonntagsprediger im Dom zu Magdeburg Gottes Wort schänden. Dialogus.* N.p., 1526. (Köhler [q.v.] 831/2081.)

Wicks, Jared, ed. and trans. *Cajetan Responds: A Reader in Reformation Controversy.* Washington: Catholic University of America Press, 1978.

Wilhelm, Graf von Isenburg. *In diesem Büchlein unterrichtet der wohlgeborn mein G. H. von Isenburg den ehrsame Rat von Köln.* N.p., n.d. (Köhler [q.v.] 1557/4039.)

———. *Kurze Erklärung der prinzipal Artikel meins G. H. von Isenburg, der halben sein Gnad als ein Ketzer wider die Billigkeit wird angegen.* N.p., n.d. (Köhler [q.v.] 1558/4041.)

———. *Kurzer Bericht und Anzeige aus heiliger, göttlicher Geschrift, wie Gott in seinen Heiligen zu loben ist.* N.p.: Jakob Schmidt, 1526. (Köhler [q.v.] 1557/4038.)

Wurm, Matthias. *Christenlich kurz Vermahnung zum andern Mal an Jakob Kornkauf, von Fasten, Feiertagen, Beichten.* Strassburg: Johannes Schwan, 1524. (Köhler [q.v.] 797/2006.)

———. *Trost Klostergefanger.* N.p., n.d. (Köhler [q.v.] 154–55/424.)

Zeuleys, Ulrich. *Daß die Heiligen für Gott nicht anzurufen, ein kurzer Unterricht.* N.p., 1524. (Köhler [q.v.] 569/1459.)

Ziegler, Clemens. *Ein kurz Register und Auszug der Bibel, in welchem man findet, was Abgötterei sei.* N.p., 1524. (Köhler [q.v.] 1566/4062.)

Zurich, Bürgermeister, Rat and Grosser Rat. *Christenlich Ansehung des gemeinen Kilchgangs zu Hörung göttlichs Wort.* Zurich, 1530. (Köhler [q.v.] 1600/4135.)

———. *Christliche Antwort dem hochwürdigen Herren Hugo, Bischof zu Konstanz, über die Unterricht beider Artikel der Bilder und der Mess.* Zurich: Hans Hager, 1524. (Köhler [q.v.] 1437/3816.)

———. *Ordnung und Erkenntnis eines ehrsamen Rats der Stadt Zürich betreffend den Ehebruch, Kindertauf, Feiertage, Gemein Gebet.* N.p., n.d. (Köhler [q.v.] 886/2233.)

Zwingli, Huldrich (Ulrich). *Die ander Antwort über etlich unwahrhaft Antworten, die Eck gegeben hat.* Zurich: Hans Hager, 1526. (Köhler [q.v.] 304/880.) In *Huldreich Zwinglis sämtliche Werke,* vol. 5, *Werke April 1526–Juni 1527,* Corpus Reformatorum. Zurich: Theologischer, 1982, 207–36.

———. *Ein Antwort, Valentino Compar gegeben.* Zurich: Hans Hager, [1525]. (Köhler [q.v.] 305–6/881.) In *Huldreich Zwinglis sämtliche Werke,* vol. 4, *Werke April 1525–März 1526,* 84–128.

———. *Auslegen und Gründ oder Schlußreden oder Artikeln.* Zurich: C. Froschauer, [1523]. (Köhler [q.v.] 58–63/162.) In *Huldreich Zwinglis sämtliche Werke,* vol. 2, *Werke 1523,* 157–66, 166–230, 231–39.

———. *Ein christenliche, fast nützliche und tröstliche Epistel an die Gläubigen zu Eslingen.* N.p., 1526. (Köhler [q.v.] 306/883.) In *Huldreich Zwinglis sämtliche Werke,* 5:272–85.

———. *Early Writings.* Edited by Samuel Macauley Jackson. New York: G. P. Putnam's Sons, 1912. Reprint, Durham, N.C.: Labyrinth, 1987.

———. *Die erst kurze Antwort über Ecken sieben Schlusreden.* N.p., [1526]. (Köhler [q.v.] 57/160.) In *Huldreich Zwinglis sämtliche Werke,* 5:188–92.

———. *Ein Gegenwurf und Widerwehr wider Hieronymum Emser.* Zurich: C. Froschauer, 1525. (Köhler [q.v.] 137/372.) *Adversus Hieronymum Emserum antibolon,* 20 August 1524. In *Huldreich Zwinglis sämtliche Werke,* vol. 3, *Werke 1524–März 1525,* 230–87.

———. *Der Hirt.* Zurich: C. Froschauer, n.d. (Köhler [q.v.] 340/959.) In *Huldreich Zwinglis sämtliche Werke,* 3:1–68.

———. *Huldreich Zwinglis sämtliche Werke.* Corpus Reformatorum. Zurich: Theologischer, 1982.

———. *Huldrych Zwingli: Writings.* Vol. 1, *The Defense of the Reformed Faith.* Translated by E. J. Furcha. Allison Park, Pa.: Pickwick, 1984.

———. *On Providence and Other Essays.* Edited for Samuel Macauley Jackson by William John Hinke. Philadelphia: Heidelberg, 1922. Reprint, Durham, N.C.: Labyrinth, 1983.

———. *Eine Predigt über die ewigreine Jungfrau Maria, die Mutter Jesus Christi, unseres Erlösers.* Zurich, 1522. In *Huldreich Zwinglis sämtliche Werke,* vol. 1, *Werke 1510–Januar 1523,* 385–428.

————. *Von wahrem und falschem Glauben.* Zurich: C. Froschauer, 1526. (Köhler [q.v.] 905–11/2265.) *De vera et falsa religione commentarius.* In *Huldreich Zwinglis sämtliche Werke,* 3:590–612.

INDEX

A

Abtuhng (Karlstadt), xi n12, 43n38

abuses in the church. *See* disputations, diets, and colloquies; indulgences

Acts of the Apostles, 32, 138–39

Acts of the Disputation (Bern Disputation, 1528), 10, 87, 87n50

Adler, Caspar, 4, 49

Adrian VI, pope, 78

Agricola, Johann, 99

Aland, Kurt, 108

All Saints' Day, 105, 106

Amsdorf, Nikolaus von, 13n1, 25

Anabaptists, 89n59

Annunciation, 33, 70, 105, 106

Ansbach visitation (1567), 103, 103n124

Answer to Valentin Compar (Zwingli), 10, 56, 59

Antichrist, 41, 43, 48

Antonites, *15*, 18

Apology of the Augsburg Confession (Melanchthon), 91–93, 93n70

Appenzell Disputation (1524), 82–83, 83n29, 112

arrogance, 32–33

art, sensuality of, 46–47, 47n53

artistic representation of saints. *See* images

Ascension, 105

Assumption, 106

Augsburg Confession (Melanchthon), 12, 90–91

Augustine, 91

Ave Maria, 70

B

Baal, 42–43, 43n38

Backus, Irena, 84

Baden–Aargau Disputation (1526), 83–86, 85n40, 112

Bagchi, David, 13n2

Bainton, Roland, 54, 60

Bamberger, Peter, 96–97, 98

Basil, 91

Bauer, Martin, 96–97n89

Baxandall, Michael, 47n53

Beier, Leonhard, 75

Benedictines, *15*

Bergendoff, Conrad, 101–2n113

Bernard, 91

Bern Disputation (1528), 10, 86–87, 112

Beyer, Christian, 90

Bible. *See* Scripture; *specific books*

Blarer, Ambrosius, 13n1, 50

Blickle, Peter, 52

Bornkamm, Heinrich, 61n31

Bossy, John, 37n9, 41n29

Brenz, Johannes, 51

    A Sermon concerning the Saints, 36

    Sermon on the Saints, x–xi

Briggitines, *15*

Brown, Peter, 39n23

Brueghel, Pieter the Elder: *Combat of Carnival and Lent,* 41n30

Bucer, Martin

    at the Bern Disputation, 86, 87

    as a clergyman, 13n1

    on pilgrimages, 37, 45

    on saints' days, 44–45

    on sinful behavior on holidays, 44

    That Images Will No Longer Be Tolerated by the God-Fearing, 30

Bugenhagen, Johannes, 13n1

Bullinger, Heinrich: *On the Origin of Errors,* 14, 14n8

Bundsgenossen (Eberlin), 55

Burke, Peter, 6, 41n30

C

Cajetan, Cardinal, 75–76
Calvin, John, 2
Campeggio, Lorenzo, 78, 91
Candlemas, 105, 106
Capito, Wolfgang, 86
Catholics, 89–91. *See also* disputations,
    diets, and colloquies
celibacy, 67, 74
Charles V, Holy Roman Emperor, 90–91
Chieregati, Bishop, 78
Christ
    as intercessor, 34–35, 86, 109
    on veneration of Mary, 33
Christian Instruction, 49–51
Christianity, 73–74, 73n34, 89–91. *See also*
    Lutherans; Protestantism; Reformation
2 Chronicles, 126
Chrysostom, 91
church visitations, 101–2n113, 101–4,
    104n124
Cistercians, *15*
Clement VI, pope, 76
Clement VII, pope, 78
clergy, 48n59, 50. *See also* Erfurt,
    Pfaffensturm in; orders
Cling, Conrad, 98
cloister and saints, 3–4
Cochlaeus, Johannes, 91
colloquies. *See* disputations, diets, and
    colloquies
Colossians, 143
Combat of Carnival and Lent (Brueghel),
    41n30
commandments. *See* First Commandment;
    Second Commandment
Commentary on True and False Religion
    (Zwingli), 10, 56
Concerning the Invocation of Saints
    (Oecolampadius), 86
Confutatio (Diet of Augsburg, 1530), 91
1 Corinthians, 24n43, 28, 141–42
2 Corinthians, 142
corruption. *See* disputations, diets, and
    colloquies; indulgences

Council of Trent (1563), 46–47
Cranach, Lucas the Elder: *Passional Christi
    und Antichristi,* 43n39
Cronberg, Hartmuth von, 6
Culsamer, Johannes, 13n1, 97, 99n104
    *Refutation of the Sermon Delivered at
        Erfurt,* 98
Curia, reform of, 78. *See also* disputations,
    diets, and colloquies
Cyprian, 91

D

Daniel, 133
Davis, Natalie Zemon, 45n44
the dead vs. the living, 38–39, 39n23,
    85–86
Deuteronomy, 30, 123–25
Dialogue between a Monk and a Baker
    (Staygmeyer), 4, *5*
*Dialogue between a Prior, a Lay Brother, and a
    Beggar* (Stanberger), *20*
Dialogue between Peter and a Peasant
    (Stanberger), 99–100
Diepolt, Johann, 66
Diet of Worms (1521), 18, 77, 87, 111
diets. *See* disputations, diets, and colloquies
Diets of Augsburg (1518, 1530), 90–93, 111
Diets of Nuremberg (1522–1524), 78,
    78n9, 87, 111
Diets of Speyer (1526, 1529), 87–88,
    88n54, 89–90, 89n59, 112
disorder, 6–7
    and the Antichrist, 41, 43, 48
    and Baal, 42–43, 43n38
    and holidays, 43–44, 44–45n44
    and powerful, unmarried women,
        47–48, 47n56
    and prostitution, 47–48
    saints as agents of, 41–42
    and the *verkehrte Welt,* 41–42n34, 43,
        43n38, 48
Disputation between a Shoemaker and a Canon
    (Sachs), 27, 79–80

disputations, diets, and colloquies
Appenzell Disputation, 82–83, 83n29, 112
Baden–Aargau Disputation, 83–86, 85n40, 112
Bern Disputation, 10, 86–87, 112
Diet of Augsburg, 111
Diet of Augsburg, 90–93, 111
Diet of Nuremberg, first, 78, 78n9, 87, 111
Diet of Nuremberg, second, 78, 78n9, 87, 111
Diet of Speyer, first, 87–88, 88n54, 112
Diet of Speyer, second, 89–90, 89n59, 112
Diet of Worms, 18, 77, 87, 111
Düsseldorf Disputation, 88–89, 112
Heidelberg Disputation, 75, 111
Leipzig Disputation, 76–77, 111
Marburg Colloquy, 89n59
Riga Disputation, 80–81, 111
Synod of Homberg, 88, 112
Waldshut Colloquy, 83
Waldshut Colloquy, 112
Zurich Disputation, first, 9, 81, 111; second, 10, 81–82, 111; third, 81, 82, 111; fourth, 81, 82, 112
Dixon, C. Scott, 103n124
Dominicans, 15, 20–21, 20n24
Douglass, Jane Dempsey, 44n44
Düsseldorf Disputation (1527), 88–89, 112

E
early modern society, 39, 41, 41n29
Eberlin, Johann
and the Bern incident, 20–21
Bundsgenossen, 55
on the cloister, 3–4
on the Franciscans, 22, 23–24
Gespräch, 44, 44n42
monastic background of, 13n1
on monasticism, 17
pamphlet in support of Luther, 16
saints' cult attacked by, 55, 55n8
on saints' days, 105–6
on sola Scriptura, 25
on superstition, 6
Eck, Johann, 76–77, 77n4, 84, 85–86
economic waste, 48–52
Edict of Worms (1521), 77–79, 87–88, 89–90
Einsiedeln (Switzerland), 9
Eire, Carlos, xi, xi n11, 2, 14n8, 72n32
Engelhard, Heinrich, 82
Ephesians, 28, 142–43
Epistle or Instruction on the Saints (Luther), 98–99, 99n100, 101–2n113, 102
Erasmus, 36, 36n1, 53
Erfurt (Thuringia)
evangelical movement in, 96–97, 97n91
Pfaffensturm in, 93–101, 95n78, 95n81, 96n83, 96n87, 98n98, 99nn100–101
evangelicals
fissures among, 89, 89nn59–60
origins/use of term, xii n
Exodus, 30, 122
Explanation of the Ninety-Five Theses (Luther), 76
Ezekiel, 132–33

F
Fabri, Johannes, 81, 84–85, 86, 91
faith vs. works. See works righteousness
feast days, 105–6. See also saints' days/ festivals
"feeding upon the dead" (Totenfresserei), 4, 6, 36, 39
Femelius, Johannes, 98
A Short Sermon concerning God's Saints, 96, 96n83, 96n87
feminization of Christianity, 73–74, 73n34
Ferber, Nikolaus, 88
Ferdinand of Austria, 78
Ferrarius, Johannes, 17–18
festivals/saints' days, 6–7, 43–45, 105–6
First Commandment, 11, 11n51, 30n66, 56, 56n12

First Reply (Zwingli), 85–86
Forchheim, Georg, 97, 98
Franciscans, *15*, 18, 20–21, 20n24, 22, 23–24
Freisleben, Johannes, 71–72, 80
Fritzhaus, Johannes, 13n1
Froschauer, Christoph, 87
Fuchs, Thomas, 83n29
Fuggers, 77n4

G
Gabriel, 70
Galatians, 142
Genesis, 122
Gengenbach, Pamphilus, 6
    Die Totenfresser, 39, 39n21, *40*
George, duke of Saxony, 76
Gespräch (Eberlin), 44, 44n42
Ein Gespräch mit einem frommen Altmütterlein von Ulm (Kettenbach), 46, 51
Goldschmidt, Sebastian, 44, 70
A Good Christian Sermon about the Exodus of the Children of God from the Antichrist's Prison (W. Linck), 43
good works. *See* works righteousness
Great Council, 10
Gregory I, pope, 61, 61n35
Greifenberger, Hans, 28, 29
Gretzinger, Benedikt, 29, 32, 66n2
Grimmental, 21, 21n27
Güttel, Kaspar, 13n1, 28, 29, 44

H
Habakkuk, 133–34
Haller, Berchthold, 84
    Schlußreden, 86–87
Hätzer, Ludwig, 9–10, 30–31
Hausmann, Nikolaus, 6
Hebrews, 38, 144
Heidelberg Disputation (1518), 75, 111
Heimpel, Hermann, 2
Heller von Korbach, Johann, 88–89
Hess, Johannes, 85n40
Hesse (Germany), 107

Heyden, Sebald, 28, 33, 33n81, 80
Hofmeister, Sebastian, 82
holidays, 43–44, 44–45n44. *See also* saints' days/festivals
Hosea, 133
Hubmaier, Balthasar, 83
Hugo, bishop of Constance, 57
Huizinga, Johan, 1–2, 3n10, 103
Hus, Jan, 84n36

I
iconoclasm, 7–8, 8n35, 9–10, 54, 62, 81–82. *See also* Zurich Disputations
idolatry, 47n54. *See also* images
images
    abolition of, 82, 87
    of female saints as prostitutes, 46–48
    and iconoclasm, 7–8, 8n35, 9–10, 62, 81–82 (*see also* Zurich Disputations)
    as idolatry, 10
    Luther on, 7–8, 46, 60–62
    reformers' criticism of, xi, xi n11
    scriptural prohibition of, 3, 9–10, 11n51, 30–32
    sensuality of, 46
    Zwingli on, 1, 10, 46, 56, 56n12, 60–61, 63, 82
Immaculate Conception, 67, 67n8
indulgences. *See also* Treasury of Merits
    and the Fuggers, 77n4
    Luther on, 62, 75, 76
    relics as a source of, xi
    Treasury of Merits as underpinning, 39
    Zwingli on, 63
In Praise of God through Mary (Oecolampadius), 54
Instruction on Vows (Karlstadt), 22
intercessor
    Christ as, 34–35, 86, 109
    Luther as, 109n22
    saints as, 34–35, 81, 85, 108–9 (*see also* saints, cult of)
    Virgin Mary as, 71, 71n28

Invocavit sermons (Luther), 7–8
Isaiah, 30–31, 128–30

J

Jackson, Samuel Macauley, 8–9
Jacobson, Grethe, 3n10
Jeanne de Jussie, 44n44
Jeremiah, 32, 32n75, 130–32
Jerome, 91
Jesus. *See* Christ
Job, 38
Johannites, *15*
John, 33, 34–35, 136–38
1 John, 145
John of Saxony, 89, 101
Jonas, Justus, 94
Joshua, 125
Jud, Leo, 82
Jude, 145
Judges, 125
Jungfrawenspiegel (Porta), 67, 106

K

Karant-Nunn, Susan, 3n10
Karlstadt, Andreas
    on the *Ave Maria,* 70
    on Baal, 42–43, 43n38
    on holidays, 44
    iconoclasm of, 7
    on images, 30–31
    Instruction on Vows, 22
    at the Leipzig Disputation, 76–77
    on Psalm 150, 28
    on saints' days, 6–7
    on the *verkehrte Welt,* 43
    Von Abtuhng der Bylder, xi n12, 43n38
    on the weak, 58n21
Katharina von Bora, 13
Kattelsburger, Nikolaus, 22
Kettenbach, Heinrich von, 13n1
    on the Edict of Worms, 79
    *Ein Gespräch mit einem frommen
        Altmütterlein von Ulm,* 46, 51

on Luther, 79
on saints as models, 66n2
on waste/neglect, 51
1 Kings, 125
2 Kings, 125–26
Knopken, Andreas, 80–81
Kolb, Franz: *Sclußreden,* 86–87
Kolb, Robert, 105, 109

L

Lambert, Franz, 9, 9n38, 88
Lamentation of a Layman (Schwalb), 54–55
Lang, Johannes, 13n1, 94, 97, 98, 99n104
Langenzenn visitation (1553), 103n124
Large Catechism (Luther), 11, 18, 38, 103
Leipzig Disputation (1519), 76–77, 111
Leviticus, 122
Linck, Heinrich, 85n40
Linck, Wenzeslaus, 13n1, 66
    *A Good Christian Sermon about the
        Exodus of the Children of God from
        the Antichrist's Prison,* 43
Lindenau, Paul, 6
living saints, as the poor, 51, 51n82
the living vs. the dead, 38–39, 39n23,
    85–86
Locher, Johann, 13n1
Lohse, Barnhard, 13n2
Lonicer, Johannes, 13n1, 18, 20, 29, 45
Lotzer, Sebastian, 49
    Twelve Articles, 49n67, 52
Lucke, Wilhelm, 55
Luke, x–xi, xi n10, 33, 136
Luther, Margarethe, 14n6
Luther, Martin
    on Bishop Benno of Meissen, 25–26,
        61n32
    and Cajetan, 75–76
    on the commandments, 30n66
    death of, 108
    at the Diet of Worms, 77
    Eberlin on, *16*
    Epistle or Instruction on the Saints,
        98–99, 99n100, 101–2n113, 102

Luther, Martin, *continued*
 and the Erfurt incident, 94–95, 94n75,
  98–99, 99nn100–101 (*see also*
  Erfurt, *Pfaffensturm* in)
 Erfurt letter of, 1, 6, 6n21, 8
 in exile, 77–78, 90
 Explanation of the Ninety-Five Theses, 76
 on godly law, 56
 on Gregory I, 61, 61n35
 on holidays, 44
 on iconoclasm, 7–8, 8n35, 62
 on images, 7–8, 46, 60–62
 on the Immaculate Conception, 67n8
 on indulgences, 62, 75, 76
 influence/popularity of, 78, 94
 as intercessor, 109n22
 Invocavit sermons, 7–8
 Kettenbach on, 79
 Large Catechism, 11, 18, 38, 103
 at the Leipzig Disputation, 76–77
 on living vs. dead saints, 55–56, 63
 on the *Magnificat,* 68, 68n17
 on marriage, 72
 marriage to Katharina, 13
 monastic background of, 13
 on monasticism, 13–14, 13n2, 18, 23
 Ninety-Five Theses, 62, 75–76, 75n (*see
  also* Heidelberg Disputation)
 nominalism of, 21–22n29
 and Oecolampadius, 53–54
 On Monastic Vows, 13n2
 on papal authority, 26, 26nn51–52
 pilgrimage of, 58, 60
 on pilgrimages, 45, 62
 on the poor as saints, 58
 Sachs on, 79–80
 saintlike attributes of, 108
 on saints, great vs. true, 64–65
 on saints as believers in Christ, 6,
  6n21, 38, 55, 58, 63, 65
 on saints' cult, 1, 3, 7, 55, 58, 61,
  61n32
 on saints' legends, 65n55
 saints venerated by, 58, 60, 60n23,
  60n25, 61n31

 on the Saxon visitation, 101–2n113,
  101–3
 Sermon on Penance, 76
 Small Catechism, 11, 11n51
 on *sola Scriptura,* 25–26
 on St. Anne, 58, 60, 61
 on superstition and saint worship, 6,
  6n22
 Tischreden, 67
 on the Treasury of Merits, 94
 on virgin martyrs, 67
 on the Virgin Mary, 54–55, 68, 68n17,
  73, 73n38, 74
 on works righteousness, 34, 61–62,
  63–64
Lutherans
 vs. Catholics, 89–91 (*see also*
  disputations, diets, and colloquies)
 Edict of Worms against, 77–79, 87–88,
  89–90
 influence of, 88
 on traditional piety, 38
 on the Virgin Mary, 67–68

M

MacKinnon, James, 88n54
Magdalene, Mary, 66
Magnificat, 68, 68n17, 70–71
Malachi, 134
Manuel, Nikolaus, 6
 Die Totenfresser, 39, 39n21
Marburg Colloquy (1529), 89n59
Mark, 135–36
marriage, 72
martyrologies, 66–67
Mary. *See* Virgin Mary
mass, 82, 87
materialism, 48–49
Matthew, 134–35
 on the keys of heaven, 26, 26nn51–52
 and papal authority, 26, 26n51, 28
 rock metaphor in, 28
 on veneration of dead saints, x–xi,
  xi n10
 on waste/neglect, 51

Mayer, Sebastian, 13n1, 17
Mechler, Egidius, 96–97n89, 98, 99n104
medieval society, 39, 41, 41n29
Melanchthon, Philipp
   Apology of the Augsburg Confession,
      91–93, 93n70
   Augsburg Confession, 12, 90–91
   at Diet of Augsburg, 90–91
   and the Erfurt incident, 99
   Offenbarung der allerheimlischsten
      Heimlichkeit der jetzigen
      Baalspriester, 49, 50
   on pilgrimages, 49
   on prayers, 102
   on the Saxon visitation, 101, 102,
      102n113
   on *sola Scriptura,* 92
Melhofer, Philipp, 32, 109
   Revelation of the Top Secrecy of Today's
      Baal Priests, 42
Micah, 133
Miracle Book, 69
Mirisch, Melchior, 13n1
Moeller, Bernd, 2
monks/monasticism, 4, 5. *See also* orders
Musa, Antonius, 96, 98
Myconius, Friedrich, 88–89
Myconius, Oswald, 108

N

Nassau–Wiesbaden visitation (1594),
   103n124
Ein neues Büchlein von der löblichen
   Disputation in Leipzig (Rubius), 77,
   77n5
A New Disputation between Two Journeymen,
   29
Ninety-Five Theses (Luther), 62, 75–76,
   75n1. *See also* Heidelberg Disputation
Nothelfer (helper saints), 17n13
Numbers, 123
nuns, 48n59
Nuremberg visitations (1560–1561, 1579),
   103, 103n124

O

Oecolampadius, Johannes, 13n1, 53–54,
   53n3
   at the Baden Disputation, 84, 85,
      85n40, 86
   at the Bern Disputation, 86
   Concerning the Invocation of Saints, 86
   iconoclasm of, 54
   In Praise of God through Mary, 54
   on the Virgin Mary, 54, 54n6
Offenbarung der allerheimlischsten Heimlichkeit
   der jetzigen Baalspriester (Melanchthon),
   49, 50
On Monastic Vows (Luther), 13n2
On the Origin of Errors (Bullinger), 14, 14n8
order. *See* disorder
orders, 13–24, 14n8, 17n10, 18n19, 20n24,
   21–22n29, 21n27
   Antonites, *15,* 18
   begging, 18, 18.19, 20
   Benedictines, *15*
   Bern incident of 1509, 20–21
   Briggitines, *15*
   Cistercians, *15*
   criticism of, 4, *5,* 17–18, 20–24,
      21–22n29
   Dominicans, *15,* 20–21, 20n24
   Franciscans, *15,* 18, 20–21, 20n24, 22,
      23–24
   fraudulent practices of, 17–18, 20–21,
      21n27
   Johannites, *15*
   Luther on, 13–14, 13n2, 18, 23
   as multiplying the objects of worship,
      21–22n29, 21–23
   Polenz on, 17
   reformers as clergymen, 13n1
   representatives of, *15*
   and works righteousness, 13, 17,
      17n10
   Zwingli on, 14, 21–22
Osiander, Andreas, 71, 106–7

Ozment, Steven, 44n42
 on belief/practice related to the dead, 4, 6, 39
 on women's labor/childbirth, 73n36
 on women's status, 72n33

P

paganlike qualities of saint cult, x–xi, 37–38, 37n8
pamphlets: number of, 1. *See also specific pamphlets*
 on saints' cult, 3, 3n11, 7
 on scriptural prohibition of images, 30–32
 on *sola Scriptura,* 24–35, 26nn51–52, 31n71, 32n75, 33n81
particularism, 88n54
Passional Christi und Antichristi (Cranach), 43n39
Peasants' War (1525–1526), 4, 52, 95n78, 101
Peringer, Diepold, 20, 28, 29, 79
1 Peter, 144–45
Pfaffensturm. See under Erfurt
Philip, landgrave of Hesse, 88, 89, 107
Philippians, 143
pilgrimages
 criticism of, xi, xi n12, 4
 decline in, 37n9
 indulgences bought during, 49
 Luther on, 45, 62
 as satanic/pagan, 37
 sinful behavior during, 45
 waste/neglect from, 49–51
 Zwingli on, 63
Polenz, Georg von, 17
the poor
 duties to vs. neglect of, 50–52
 as images of God, 56
 reformers on, 56–57, 58, 63
 as saints, 51, 51n82, 58
 saints' feeding of, 52n84
 Zwingli on, 56–57, 63

pope
 authority of, 26, 26nn51–52, 28, 106
 teachings of, 51
 as the "Whore of Babylon," 47
popular culture/religion, ix–x, 41, 41n30
Porta, Conrad
 Jungfrawenspiegel, 67, 106
 on the Virgin Mary, 67–68, 74
Potter, G. R., 9n38, 84
prayers, 67, 70–71, 73, 73n36, 102
Preuß, Horst Dietrich, 67n8
priests/clergy, 48n59, 50. *See also* Erfurt, *Pfaffensturm* in; orders
Probst, Jakob, 99
prophecies, 106–7
prostitution, 47–48
Protestantism
 Christocentric focus of, 72–73
 Lutheran, influence of, 88
 origins/use of term, xii
 Reformed, influence of, 88
 Virgin Mary marginalized in, 74. *See also* Lutherans; Reformation
Protestation (Diet of Speyer, 1529), 89–90
Psalms, 28–29, 31–32, 126–28

R

Reformation: in Bern, 87.
 opposition to, 103–4, 104n125 (*see also* disputations, diets, and colloquies; saints, cult of)
 and women's status, 72, 72n33
reformers, 53–65. *See also* Luther, Martin; pamphlets; Zwingli, Huldrich; *other specific reformers and issues, such as* orders *and* pilgrimages
 on artistic representation of saints, xi, xi n11 (*see also* images)
 on church expenditures/waste, 56–58
 on the cloister, 3–4
 on cult of images, xi, xi n11
 on disorder, 6–7
 diversity among, 53
 humanist, 53

reformers, *continued*
  on images, 60–62, 63
  on indulgences, 62–63
  monastic background of, 13, 13n1
  on paganlike qualities of cult of saints,
    x–xi
  on pilgrimages, 62–63 (*see also*
    pilgrimages)
  on the poor, 56–57, 58, 63
  on relics, xi, xi n11
  on saints as superseding Christ, 4
  saint veneration gradually abandoned
    by, 54–55
  on scriptural authority, 55
  on shrines, xi
  on works righteousness, 61–62, 63–
    64.
Refutation of the Prophets of Baal (Reuter), 42
Refutation of the Sermon Delivered at Erfurt
  (Culsamer), 98
relics, xi, xi n11
religion, 1, 89–91. *See also* Christianity;
  Lutherans; orders; Reformation; *sola*
  Scriptura
Reuter, Simon, 13n1, 50
  Refutation of the Prophets of Baal, 42
Revelation, 32–33, 145–46
Revelation of the Top Secrecy of Today's Baal
  Priests (Melhofer), 42
Riga Disputation (1522), 80–81, 111
rock metaphor, 28
Roman Catholics, 89–91. *See also*
  disputations, diets, and colloquies
Romans, 35, 139–41
Römer, Johannes, 55
Roper, Lyndal, 3n10, 68, 72n33, 74
Rothkrug, Lionel, 2
Rubius, Johannes: *Ein neues Büchlein von der*
  löblichen Disputation in Leipzig, 77, 77n5

S
Sabbath, 44
Sachs, Hans, 24–25
  Disputation between a Shoemaker and a
    Canon, 27, 79–80

Sacramentarian Controversy, 89n59
saints. *See also* saints, cult of; *specific saints*
  as believers in Christ, 6, 6n21, 38, 55,
    58, 63, 65
  and cloister, 3–4
  great *vs.* true, 64–65
  intercession of, 34–35, 81, 85, 108–9
    (*see also* saints, cult of)
  legends about, 65n55
  as living images of God, 63
  Luther's veneration of, 58, 60, 60n23,
    60n25, 61n31
  as models, 64, 65, 66–67, 66n2, 106,
    107–8
  the poor as, 51, 51n82, 58
  prophecies of, 106–7
  sinfulness of, 64–65, 108
saints, cult of
  dismissal of/focus on, 1–3, 3n10, 7,
    75, 79–80, 93 (*see also*
    disputations, diets, and
    colloquies; pamphlets
  and the Erfurt incident, 9n104,
    95–96, 95n81, 96n83, 96n87, 98,
    99–101
  laity's acceptance of, 2
  Luther on, 1, 3, 7, 55, 58, 61, 61n32
  persistence of, 105–9, 107n13, 109n22
  presence of, 1–12, 3nn10–11, 6n24,
    6nn21–22, 8n35, 103–4
  rise of, 41
  and salvation, 72n32
  as satanic/pagan, x–xi, 37–38, 37n8
  Scripture on (*see* Scripture; *specific*
    books of Bible)
  as superseding Christ, 4
  in Switzerland, 8–11
  ubiquity of (*see* disputations, diets, and
    colloquies)
  women's involvement in, 2–3, 3n10
  Zwingli on, 1, 3, 7, 37n8, 55–58
saints' days/festivals, 6–7, 43–45, 105–6
saint worship/veneration. *See* saints, cult of
salvation, 72n32
Salve Regina, 67, 71–72, 71n27, 80, 107
1 Samuel, 125

2 Samuel, 125
Sargent, Steven D., 37n9
Sattler, Michael, 13n1
Saxon visitation (1527–1528), 101–2n113,
    101–4
Schappeler, Christoph, 49
    Twelve Articles, 49n67, 52
Schenck von Stauffenberg, Jakob, 33, 68
Schilling, Johannes, 21–22n29, 107
Schlußreden (Zwingli), 21–22, 38–39, 46,
    56–57, 81. *See also* Zurich Disputations
Schmid, Konrad, 13n1, 66, 82, 87
Schriftprinzip, 84, 84n36
Schwalb, Hans, 52n84
    Lamentation of a Layman, 54–55
Schwanhauser, Johannes, 37–38
Schwarzenberg, Johann von, 49
Sclußreden (Haller and F. Kolb), 86–87
Scribner, R. W
    on the Erfurt incident, 98n98,
        99n101, 101
    on prophecies, 107
    on saint cult's persistence, 108
    on the *verkehrte Welt*, 41–42n34
Scripture, x–xi. *See also sola Scriptura; specific
    books of Bible*
    on apocryphal vs. traditional saints, 3
    on images, prohibition of, 3, 9–10,
        11n51, 30–32
    on saints' cult, 3, 55.
Second Commandment, 11n51, 30n66,
    56n12
Seibelsdorf visitation (1573), 103n124
sensuality, 45–47
A Sermon concerning the Saints (Brenz), 36
Sermon on Penance (Luther), 76
Sermon on the Saints (Brenz), x–xi
A Sermon on Worship, 29
The Shepherd (Zwingli), 56
A Short Sermon concerning God's Saints
    (Femelius), 96, 96n83, 96n87
Shrine of the Beautiful Maria (Regensburg,
    Germany), 62, *69*
shrines, xi
Sickingen, Franz von, 22, 29
sinful behavior, 43–44, 45, 64–65, 108

Small Catechism (Luther), 11, 11n51
sola Scriptura (authority of Scripture alone),
    3, 24–35, 30n66
    Eberlin on, 25
    Luther on, 25–26
    Melanchthon on, 92
    pamphlets on, 24–35, 26nn51–52,
        31n71, 32n75, 33n81
Spalatin, Georg, 88
St. Anne, 58, 60, 61
St. Anthony's *Brief*, 18, 18n18
St. Benno, bishop of Meissen, 25–26,
    61n32
St. Elizabeth, 107
St. Hildegard, 106
St. John the Baptist Day, 105, 106
St. Margaret, 3n10
St. Mary Magdalene Day, 106
St. Peter, 26, 26n51
St. Stephen's Day, 106
Sts. Felix and Regula Day, 106, 106n4
Sts. Peter and Paul Day, 105
Stanberger, Balthasar
    *Dialogue between a Prior, a Lay Brother,
        and a Beggar*, 20
    Dialogue between Peter and a Peasant,
        99–100
Stationierer, 18, 18.19
Staupitz, Johannes von, 75n
Staygmeyer, Hans, 52n84
    Dialogue between a Monk and a Baker, 4,
        5
Stifel, Michael, 13n1
Stör, Thomas, 51
Strauss, Gerald, 103–4, 104n125
superstition, 6n24
    Brenz on, 36
    Erasmus on, 36, 36n1
    and "feeding upon the dead," 4, 6, 36,
        39
    and the living vs. the dead, 38–39,
        39n23
    Luther on, 6, 6n22
Switzerland, 46
Synod of Homberg (1526), 88, 112

T

Terminierer, 18.19
That Images Will No Longer Be Tolerated by the
God-Fearing (Bucer), 30
1 Thessalonians, 143
Thomas, Keith, 6n24
1 Timothy, 35, 143–44
Tischreden (Luther), 67
tithes, 52
Titus, 144
Die Totenfresser (Gengenbach), 39, 39n21,
40
Die Totenfresser (Manuel), 39, 39n21
Totenfresserei ("feeding upon the dead"), 4,
6, 36, 39
Treasury of Merits, 39, 65, 75–76, 94
Twelve Apostles' Day, 106
Twelve Articles (Lotzer and Schappeler),
49n67, 52

U

Ühlfeld visitation (1582), 103n124
Unigenitus, 76
Usingen, Bartholomaeus Arnoldi von, 91,
97–98, 98n98

V

verkehrte Welt (world turned upside down),
41–42n34, 43, 43n38, 48
Virgin Mary, 65–74
    the Annunciation, 33, 70
    and the Ave Maria, 70
    celibacy of, 74
    credulity of, 68, 70
    cult of, 3n10, 68, 70, 73, 73n34
    as an exemplar, 74
    humility of, 68, 70, 71–72
    Immaculate Conception of, 67, 67n8
    as intercessor, 71, 71n28
    Luther on, 54–55, 68, 68n17, 73,
        73n38, 74
    and the Magnificat, 68, 68n17, 70–71
    marginalization by Protestants, 74
    modesty of, 68, 70
    motherhood of, 68, 73
    Oecolampadius on, 54, 54n6
    Porta on, 67–68, 74
    prayers/songs to, 67, 70–71
    and the Salve Regina, 67, 71–72,
        71n27, 80, 107
    scriptural references to, 33, 33n81
    veneration of, 33, 33n81
    Visitation to Elizabeth, 74
    women's prayers to during labor/
        childbirth, 73, 73n36
    Zwingli on, 70
visitations to churches, 101–2n113, 101–4,
    104n124
Von Abtuhng der Bylder (Karlstadt), xi n12,
    43n38

W

Waldshut Colloquies (1524, 1526), 83, 112
Wallmersbach visitation (1553), 103n124
Wandel, Lee Palmer, 47, 47n54, 48–49,
    51n82
Warner, Marina, 73n34
waste/neglect, 49–51
Weber, Max, 6n24
Weidenbach visitation (1579), 103n124
Wiesner, Merry E., 2, 47n56, 73
Wilhelm, Graf von Isenburg, 29, 32n75,
    33–34, 66n2
Wimpina, Konrad, 91
Wirsberg visitation (1558), 103n124
Wolfgang, prince of Anhalt, 89
women
    labor/childbirth of, 73, 73n36
    physicality of, 47n53
    powerful, unmarried, 47–48, 47n56
    saint cult involvement of, 2–3, 3n10
    silence of, 24, 24n43
    status during Reformation, 72, 72n33
    and the Virgin Mary, 73, 73n34
works righteousness
    Luther on, 34, 61–62, 63–64
    and orders, 13, 17, 17n10, 34
Wurm, Matthias, 22

Z

Zeuleys, Ulrich, 32
Zeuner, Wolfgang, 6
Zili, Dominik, 85n40
Zurich, 46, 106, 106n4
Zurich Council, 57–58
Zurich Disputations (1523–1524), 9–10,
    81–82, 111–12
Zwilling, Gabriel, 7
Zwingli, Huldrich
    Answer to Valentin Compar, 10, 56, 59
    on the *Ave Maria,* 70
    at the Bern Disputation, 86–87
    Commentary on True and False Religion,
        10, 56
    death of, 10
    at Einsiedeln, 9
    First Reply, 85–86
    humanism of, 38
    on iconoclasm, 9
    on idolatry, 31–32
    on images, 1, 10, 46, 56, 56n12,
        60–61, 63, 82
    on indulgences, 63
    influence of, 82
    on intercession of the saints, 81
    vs. Lambert, 9
    on living vs. dead saints, 55–56
    on monasticism, 14, 21–22
    music/worldly pleasures enjoyed by, 46
    and Oecolampadius, 54
    on pilgrimages, 63
    on the poor, 51n82, 56–57, 63
    on saints as living images of God, 63
    on saints as models, 66n2
    on saints' cult, 1, 3, 7, 37n8, 55–58
    on the sanctified on earth, 38–39
    Schlußreden, 21–22, 38–39, 46, 56–57,
        81 (*see also* Zurich Disputations)
    and the *Schriftprinzip,* 84, 84n36
    The Shepherd, 56
    on sinful behavior, 43–44
    on the Virgin Mary, 70
    in Zurich, 8–9
    at the Zurich Disputations, 81–82

DATE DUE
